IRISH LITERARY AND
MUSICAL STUDIES

IRISH LITERARY AND MUSICAL STUDIES

BY

ALFRED PERCEVAL GRAVES

("CANWR CILARNÉ")

Essay Index Reprint Series

BOOKS FOR LIBRARIES PRESS
FREEPORT, NEW YORK

First Published 1914
Reprinted 1967
Second Reprinting 1970

PR 8761
G7

INTERNATIONAL STANDARD BOOK NUMBER:
0-8369-0494-X

LIBRARY OF CONGRESS CATALOG CARD NUMBER:
67-23224

PRINTED IN THE UNITED STATES OF AMERICA

DEDICATION

These Essays on Irish and Celtic Poetry and Music, and these Reminiscences and Studies of the writings of Nineteenth Century Irish Poets and Musicians—Mangan and Bunting, known to, and Petrie, beloved of my father—Joseph Sheridan Le Fanu, Sir Samuel Ferguson and William Allingham, his friends and mine from my boyhood to middle manhood—of Tennyson, to whom my uncle, Robert Perceval Graves, had been host at Windermere, and to whom I was guest at Kilkee—and, lastly, of Patrick Weston Joyce, for forty years my generous musical and literary ally—I dedicate to my good friends and colleagues, " those kindred Irish spirits banded together to tend the flame of national pride in the heart of London," the members of the Irish Literary Society.

A. P. G.

July 31, 1913.

PREFACE

THE Irish Literary and Musical Studies contained in this volume consist of revised versions of lectures delivered from time to time before the Irish Literary Society of London, the Royal Literary Society, the National Literary Society of Dublin, the National Eisteddfod at Carnarvon, the students of Alexandra College, Dublin, and the Belfast Philosophical Society; also of revised versions of articles and reviews in *The Contemporary Review* ("Celtic Nature Poetry"), *The Dublin Review* ("Early Irish Religious Poetry" and "The Preternatural in Early Irish Poetry"), *The Cornhill Magazine* ("Tennyson in Ireland" and "James Clarence Mangan"), *The Spectator* ("The English Spoken in Ireland," "The Religious Songs of Connacht," "An Irish Wonder Book" and "Edward Bunting"), and *A Treasury of Irish Literature in the English Tongue* ("Sir Samuel Ferguson"), published by Smith, Elder and Co., to whose editors and publishers I gratefully acknowledge permission to republish them.

My original verse translations from the Irish contained in the articles on "Celtic Nature Poetry," "Early Irish Religious Poetry," and "The Preternatural in Early Irish Poetry," and many others, by my own and other hands, will appear in an anthology of English verse renderings of Irish Poetry entitled *Harpstrings of the Irish Gael*, with some twenty illustrations in colour, Celtic capital letters, and a cover of Celtic design by George Morrow, to be published coincidently with this volume by the Devin-Adair Company of 437, Fifth Avenue, New York.

ALFRED PERCEVAL GRAVES.

ERINFA, HARLECH, N. WALES.
July 31, 1913.

CONTENTS

	PAGE
TENNYSON IN IRELAND	1
THE ENGLISH SPOKEN IN IRELAND	12
JAMES CLARENCE MANGAN	19
SIR SAMUEL FERGUSON	36
JOSEPH SHERIDAN LE FANU	51
WILLIAM ALLINGHAM	70
EARLY IRISH RELIGIOUS POETRY	101
THE RELIGIOUS SONGS OF CONNACHT	122
CELTIC NATURE POETRY	128
THE PRETERNATURAL IN EARLY IRISH POETRY	143
DR. JOYCE'S IRISH WONDER BOOK	166
FOLK SONG	175
EDWARD BUNTING	191
GEORGE PETRIE AS AN ARTIST AND MAN OF LETTERS	200
GEORGE PETRIE AS AN ANTIQUARY	214
GEORGE PETRIE AS A MUSICIAN AND AMONGST HIS FRIENDS	231

IRISH

LITERARY AND MUSICAL STUDIES

TENNYSON IN IRELAND

A Reminiscence

It was the summer of 1878. A gale from the south-west, after breaking suddenly over the iron-bound coast of Clare, and raging against it furiously for forty-eight hours, had just died away.

Scarcely a breath of air was stirring, and the August sky was intensely blue. Yet the great Atlantic billows, gathering out of the sea distance at ever increasing intervals, still boomed and smoked against the cliffs—the last sullen thunders of ocean's retreating insurgency.

But the proverbial ill wind that had kept all but the most venturesome spirits close prisoners in the "lodges" of Kilkee had blown the storm-loving Tennyson over from Foynes, where he and his son Hallam were the guests of Lord and Lady Monteagle.

So far back as September 1842 he had written to Aubrey de Vere from Killarney: " I have been to your Ballybunion Caves, but could not get into the finest on account of the weather." But in one of these caves, so his son now records, "he made the following lines, which occur in *Merlin and Vivien* :

> So dark a forethought rolled about his brain,
> As on a dull day in an ocean cave
> The blind wave feeling round his long sea-hall
> In silence."

In the year 1848 he had written to de Vere, "I hear that there are larger waves at Bude than on any other part of the British coast; and I must go hither and be alone with God"; but his friend persuaded him to come to Ireland, where the waves are far higher and the cliffs often rise to 800 feet, and in one spot, Slieve League, to 2,000.

On his way to Valencia he slept at Mount Trenchard, the residence of Lord Monteagle, and, de Vere continues, "I led him to the summit of Knock Patrick, the farthest spot in the south-west to which Ireland's apostle, patriarch, and patron advanced.

". . . The sunset was one of extraordinary but minatory beauty. It gave, I remember, a darksome glory to the vast and desolate expanse with all its creeks and inlets from the Shannon, lighted the green islands in the mouth of the Fergus, and fired the ruined castle of Shanid, a stronghold of the Desmonds. . . .

"The western clouds hung low, a mass of crimson and gold; while from the ledge of a nearer one, down plunged a glittering flood empurpled like wine. The scene was a thoroughly Irish one, and gave a stormy welcome to the Sassenach bard. The next morning he pursued his way alone to Valencia. He soon wrote that he had enjoyed it. He had found there the highest waves that Ireland knows, cliffs that at one spot rise to the height of 600 feet, tamarisks and fuchsias that no sea-winds can intimidate, and the old ' Knight of Kerry,' as chivalrous a representative of Desmond's great Norman House as it had ever put forth."

And now, a generation afterwards, and having found his full fame in the interval, Tennyson was paying his third and last visit to Ireland, and again revisiting " Kilkee by the great deeps," for a letter from him to de Vere in October 1848 containing this phrase seems to show he had visited the spot in the previous summer, when the guest of his brother poet at Curragh Chase.

" I am glad," he writes, " that you have thought of me at Kilkee by the great deeps. The sea is my delight."

The intelligence of Tennyson's arrival at Moore's Hotel had spread rapidly, and on the splendid forenoon in question it was very noticeable what a number of the Laureate's slim green volumes were in evidence on the terraces and up the cliff side in the hands which had been swinging a racquet in the fine weather of a few days before.

"These Limerick girls," remarked a local wit, " are growing more fickle than ever. Yesterday they had lawn-tennis on. To-day they have Alfred Tennyson."

Bathing had been out of the question for a couple of days, so it was with a keen sense of exhilaration that I, a visitor to Kilkee at the time, again found myself on the Duggena spring-board. I plunged, and was in mid career, when, rounding a reef corner, I all but knocked heads with another swimmer.

" Beg your pardon, sir."

" Not at all, sir! but—yes! What! *You* here? Why, how long have you been in these parts? "

" About ten days, J. G. ! "

" Very odd, we've not met before, then ? "

" Not at all. I've been purposely avoiding you."

" That doesn't sound very friendly."

" Perhaps not, but my intention was particularly so."

" Explain ! "

" Well, the fact is, I heard you were showing Tennyson the sights; and knowing how shy he is of strangers, I thought the most friendly thing I could do was to steer clear of your party."

" My dear fellow, I'll make that all right."

And he did within a few hours; for that afternoon I got a note from him saying, " Tennyson hopes you will spend the evening with us. Don't bother about dressing. Come just as you are, if not exactly just as you were when last we met."

The writer was my old friend John George Butcher, now a well-known figure at the English Bar and in the House of Commons.

On the outbreak of the storm he and his two sisters had run over from Mount Trenchard, their brother-in-law Lord Monteagle's country seat, in company with Tennyson and his son Hallam, and I found this party awaiting me at Moore's Hotel. Tennyson received me, beaming, evidently thorougly amused at my marine encounter with Butcher that morning. He offered me a long pipe, pressed me into a chair at his right hand, and plunged into animated conversation.

His personality more than satisfied me, though I had been led to anticipate much from Mrs. Cameron's and Rejlander's artistic photographs.

"The large dark eyes, generally dreamy, but with an occasional gleam of imaginative alertness," as de Vere describes them, still varied between haunting softness and eager brightness ; "the great shock of rough dusky dark hair," that Carlyle wrote of in 1842, had been somewhat subdued, but far from subjugated by time ; it revealed more of the poet's "high-built brow," but its raven hue was unimpaired. "The massive aquiline face" was still "most massive, yet most delicate," and still of a healthy bronze. His gestures were free and spontaneous, his voice full and musical. It was impossible to believe he was in his seventieth year.

His accent and speech both surprised me. I was quite prepared for the fastidious articulation and premeditated hesitation in the choice of words to which so many distinguished English University men are prone. There was a rich burr in his accent, Lincolnshire, I suppose, and a pungent directness in his utterance which were as refreshing as they were unlooked for.

Then he evidently possessed the rare knack of getting the very best out of his fellow talkers at the same time that he gave them much more than he got for it. At this interval of time I cannot, of course, do more than record the general drift of our conversation and the opinions he expressed; his exact words have escaped me, except in an occasional instance. First we talked of the sea, and here he spoke notably. He said that a great storm, such as we had witnessed, was a wonderful and terrible sight of impotent passion, and he quoted St. Jude's words, " Raging waves of the sea, foaming out their own shame." But he had once seen roll in out of the Atlantic, suddenly, over a still sea and under a still sky, a succession of stupendous billows, earthquake waves perhaps, which completely engulfed the shore, and whose awful serenity impressed his imagination far more deeply than any tempest he had ever experienced. It is easy for all who have heard him thus discourse to believe, as we are now told by his son, that he claimed a Norse ancestry, " that he loved the sea for its own sake, and also because English heroism has ever been conspicuous on shipboard," and that he " gloried," therefore, in having made these lines in *Boadicea :*

Fear not, isle of blowing woodland, isle of silvery parapets !
Thine the liberty, thine the glory, thine the deeds to be celebrated,
Thine the myriad-rolling ocean, light and shadow illimitable ;

and—

Roared as when the roaring breakers boom and blanch on the precipices.

When thus talking of the storm to me he rolled out a line from Homer, and challenged Butcher, a fine Greek scholar, to say where it came from. I should imagine that it was

ἐξ ἀκαλαρρείταο βαθυρρόου ὠκεάνοιο,

a favourite example to him of sounding lines, according to his son. This line and the well-known

βῆ δ' ἀκέων παρὰ θῖνα πολυφλοίσβοιο θαλάσσης,

he would say, are grander in our modern Northern pronunciation than in the soft Southern talk of the Greeks,
with a difference as between the roar of the Northern sea
and the hissing of the Mediterranean.

The rugged, open-throated, deep-chested vocalisation of
his own north-eastern folk, which he himself so finely
illustrated by his chanting of verse, when gathered into the
grandly rolling Yorkshire choruses, affords a similar contrast
to the smoother and softer but thinner and sharper concerted
singing of southern England.

In this connection his son's biography of Tennyson may
well be quoted :

" He never cared greatly for the sea on the south coast
of England; not a grand sea," he would say, "only an
angry curt sea. It seems to shriek as it recoils with the
pebbles along the shore ; the finest seas I have ever seen
are at Valencia, Mablethorpe, and in West Cornwall. At
Valencia the sea was grand, without any wind blowing and
seemingly without a wave ; but with the momentum of the
Atlantic behind, it dashes up into foam, blue diamonds it
looks like, all along the rocks, like ghosts playing at hide
and seek. When I was in Cornwall it had blown a storm
of wind and rain for days, and all of a sudden fell into
perfect calm ; I was a little inland of the cliffs ; when after
a space of perfect silence, a long roll of thunder, from some
wave rushing into a cavern I suppose, came up from the
distance, and died away. I *never* felt silence like that."

He talked a good deal of that visit to Kerry, of the
scenery and of the people.

It was in 1848, the year of revolutions, and the political
electricity had even penetrated to Valencia ; and Tennyson,
while studying the Alantic breakers from the mountain, was
cautiously followed up by a conspirator, attracted no doubt
by his distinctly un-English dress and appearance. The
man finally closed upon Tennyson and whispered in his
ear, " Be you from France ? " I could narrate a similar

experience. When in Fenian times my father (afterwards the Bishop of Limerick) and I were belated during an archæological ramble in an Irish-speaking part of Kerry, our nocturnal appearance at a remote homestead led to a guarded inquiry whether the French fleet were in the Bay, as reported—so expressed as to convey the belief that our coming was in some way connected with it.

Tennyson was evidently greatly interested in the Irish play of character, and in its dramatic as well as its humorous side. He told us of his drive to see a waterfall on Hungry Hill, and of an amusing conversation he had with the carman, a Celt of the type of Daniel O'Connell, or—to take an instance from our day—of Denis O'Sullivan, the "Shamus O'Brien" of Stanford's opera, so distinguished-looking indeed that when he claimed the closest connection with the great old families of McCarthy More and The O'Sullivan Bear, and emphasised the statement by the production of a ponderous old seal containing their arms quartered together, Tennyson felt quite inclined to believe his final contention that if he had his rights he should be reigning in these parts. "He looked an Irish chief," said Tennyson; and though the poet did not tell me so at the time, his driver, it appears, on being rallied by the waiter after returning to the inn from which they had driven, for talking to the gentleman of his "great blood," drew himself up, answering, "The gentleman *is* a gentleman, every inch of him." *Noblesse oblige*, and on that drive in search of one waterfall it had rained such cataracts that they were fain to take shelter in a wretched little roadside shealing occupied by a poor woman and her little son Johnny. To use Tennyson's own words as given by his son :

"The 'King of Connaught' dried my stockings and went to sleep on a bench. The woman drew me up a stool to the turf fire with the courtly air of a queen. While he was asleep, I heard the mother say to the boy ' Johnny,' several times (she didn't speak a word of English). The

King awoke, and, as we were going out, I said, 'Johnny,' and the little boy with a protuberant paunch (protuberant, I suppose, from eating potatoes) ran forward and I gave him a sixpence. The woman, with her black hair over her shoulders, and her eyes streaming with tears, passionately closed her hands over the boy's hand in which was the sixpence. When the King and I climbed into the car, I, in my stupid Saxon way, thinking it was the beggarly sixpence that had made the woman grateful, expressed my astonishment at such gratitude. ' It was not the sixpence, your honour, it was the stranger's gift.' "

My recollection of the story as told to me is a slight variant upon this version. According to it the woman cried out something in Irish, and Tennyson asked the driver for its meaning when they got outside, on which he replied, "She was blessing God, your honour, that the child's hand had been crossed with silver by the dark-haired stranger." And certainly I don't remember in Tennyson's version of the story as told me that claim to the kingdom of *Connaught* was made by the driver. Even in fun a McCarthy or an O'Sullivan would never have advanced such a claim. Tennyson saw I was much affected by his story, which was very strikingly told, and said, " There ! you must make a poem out of ' the Stranger's Gift.' " He went on to say that he much desired to write an Irish poem, and was on the look-out for a suitable subject. Could I make a suggestion ?

I ran over in my mind the themes with which I was familiar, and suddenly bethought me of my friend Dr. Joyce's *Old Celtic Romances*, some of which he had shown me in manuscript and which were to be published in a few months' time.

I told him of these, and undertook that he should have an early copy of the book. When it appeared I took care to fulfil my promise. Tennyson's *Voyage of Maeldune* was the outcome. In his notes quoted by his son he writes, " I read the legend in Joyce's *Celtic Legends*" (it should be

Joyce's *Old Celtic Romances*), "but most of the details are mine." His biographer adds, "By this story he intended to represent in his own original way the Celtic genius, and he wrote the poem with a genuine love of the peculiar exuberance of the Irish imagination."

When telling Tennyson of Joyce's book, several of the tales in which relate to Finn and his heroic companions, I had hoped he would have treated one of them, by choice *Oisin* (Ossian) *in Tirnanoge* (The Land of Youth) rather than *The Voyage of Maeldune.* For the mention of Ossian had started him off into an expression of admiration for some passages in Macpherson's work for which I was not prepared.

" Listen to this," he said :

" ' O thou that rollest above, round as the shield of my fathers ! Whence are thy beams, O sun ! thy everlasting light ? Thou comest forth in thy awful beauty ; the stars hide themselves in the sky ; the moon, cold and pale, sinks in the western wave ; but thou thyself movest alone. Who can be a companion of thy course ? The oaks of the mountains fall ; the mountains themselves decay with years ; the ocean shrinks and grows again ; the moon herself is lost in heaven ; but thou art for ever the same, rejoicing in the brightness of thy course. When the world is dark with tempest, when thunder rolls and lightning flies, thou lookest in thy beauty from the clouds, and laughest at the storm. But to Ossian thou lookest in vain, for he beholds thy beams no more ; whether thy yellow hair flows in the eastern clouds, or thou tremblest at the gates of the west. . . .' "

" Is it not fine ? " he said. I owned it was, but have never ceased to regret that the much finer, older, and truer Irish Ossianic gold, such as that, for example, which glitters in the pages of Standish Hayes O'Grady's *Silva Gadelica* had not been earlier open to him. Had it been, I make no doubt he would have given us a saga immeasurably more true to the Celtic spirit than his *Voyage of Maeldune* delightful though that poem is in itself, and deeply interesting though it is as a great English poet's attempt to express the Celtic genius. To compare Tennyson's finished poem with the Irish tale from which he took it is a novel experience. I own I share Mr. Stopford Brooke's opinion as to which of them is the simpler and the more convincing.

Tennyson's other Irish poem, *To-morrow*, was founded on the story told him by Aubrey de Vere: " The body of a young man was laid out on the grass by the door of a chapel in the West of Ireland, and an old woman came and recognised it as that of her young lover, who had been lost in a peat bog many years before ; the peat having kept him fresh and fair as when she last saw him."

His son notes: " He corrected his Irish from Carleton's admirable *Traits of the Irish Peasantry*, a proof of the poet's extraordinary laboriousness, and a crying comment on the want of an Anglo-Irish or Hiberno-English dialect dictionary. Tennyson certainly could not have written that intensely dramatic poem had he not been deeply sensible of the tragic side of Irish peasant life as he saw it with his own eyes so shortly after the potato famine. How gracefully, too, he presses into his service the poetic imagery of the Western Gael. It is, moreover, an interesting assertion of his belief in the artistic value of Irish dialect in verse ; *Irish Doric*, as he once wrote of it to me.

But to go back to our conversation, which had turned upon the preternatural, whether through the superstitious touch in the story of *The Stranger's Gift* or because something was said of Macpherson's ghost machinery, I cannot recollect. Tennyson acknowledged to having taken a very deep interest in spiritualism, but he added that, though he could not account for some of the phenomena he had witnessed, investigation had led him to no valuable results, and he had therefore dropped it. Truth and falsehood were evidently woven strangely together in the minds of the mediums, who he believed corresponded to the mediæval witches. He instanced in support of this view the record of an old witch trial at which violent manifestations occurred in full court similar to the so-called "spirit rappings" of recent *séances*.

He went on to say that witches had, under torture, confessed to the most preposterous doings, such as having suckled young devils.

The talk then turned to national education, and he seemed eager for practical instances of its enlightening effects upon the people, derived from my personal knowledge as an inspector of schools. A generation previously he had said that "one of the two great social problems impending was the housing and education of the poor man before making him our master; the other was the Higher Education of Women," to which his *Princess* served as a pioneer.

"Wasn't the Bard great?" said Butcher when we met next morning.

Readers of his son's noble memoir, all the world over, will answer that question as emphatically as I did.

THE ENGLISH SPOKEN IN IRELAND *

DR. JOYCE's literary vitality is as remarkable as his literary versatility. Sixty years ago he was contributing Irish folk-songs and notes on Irish dances to Dr. Petrie's *Ancient Music of Ireland*. In his spare hours when an active teacher, Professor, and Training College Principal he produced what have since become standard works on Irish school method and Irish names of places ; and since his retirement from the Government Service some twenty years ago he has kept his literary energy fresh by turning from folk-lore to folk-song, and from archæology to history. His Irish historical writings exhibit close research and impartial judgment. His *Old Celtic Romances* inspired Tennyson's *Voyage of Maeldune;* and, when the artistic vigour of Sir Edward Burne-Jones had, for the time being, failed, the study of these Romances gave it renewed life, by the painter's own confession.

To Dr. Joyce's first collection of Irish folk-songs Sir Charles Stanford and Dr. Charles Wood are indebted for Irish melodies harmonised by them, and popularised by the singing of Mr. Plunket Greene ; and Dr. Joyce has quite recently edited his musical *opus magnum*, a collection of no less than eight hundred and forty-two Irish airs and songs hitherto unpublished. And now, taking a fresh departure, he presents us, in a popular form, with the first detailed analysis and systematic classification of Anglo-Irish speech.

* *English as We Speak it in Ireland*. By P. W. Joyce, LL.D., M.R.I.A., etc. London : Longmans and Co. [2s. 6d. net.]

He has been for more than twenty years quietly gathering the materials for this book, with unique qualifications and opportunities for the undertaking. For he spoke both Irish and English as a boy, and during his days at Marlborough Street Training College had unequalled chances for inquiry into the differences of speech exhibited by the students under his care, who came from " all the four corners of Erin." But he did not make any serious preparation to write upon the English spoken in Ireland till 1892, when he invited, through the medium of the Press, the contribution of collections of dialectical words and phrases to a projected book on the subject. In response to this appeal he received such collections from no less than a hundred and sixty-four persons in all parts of Ireland and Great Britain, and even in America, Australia, and New Zealand. He has, furthermore, studied the works of the leading writers who make use of different forms of Anglo-Irish and Hiberno-English dialect, and quotes from them at large. Finally, he has digested, and refers to, all the articles and pamphlets on the subject of his book published up to date.

Dr. Joyce's treatment of this considerable mass of material is both scholarly and attractive. The book contains many humorous personal reminiscences, more especially in the chapters devoted to " The Devil and his Territory," " Swearing," " Proverbs," " Exaggeration and Redundancy," and " The Memory of History and Old Customs," all of which are pervaded with the peculiarly dry form of fun for which Dr. Joyce has established a reputation. But the special value of his volume is its authoritative explanation of the origin and building up of the forms of English spoken in Ireland.

Dealing with the sources of " Anglo-Irish dialect," he shows that the influences of Irish pronunciation, vocabulary and idiom, and of Elizabethan English and of Lowland Scotch, have largely affected that form of speech. According to him, the Irish language has determined the popular, though not the educated, pronunciation of the English letters " t," " d," " s," and " z," in imitation of their Irish sounds as in " butther " (butter), " thrue " (true), " fisht " (fist), " drizzhling" (drizzling).   Irish Gaelic has also introduced into Anglo-English many single words, some of which —such as " shamrock," " whisky," " bother," " blarney," " galore," and even " smithereens"—are now current wherever English is spoken.

But more interesting to the linguist, and to those who wish to write correct Hiberno-English, is Dr. Joyce's chapter on the idioms from the Irish language imported into Anglo-Irish speech.   These peculiarities may be classified as prepositional, pronominal, adverbial, verbal and general.   Of the prepositional peculiarities, the following examples will suffice :—" There is snow *in it*" is used for " There is snow there," the Gaelic preposition *ann* denoting "in existence."   "The tinker took fourpence *out of* the kettle,"—*i.e.*, he earned fourpence by mending it.   " I once heard a grandmother," writes Dr. Joyce, " an educated Dublin lady, say, in a charmingly pretty way, to her little grandchild who came up crying : ' What did they do to you *on me* (to my harm)?   Did they beat you *on me ?*'"   This is just the sense of the Irish preposition *air* (on) before a personal pronoun or personal name after an active verb.

The reflexive pronouns " myself," " himself," etc., have meanings borrowed from the Irish to be found in such phrases as " The birds are singing for themselves," " I felt dead (dull) in myself."   The personal pronoun has a curious use in Irish-English which comes straight from the Gaelic, as, for example, " I saw Thomas *and he sitting* by the fire."   Hence Charles Wolfe, an Irishman, in his " Burial of Sir John Moore " writes :

> We thought, as we hollowed his narrow bed,
>   And smoothed down his lonely pillow,
> That the foe and the stranger would tread on his head,
>   *And we far away* on the billow.

The following are instances of adverbial peculiarities in Hiberno-English : The Irish *Is amhlaidh* (it is the way), meaning " thus " or " how " or " in order that," is responsible for such expressions as these : " What do you want, James ? " " 'Tis *the way*, ma'am, my mother sent me for the loan of the shovel." " I brought an umbrella *the way* I wouldn't get wet." In colloquial Irish the words " even " and " itself " are expressed by *fein*, but the Anglo-Irish avoid the word " even " and incorrectly use " itself " in its place,—*i.e.*, " If I had that much *itself*," meaning " If I had *even* that much." The English " when " is expressed in Gaelic by *an uair*, the hour or the time ; hence " The time you arrived I was away in town."

Verbal peculiarities from the Irish are the use of the narrative infinitive, a construction common to the old Irish annals, and still fast-rooted in Irish folk speech,—*e.g.*, " How did the mare get that hurt ? " " Oh ! Tom Cody *to leap her* over the garden wall, and she *to fall* on her knees on the stones." The Irish Gaelic is without the perfect and pluperfect tenses, and the Irish people do not know how or do not care to use them in their English, but feeling their need of them supply it by a periphrasis. Thus when we should say, " I have finished my work," they say, " I am after finishing my work," which is a direct translation from the Irish. Or they wrongly use the preterite—*i.e.*, " I done my work "—or they incorrectly resort to the present progressive—*i.e.*, " I am sitting " (for " I have been sitting ") " waiting for you for the last hour."

" Corresponding devices," writes Dr. Joyce, " are resorted to in order to escape the use of the pluperfect, such as, ' An hour before you came yesterday I finished ' (for ' I had finished ') ' my work.' " The Irish language has a consuetudinal tense which the Irish people so much miss from the English tongue that they have manufactured one by the use of the verbs " do " and " be,"—*i.e.*, " There *does be* a meeting of the Company every Tuesday," that is to say, the meeting is held regularly on that day. Sometimes " be " is used alone,—*e.g.*, " My father *bees* at home in the morning," *i.e.*, is regularly at home.

The following sentences strung together in the narrative form from Dr. Joyce's pages will show how Irish idioms abound in the English spoken in Ireland :

> That was well and good, but the lion let such a roar out of him that she had like to be killed with the fright, and she was no fool of a girl neither ; when up comes along Dicky Diver, the boy she was to be married on, with his regulation rifle and it wasn't long after that the lion got death from him. And if they didn't live happy ever after, that we may !
>
> The day was rising (clearing) when I called in on the Murphys. " Is himself within ? " I axed the servant girl. " He is so and herself too !" says she. With that I went in through the half-door. The woman had a nose on her (was looking sour) and neither of the two axed me had I a mouth on me (would I like some refreshment). Then I drew down with them (introduced the subject) about the money.

Dr. Joyce thus accounts for the Irish and Scotch use of " will " and " shall " as a survival from Elizabethan times. Hamlet says :—" I will win for him an I can ; if not, I will gain nothing but my shame and the odd bits." The second " will " exactly corresponds with the Irish and Scotch use. So also as regards " shall." Its old and correct use, which indicated obligation, has been discarded in England since Shakespeare made Macbeth, on being requested by his wife to " Be bright and jovial among your guests to-night ! " reply to her : " So shall I, love ! " But this use of the " shall " is preserved in Ireland, for if you ask an attentive Irish " boots " to call you early, he replies : " I shall, Sir." On the other hand, *Punch's* Irish waiter's use of " will," as he stands with his hand on a dish-cover inquiring : "*Will* I strip, ma'am ? " appears, like Topsy, to have " growed " of itself, and is therefore incorrect English. Dr. Joyce has not accounted for the equally common Irish confusion of " would " and " should," and it is to be hoped that he will do so in a second edition of his book, which should be assured,

Dr. Joyce points out that the correct English sound of the diphthongs *ea* and *ei*, and of long *e*, was the same as long *a* in "fate" from Elizabethan to comparatively recent times. Thus Cowper rhymes "sea" with "way"; Tate and Brady rhyme "conceive" with "grave"; while Pope rhymes "race" with "Lucrece" and "sphere" with "fair." On the other hand, the correct old English pronunciation of *ie* and *ee* has not changed in Ireland; therefore Irish people never say *praste* for priest, *belave* for believe, *indade* for indeed, or *kape* for keep, as writers of shoddy Anglo-Irish think they do.

"Vocabulary and Index" is a somewhat misleading heading to Dr. Joyce's twelfth chapter, which certainly contains a fairly full vocabulary, but is in no sense an index to the text of the preceding chapters, though such an index was to be looked for in a book of this kind.

There is no Irish Dialect Society to contest Dr. Joyce's use of the term "Anglo-Irish dialect" as a general description of the English spoken in Ireland. But doubtless the representative scholars of the Irish-speaking provinces would hold that each of them has impressed a dialect of its own upon the English spoken within its borders.

Then the Anglo-Irish of much of County Wexford was undoubtedly of West Saxon origin, and we imagine that Sir John Byers has something to say for the existence of more than one Scoto-Irish dialect in Ulster, as doubtless would Mr. Henry Hart and Mr. W. J. Craig, the Shakespearean scholars, had they lived to produce their important glossary of North of Ireland words.

The curious resemblance of many English proverbs, folk-sayings, and primitive forms of expression to Anglo-Irish examples drawn from the Gaelic raises the interesting questions whether some of these may not date back to days when British-Celtic must have considerably affected Anglo-Saxon speech. These proverbs, sayings, and idioms may, indeed, go back to a time when a Celtic speech,

cognate to the Irish, pervaded England.   That it died hard
in this country is now beginning to be conceded. For, quite
apart from the obvious influence of the Cumbrian, Cambrian,
and Cornish Celtic dialects upon the English North-Western,
Border, and South-Western counties, it is now held by some
that British speech lingered on in the North York moors
till after the Norman Conquest, whilst so far East as Lincolnshire we find in the shepherds' tallies traces of a Celtic
language.

We should like to have followed Dr. Joyce through the
chapters in which he illustrates the *ingenium perfervidum
Scotorum* by such comparisons as " My stomach is as dry
as a lime-burner's wig," and such proverbs as " If you give
away an old coat, don't cut off the buttons " ; or dwell upon
his disquisition on the Irish methods of " dodging a curse,"
as exemplified in the well-known expression, " The dear
knows," or more correctly, " The deer knows " (*Thauss ag
fee*), by which *Thauss ag Dhee* (God knows) is avoided ; or
quote some of the delicious anecdotes with which his pages
abound.   But space forbids, and we conclude by warmly
recommending his book to all would-be writers and tellers
of Irish stories as by far the most authoritative guide to the
English spoken in Ireland that has yet appeared.

JAMES CLARENCE MANGAN

THE growing cult of James Mangan, or James Clarence Mangan, as he renamed himself, who died sixty-seven years ago in Dublin, has been recently marked not only by a sympathetic " Study " of Mangan by Louise Imogene Guiney, the American poetess, prefacing an admirable selection from his poems, but also by Mr. D. J. O'Donoghue's complete edition of his poems and very detailed biography. The reasons for the slow recognition he has received in this country are not far to seek. He wrote in Ireland, and entirely for Irish periodicals. His poems were never collected during his lifetime, and ill-collected at his death. Again, while he was regarded as a writer of genius by the few Dublin contemporaries to whom his authorship of poems, very variously subscribed, was familiar, even the Irish public, owing to his natural modesty and his solitary habits, knew practically nothing of him.

But his work was too good to remain buried in old magazines ; indeed, the best of it is, by its rich colouring and weird melody, even more calculated to delight our times than his own.

Mangan did not find life worth living. " You shall tramp the earth in vain for a more pitiable object than a man of genius with nothing to back it," he himself writes, doubtless thinking of his own case. For the possession of extraordinary gifts amid such wretched surroundings as he had to face called for a stubborn heroism of which his gentle, sensitive nature was incapable, and he went down, though not without a struggle, leaving us a legacy of passionate, poetic melancholy, here and there, however, shot through by gleams of wit and humour which mark him for a true Irishman, and of which the following is a fair example :

A FAST KEEPER

My friend, Tom Bentley, borrowed from me lately
  A score of yellow shiners. Subsequently
  I met the cove, and dunned him rather gently ;
Immediately he stood extremely stately,
And swore, "'pon honour," that he " wondered greatly."
  We parted coolly. Well (exclaimed I ment'lly),
  I calculate this isn't acting straightly ;
You're what slangwhangers call a scamp, Tom Bentley.

In sooth, I thought his impudence prodigious ;
  And so I told Jack Spratt a few days after ;
  But Jack burst into such a fit of laughter.
" Fact is " (said he), " poor Tom has turned religious."
  I stared, and asked him what it was he meant.
  " Why, don't you see," quoth Jack, " *he keeps the Lent* ? "

The eldest son of a Dublin grocer, James Mangan was born, in the year 1802, into the same circumstances under which Thomas Moore had seen the light in the very same locality four-and-twenty years before.

Like Moore, moreover, he was destined to write Irish national lyrics of great beauty and Oriental poems of a very striking character, though in each instance the quality of Mangan's verse differs absolutely from Moore's.   One more parallel.   He possessed a vein of whimsicality as delicate as Moore's, which, had he worked it judiciously, would have given him as high a reputation as a poetical satirist.

But here all likeness between the two poets ceases. Moore had a happy home in childhood, Mangan a most unhappy one.   Though crediting his father with some fine traits of character, Mangan writes that, unlike Moore's, " he never exhibited the qualities of guardian towards his children," whom he treated habitually as a huntsman would treat refractory hounds.   It was his boast, uttered in pure glee of heart, "that we would run into a mousehole to shun him." But with "this rigorous conception of the awe and respect due to him as head of the family," as Mr. O'Donoghue puts it, he combined a wrong-headed generosity and credulity which gradually dissipated his respectable fortune in foolish loans and silly speculations, and in the end reduced him to absolute ruin. Thus it came about that at the age of fifteen, when James Mangan's great promise as a schoolboy should have been inducing his father to give him those continued educational advantages which lifted young Moore to honour and affluence, Mangan was helping to support his broken-down parents by monotonous drudgery at a scrivener's desk, in rude and unsympathetic company.

For his mother's sake he went through with the un-palatable duty. But he deeply resented his father's action in the matter. Indeed, the very recollection of it in after-years threw him into a paroxysm of self-pity. Yet it must be confessed that when in this condition Mangan had a way of making his strong imagination take the place of his weak memory, or of describing things not as they happened, but as they should have happened in his morbid opinion. He therefore exaggerates his hours of work and the chaff of his fellow-clerks, in what Mr. O'Donoghue proves was a highly respectable office, into an appalling record of white slavery amongst a herd of obscene savages.

Is Mangan hysterically playing upon our feelings of pity and his own sense of self-importance? Or is he dealing with matters of fact on the non-moral, if artistic, principle which he thus enunciates when treating of matters of opinion in a sketch of Dr. Petrie, the famous Irish archæologist?—

I take a few facts, not caring to be overwhelmed by too many proofs that they are facts; with them I mix up a dish of the marvellous—perhaps an old wife's tale—perhaps a half-remembered dream or mesmeric experience of my own—and the business is done. My conclusion is reached and shelved, and must not thenceforward be

disturbed. I would as soon think at any time afterwards of questioning
its truth as of doubting the veritable existence of the Barber's five
brothers in *The Arabian Nights* or the power of Keyn Alasnam, King
of the Genii.   There it is, and an opponent may battle with me
anent it, if he pleases.   I manage to hold my ground by the help ot
digressions and analogies.

Till his eight-and-twentieth year Mangan did clerical
work by day, and studied and rambled and rhapsodised
alone by night, building up his education in desultory
fashion on the good foundation of Latin and modern
languages laid for him during his school-days by Father
Graham, a very learned scholar of the best continental
training.

He read much English literature, and enjoyed declaim-
ing aloud from Shakespeare and Byron ; but the dreamy
philosophy and romance of the German poets attracted him
most, and he threw himself deeply into their study.   He
was also an eager reader of mediæval works of magic and
mystery.   And so, a slender, picturesque figure, with deep
blue eyes, golden hair, and fine but strangely pallid features,
he haunted the bookshops and bookstalls, turning over the
pages of old black-letter, in search of the mystical and
marvellous.

He looked—he could not help looking—a character
and having discovered the fact, he apparently amused himself by playing the part.

In 1818—that is to say, when he was sixteen years of
age—Mangan's verse began to appear in the poets' corners
of the Dublin and Belfast almanacks, in the shape of
charades, acrostics, and rebuses, at that time greatly in
fashion ; and till 1826 he was a frequent and popular
contributor to these annuals.

Under countless pseudonyms he thus indulged his love
of mystery and enigma, and gratified his taste for literary
sleight of art by outrhyming all his rivals in original metres
of the most complicated kind, as Mr. O'Donoghue points

out. The faculty for alliteration and rhyme, for pause and cadence thus developed, on the whole affected his after-work for good; though we must also attribute to the almanack influence, as suggested by Mr. O'Donoghue, the forced double rhymes and the forced gaiety that occasionally vitiate it.

After a twelvemonth of deep religious depression, from which his spiritual advisers rescued him by judiciously prescribing his resort to "cheerful and gay society," Mangan, who had been reading much but writing little, became a leading poetical contributor to *The Comet*, a very cleverly but bitterly written "anti-tithe" weekly.

The conductors of *The Comet* were Philistines, and had little sympathy with Mangan's higher flights ; though he had the courage to press upon them poems of such promise as "The Dying Enthusiast" and "Life is the Desert and the Solitude," and so specimens of his whimsical prose and verse figure most frequently in that journal.

John Sheehan, its editor, and his cronies treated Mangan to a full share of the coarse chaff which they mistook for wit, ridiculing him for his peculiarities, voting him "a spoon" because he did not or could not retort in the same vein, and finally insulting him into a severance of his connection with *The Comet*, before its final collapse under a Government prosecution.

But the establishment of *The Dublin Penny Journal* gave him a better literary connection, which he continued to extend until he had established himself as a regular contributor to *The Dublin University Magazine*, then under Charles Lever's editorship.

The vogue for German literature, largely attributable to Carlyle's influence, made good translations from the German poets peculiarly acceptable about this time ; and this special need was Mangan's opportunity as a sympathetic student of these authors, and now a considerable master of verse. He availed himself of it fully, and at first quite seriously. He

evidently took infinite pains to reproduce the spirit of each
original with which he dealt.   In the rare instances where
the character of the original lent itself to almost literal
translation into English he so rendered it with superlative
skill, if anything *out Schillering* Schiller in some of his
versions of that poet, as Coleridge may be said to have done
in part of his *Wallenstein.*   But as a rule he was an
adapter rather than a translator, " treating his victims on the
same principle, though without the same justification, as
Burns treats the floating Scotch ballads," as Miss Guiney
justly points out.   For " the children of conventional art "
suffer more from Mangan's re-dressing than the Scotch
children of Nature do from Burns's genius for readjusting
and beautifying.   Take the following from the German of
Otto Runge as an instance of Mangan's happiest manner as
a translator :

HOLINESS TO THE LORD.

There blooms a beautiful Flower, it blooms in a far-off land ;
Its life has a mystic meaning for few to understand ;
Its leaves illumine the valley, its odour scents the wood ;
And if evil men come near it, they grow for the moment good.

When the winds are tranced in slumber, the rays of this luminous
  Flower
Shed glory more than earthly o'er lake and hill and bower ;
The hut, the hall, the palace, yea, earth's forsakenest sod,
Shine out in the wondrous lustre that fills the heaven of God.

Three Kings came once to a hostel wherein lay the Flower so rare,
A star shone over its roof, and they knelt adoring there ;
Whenever thou seest a damsel whose young eyes dazzle and win,
O, pray that her heart may cherish this Flower of Flowers within !

The original German poem is too vague to be really
effective ; yet, while scarcely altering a word in his translation,
Mangan has by a suggestive title and an almost imper-
ceptible touch here and there given it a perfect meaning.
Surely, too, Mr. O'Donoghue is right in saying that Mangan's
version of Eichendorff's miller's daughter is much superior
to the better known English translation of it.

A tendency thus to edit and improve his originals, notably in the case of minor German poets, gradually grew upon him. Having become an acute critic of their weaknesses, and having readers to cater for who would have been intolerant of their occasional lapses into dulness and sentimentality, Mangan now began to embroider them with a free hand. This is his droll comment on the situation :

> Most to be commiserated of all is his (the German poet's) English translator, who, having the severest judges in Europe for his critics, is often reduced to the necessity of either making himself ridiculous by his desperate fidelity, or criminal by his departures from it, however marvellously these may improve the original. The entire weight of the blame rests upon the authors from whom we versify. We cannot, like the experimentalist in "Gulliver," undertake to extract a greater number of sunbeams from a cucumber than it is in the habit of yielding. . . . It is our business to cast a veil over the German poet's blemishes, and bring forward nothing but his excellences, or what we presume to be such.

Of course this is sheer paradox, but it veiled this very pertinent position : Translations from the German are my bread-and-butter. If I cannot make them interesting, I must do without bread-and-butter. I can only make them interesting by improving them or improving them away. This process sustains and amuses me, so I shall continue it.

Of the German poet in general he remarks : " He begins in a tone of thunder, as if he would bring heaven and earth into collision, but while you are waiting to see what will come of it, he calls for his pipe, and you thenceforth lose him in the fog." And Ludwig Tieck, " man-milliner to the Muses," is thus delicately touched off in particular : " He simpers and whimpers, and yet one cannot tell whether he would be thought glad or sad. He plays the poetical coquette between Fortune and Misfortune. . . . He is knocked down by a bulrush every half-minute in the day, and reverently kisses the face of his Fatherland fourteen hundred and forty times in twelve hours."

Thus he improved and improved German minor poets as his stock for translation deteriorated, until he improved them almost entirely away, and finally began to publish, as poems from the German of " Dreschler " and " Selber," and other non-existent authors, lyrics of his own, more or less influenced by his German studies.

This practice he carried on with even greater effrontery when he began to put forth so-called translations of Oriental poetry. Indeed, it seems to puzzle Mangan's researchful biographer, Mr. O'Donoghue, where his *Literæ Orientales* are original and where reflected from an Eastern source, or refracted through a German medium. Mangan slily attributes this explanation of his own altruistic attitude on the whole question to Edward Walsh :

My poor friend Clarence has perpetrated a great number of literary sins, which, taken together, would appear " the antithesis of plagiarism." It is a strange fault, no doubt, and one that I cannot understand, that Mangan should entertain a deep diffidence of his own incapacity to amuse or attract others to anything emanating from himself. . . . People have called him a singular man, but he is rather a plural one—a Proteus. . . . He has been much addicted to the practice of fathering upon other writers the offspring of his own brain. . . . I cannot commend it. A man may have a right to offer his property to others, but nothing can justify his forcing it upon them.

When remonstrated with by Dr. Anster for thus depriving himself of the credit of such fine original work as was contained in a sham translation of Hafiz, he replied, " Any one could see that it was only Half-his."

But whatever their origin, there is no doubt of the rare poetical quality of much of Mangan's so-called Eastern poems. Let the following serve for an example :

THE KARAMANIAN EXILE.

I see thee ever in my dreams,
Karaman !
Thy hundred hills, thy thousand streams,
Karaman, O Karaman !

As when thy gold-bright morning gleams,
As when the deepening sunset seams
With lines of light thy hills and streams,
Karaman !
So thou loomest on my dreams,
Karaman !
On all my dreams, my homesick dreams,
Karaman, O Karaman !

The hot bright plains, the sun, the skies,
Karaman,
Seem death-black marble in mine eyes,
Karaman, O Karaman !
I turn from summer's blooms and dyes,
Yet in my dreams thou dost arise
In welcome glory to mine eyes,
Karaman !
In thee my life of life yet lies,
Karaman !
Thou still art holy in mine eyes,
Karaman, O Karaman !

Mangan had meanwhile got fresh employment as a clerk, first in various Dublin attorneys' offices, and then under the Irish Ordnance Survey ; but when that department was for the time being closed, he practically supported himself by his pen.   In this latter office, like Charles Lamb, in whose " dry drollery " he took a congenial delight, he was a late-comer if not an early-goer, varying in his moods between long spells of dejected silence and brief outbursts of what Mitchell well describes as " fictitious jollity."   For although then more comfortably off than he had ever been, and in the midst of considerate friends, his will was becoming gradually weakened by some form of stimulant, to which he declares his wretched health and slavish work had first driven him.   Was this stimulant opium, or " red rum," or both ?

Mr. O'Donoghue maintains that he had shaken off the habit of opium-eating, contracted when he was at the scrivener's office, only to fall a victim to drink.

Dr. Sigerson and other medical experts declare that the evidence derived from his handwriting, which remained quite steady until the last, proves him never to have become an actual drunkard. And Miss Guiney holds that "this singular misconception is due to his own denial of his real folly," opium-eating, of which "secretiveness is the sign-manual," and the indulgence in which would account for the unmistakable alabaster shine upon his features, his fixed eyes, his incoherent life, and, above all, his strangely coloured and visionary poems, and such dreams as he here describes : " The Gorgon's head, the triple-faced hell-dog, the handwriting on Belshazzar's palace wall, the fire globe that turned below the feet of Pascal, are all bagatelles beside the phantasmagoria which evermore haunt my brain and blast my eyes."

Some of his most characteristically ecstatic poems were written at the very close of his career, which would indicate that opium, not alcohol, was still his master, in spite of Father Meehan's evidence.

Take this passage from *A Vision of Connaught in the Thirteenth Century*, and compare it with Coleridge's *Kubla Khan*, and the internal evidence in favour of a still prevailing opium influence will be hard to gainsay :

> Then saw I thrones,
> And circling fires,
> And a dome rose near me, as by a spell,
> Whence flowed the tones
> Of silver lyres,
> And many voices in wreathèd swell ;
> And their thrilling chime
> Fell on my ears
> As the heavenly hymn of an angel-band ;
> " It is now the time,
> These be the years,
> Of Cuhal Mor of the Wine-red Hand ! "

It has been suggested that disappointment in love, as much as his ill-health and unhappy youth, turned Mangan into an opium-eater.   The evidence, however, goes strongly against this theory.   He fell into a splenetic mood after Miss Margaret Stacpoole discouraged his attentions, and railed at her as " Caroline."   But he got over his resentment, and resumed acquaintance with her as a friend, as Sir Charles Gavan Duffy distinctly proves, and gave other unmistakable symptoms that the wound had never been a deep one.   " We must remember, moreover," with Miss Guiney, " that a poet's despair cannot gracefully charge itself to dearth of beef, unpleasant kinsfolk, and headaches out of a morphine phial.   Hence woman and the love of woman come in as the *causa rerum*, even in a Mangan."

This is his portrait at the time, touched in from several contemporary sources :

Of middle height, he is slightly stooped and attenuated as one of Memling's monks. . . . His hair is white as new-fallen snow, which gives him the appearance of age before he is old.   His eye is inexpressibly deep and beautiful, his forehead unwrinkled and white. Pressed closely over his brows is a hat with such a quaint-shaped crown, such a high, wide-boated leaf as has rarely been seen off the stage ; his little coat, tightly buttoned, is covered with a shabby cloak that once has been blue, the tightest to the form that can be imagined.   He moves seemingly with pain—his last hour is not far off.   He speaks ! You cannot choose but listen to his low, touching voice.   That man, so weak, so miserable, whom you meet alone in life, seeking companionship in darkness, is James Clarence Mangan !

Let us follow his failing life to its unhappy close.   That he had struggled hard to resist intemperance, whatever its mastering form may have been, is clear.   Ever and again he fought off his temptation, flying from it to the protection of such good friends as Father Meehan—from whom he took the pledge at last ; but, alas ! only to break it again.

But though falling more repeatedly in these latter days, he worked as hard, and indeed with a higher purpose, in the lucid intervals that were left him.

During the last few years he had come under the spell of the Young Irelanders, and had contributed fine rhetorical verse and several noble laments to the *Nation*, though he had never personally identified himself with its political views. But he had been stirred to the expression of strong patriotic feeling, and this culminates in the broken man's pathetic offer of his open services to John Mitchell when, on the eve of his revolutionary movement, he seceded from the *Nation* and founded the *United Irishman*. Mitchell generously put aside, but never forgot, this offer.

Patriotic and devotional verse and a certain amount of rough-and-ready translation from the Irish, for the supply of the very necessaries of life, occupied Mangan's closing days.

The Irish Famine, whose horrors are reflected in his *New Year's Lay*, had profoundly affected his imagination. It was followed by the cholera, and by this, in the course of one of his numerous disappearances from all knowledge of his friends, Mangan was stricken. He recovered, and was too soon allowed to leave one of the temporary cholera-sheds at Kilmainham to which he had been removed; for collapse followed, and he was finally carried from a wretched cellar in Bride Street to the Meath Hospital, where he died seven days after admission.

His true friend, Father Meehan, thus describes the end :— ' On taking a chair at his bedside the poor fellow playfully said : ' I feel that I am going; I know that I must go, " unhousel'd " and " unaneal'd," but you must not let me go "unshriven" and "unanointed."'" "Poor fellow!" writes the same good priest elsewhere, " he did occasionally take what he ought not to have taken ; but be his faults what they may have been, he was a pure man, never lowering himself to ordinary debaucheries or sensuality of any sort. He prayed and heard mass almost every day, and occasionally knelt at the altar-rail."

In this connection some of Mangan's devotional verse may fitly be quoted from Mr. O'Donoghue's volume.

I raise my thoughts in prayer to God,
 I look for help to Him alone
  Who shared our lot—
The Mighty One of Heaven, who trod
 Life's path as Man, though earth—His own—
  Received Him not !

I turn to Him, and ask for naught
 Save knowledge of His heavenly will,
  Whate'er it be ;
I seek no doubtful blessings, fraught
 With present good, but final ill
  And agony :

Come Death or Life, come Woe or Weal,
 Whate'er my God elects to send
  I here embrace ;
Blest while, though tortured on the wheel,
 I forfeit not, or worse, mis-spend
  His holy Grace.

The fount of Happiness—the source of Glory—
Eternity is in Thy hands and Power—
Oh ! from that sphere unrecognised by our
 Slow souls, look down upon a world which, hoary
In evil and in error though it be,
 Retains even yet some trace of that primeval
 Beauty that bloomed upon its brow ere Evil
And Error wiled it from Thy Love and Thee !
Look down, and if, while human brows are brightening
 In godless triumph, angel eyes be weeping,
Publish Thy will in syllables of Lightning
 And sentences of Thunder to the Sleeping !
Look down, and renovate the waning name
 Of Goodness, and relume the waning light
Of Truth and purity !—that all may aim
 At one imperishable crown—the bright
Guerdon which they, who by untired and holy
 Exertion overcome the earth, inherit—
The Self-denying, the Peaceable, the Lowly,
 The truly Merciful, the Poor in Spirit.

When his body lay in the mortuary Dr. William Stokes
had a cast taken of his face, and Frederick, afterwards Sir

Frederick Burton, made the remarkable sketch of Mangan after death which now hangs in the Irish National Portrait Gallery.

I had a conversation with Sir Frederick about this at the Athenæum Club, when he told me that he had once seen Mangan in life in the company of " dear old Petrie." Mangan left the room, and Burton, struck by his face, asked " Who was that ? " " Mangan, the Poet," replied Petrie. He had at that time, according to Burton, a profusion of reddish hair tangled over his forehead, and his nose though good was blunt. The corpse had luxuriant grizzled hair and a noble forehead ; the nose was a fine aquiline. " For the *rigor mortis*," explained Burton, " often draws the skin over the cartilage and produces an effect in death that did not exist in life." Thus poor Mangan was elusive to the last, and we do not possess his true portrait after all.

What are the poetical influences under which Mangan fell ?   What are his poetical methods ?   What is his distinctive poetical note ?   And how far is its predominance likely to ensure him poetic immortality ?

Apart from the German poets, he is in his early and middle period most reminiscent of Byron ; here and there we find in him a Shakespearean touch ; and occasional echoes of Coleridge, Keats, Shelley, and Tennyson encounter us in his writings—notably Coleridge, whom Mangan further resembled in his wonderful faculty for brilliant monologue ; *testibus* Sir Charles Gavan Duffy and others.

Mangan, writes Mitchell, would sometimes remain in conversation of his own for an hour ; for though extremely silent, shy, and reserved habitually, yet, with those in whom he confided, he was much given to strange and desultory talk, which seemed like the soliloquy of a somnambulist.   His blue eyes would then dilate, and light up strangely the sepulchral pallor of his face.

" Of his manner and his conversation," writes O'Daly,

" it would be impossible to give a correct idea ; they may be best described by an extract from his favourite Schiller :

His dreams were of great objects,
He walked amidst us of a silent spirit,
Communing with himself ; yet I have known him
Transported on a sudden into utterance
Of strange conceptions ; kindling into splendour,
His soul revealed itself, and he spake so
That we looked round, perplexed, upon each other,
Not knowing whether it was craziness,
Or whether it were a god that spake in him."

It has been explained how by force of circumstances he became a translator, adapter, improver, and improver away of Continental, Oriental, and, we should add, Irish poetry. To disentangle from his so-called translations what is Mangan's would, no doubt, be a troublesome task in many instances, but it should be a highly interesting one to a linguistic man of letters. Add to this remarkable peculiarity of method another. Stress of circumstances—sudden journalistic exigencies, for example—led him to put forth verse in an unfinished form. He, however, kept a parental eye upon a poem he valued, and he reproduced it from time to time in periodical after periodical with continually improving finish, or recast it altogether. The most memorable example of this habit is his treatment of his greatest poem, *My Dark Rosaleen.*

This is based on an Irish ode by a minstrel of the O'Donnell clan, contemporary with Shakespeare, of which the literal English translation is given by Miss Guiney at length in her study of Mangan, and there contrasted with his successive versions of it. Mangan felt that he had not done the theme justice, and worked at it with true artistic fervour until he wrought it into his masterpiece; for, as Miss Guiney truly says, " between *My Dark Rosaleen* and the preceding lyrics made from *Roisin Dubh* by the same hand is a difference—all the difference there can be between the thing cunningly wrought and the thing divinely inspired." But the great body of his verse Mangan did not treat in this way. As a consequence there is a very great variety of quality in its very considerable quantity.

When did Mangan acquire a distinctive poetical note, and what was its peculiar character? Before the year 1840 he had begun to experiment with " the refrain," as he had before experimented in rhythms that were absolutely novel. Some of the best of these refrains and rhythms, which contain a mystical music all their own, occur in his so-called translations. Edgar Allan Poe, a fellow-Celt, is generally credited, in the *Raven*, with that modern adaptation of the refrain which consists of repeating it with musical variations. Indeed, Poe himself states that this use of the refrain in that poem was his first experiment of the kind. Now the *Raven* was not published till 1845, whereas from 1839 onward Mangan, as Miss Guiney points out, "bestowed upon almost everything he wrote the curious involved diction in question." For example, the *Winniger Winehouse*, slightly improved from Hoffman of Fallersleben, has the refrain :

> As thinking but doubles men's troubles,
> 'Tis shirked in the emerald parlour ;
> Tho' banks be broken and war lour,
> We've eyes alone for such bubbles
> As wink on our cups in the Winehouse,
> Our golden cups in the Winehouse
> (As poets would feign), but 'tis glasses we drain
> In the sanded Winniger Winehouse.

This art-effect runs through Mangan's so-called Oriental poems, and its use in the *Karamanian Exile* so caught the fancy of the author of *Maryland, my Maryland!* as to have inspired that famous lyric.

Lastly, to what extent is Mangan's poetry likely to live ? It obviously cannot endure in the bulk, however musical and individual its character, owing to its want of careful technique, its everlasting dreariness of subject, and its tendency to repetition run mad, which spoils the effect of even such a delightful piece of satire as *The Woman of Three Cows*. A few of his Irish poems, including *My Dark Rosaleen*, *The Lament for Banba*, the *Vision of Connaught in the Thirteenth Century*, his version of O'Hussey s Ode to the Maguire, and his desolate *Siberia* cannot perish from Anglo-Irish literature. Some of his German translations and so-called translations from the Turkish, such as *Gone in the Wind*, the *Karamanian Exile*, and the *Howling Song of Al Mohara*, will survive, through their perfection of colour, form and music ; and the interest attached to the author of these poems should, for their subjective interest, preserve *The One Mystery* and *The Nameless One*.

For these and other poems of charming, though not of consummate, quality we refer our readers to Miss Guiney's selection from Mangan, certainly the best that has yet been got together, though perhaps hardly complete without a few additional poems recently hunted up by the indefatigable Mr. O'Donoghue from odd corners of old Irish periodicals. With one of these—apparently Mangan's epitome of his own unhappy life—this essay may fitly conclude :

REST ONLY IN THE GRAVE.

I rode till I reached the House of Wealth :
'Twas filled with Riot and blighted health.

I rode till I reached the House of Love :
'Twas vocal with sighs beneath and above !

I rode till I reached the House of Sin :
There were shrieks and curses without and within.

I rode till I reached the House of Toil :
Its inmates had nothing to bake and boil.

I rode in search of the House of Content,
But never could reach it, far as I went.

The House of Quiet, for strong and weak,
And Poor and Rich, I have still to seek.

That House is narrow and dark and small,
But the only Peaceful House of all.

SIR SAMUEL FERGUSON

SIR SAMUEL FERGUSON was unquestionably the Irish poet of
the past century who has most powerfully influenced the
literary history of his country.   It was in his writings that
was decisively begun the great work of restoring to Ireland
the spiritual treasure it had sacrificed in losing the Gaelic
tongue.   He was, however, no mere antiquarian.   He was
also a scholar, and a patriot in the highest sense of the
word.   He had friends in all parties, for he was in no sense
a political partisan.   Indeed, though with strong Irish
National feeling—of which he gave evidence in some of his
earlier ballads, and which came to the front in his successful
defence of Richard Dalton Williams, the Young Ireland
poet, when tried for treason-felony—he felt that the
highest duty he owed his country was that of a poet and
prose writer above party.   But in his poetic capacity, as
pointed out by Mr. W. B. Yeats, "he was wiser than Young
Ireland in the choice of his models; for while drawing not
less than they from purely Irish sources, he turned to the
great poets of the world for his style," and notably to
Homer : and the result is that, as Roden Noel puts it,
" *Congal* and his shorter Irish heroic poems combine in a
striking manner the vague, undefined shadowy grandeur,
the supernatural glamour of northern romance, with the
self-restraint, distinct symmetrical outline, ordered proportion
and organic construction of the Greek classic."   More than
this, as his brother poet and friend, Aubrey de Vere, urges,
"its qualities are those characteristic of the noble, not the
ignoble poetry—viz., passion, imagination, vigour, an epic
largeness of conception, wide human sympathies, vivid and

truthful description—while with them it unites none of the vulgar stimulants for exhausted or morbid poetic appetite, whether the epicurean seasoning, the sceptical, or the revolutionary."

Ferguson differs from those who regard the realm of poetry as another world detachable from this—a life mystical, non-human, non-moral—the life, if you will, of fairy, demon, or demi-god. Indeed, he was in no danger of falling into this illusion. He was absolutely human and practical; broad and sympathetic-minded both. Yet for entire success as a poet in his particular day he had to struggle against difficulties constitutional, accidental, and of his own seeking. His very versatility rendered difficult that entire devotion of his energies to his art, of which Tennyson is the great modern example. He could not spare the time, even had he possessed the taste, for that fastidious word-for-word finish in verse to which the late Laureate accustomed the critics, and through them the educated public, which undoubtedly, for the time being, militated against the success of Ferguson's poetry.

Then he was deliberately facing the fact that the Irish themes he had set his heart upon had no public behind them. A generation before, they would have had the support of a cultured and unprovincialised Irish upper class; a generation later they would have claimed attention, in Ferguson's hands, as the noblest outcome of the Irish literary revival. He was therefore both before and after his time, and realised his position to the full. Indeed, when I once spoke to him with regret of the neglect of all but Irish political literature, he acknowledged it, but with the quiet expression of his confidence that " his time would come." Edward Dowden explains the fact that *Congal* had not hit the popular taste in the following passage of a letter to Sir Samuel :

A poem with epic breadth and thews is not likely to be popular now. A diseased and over-sensitive nerve is a qualification for the writing of

poetry at present, much more than a thoughtful brain or strength of
muscle. Some little bit of novel sensibility, a delight in such colours
as French milliners send over for ladies' bonnets, or the nosing of
certain curious odours, is enough to make the fortune of a small poet.
What seems to me most noteworthy in your poems is the union of
culture with simplicity and strength. Their refinement is large and
strong, not curious and diseased; and they have spaces and movements which give one a feeling like the sea or the air on a headland. I
had not meant to say anything of *Congal*, but somehow this came and
said itself.

Nothing could be more truly appreciative of Ferguson's
work than this. That fine saying, " Your poems have spaces
and movements which give one a feeling like the sea or the
air on a headland," may be here illustrated by one of the
greatest passages in *Congal;* indeed, it in all probability
suggested the criticism to Dr. Dowden. It may be quoted,
moreover, as a telling example of how Ferguson's careless
or rough treatment of detail is carried off by the largeness
of his conception and movement :

He looking landward from the brow of some great sea-cape's head,
Bray or Ben Edar—sees beneath, in silent pageant grand,
Slow fields of sunshine spread o'er fields of rich, corn-bearing land,
Red glebe and meadow margin green commingling to the view
With yellow stubble, browning woods, and upland tracts of blue ;
Then, sated with the pomp of fields, turns seaward to the verge
Where, mingling with the murmuring wash made by the far-down
    surge,
Comes up the clangorous song of birds unseen, that, low beneath,
Poised off the rock, ply underfoot ; and, 'mid the blossoming heath,
And mint-sweet herb that loves the ledge rare-air'd, at ease reclined,
Surveys the wide pale-heaving floor crisped by a curling wind ;
With all its shifting, shadowy belts, and chasing scopes of green,
Sun-strown, foam-freckled, sail-embossed, and blackening squalls
    between,
And slant, cerulean-skirted showers that with a drowsy sound,
Heard inward, of ebullient waves, stalk all the horizon round ;
And, haply, being a citizen just 'scaped from some disease
That long has held him sick indoors, now, in the brine-fresh breeze,
Health-salted, bathes ; and says, the while he breathes reviving bliss,
" I am not good enough, O God, nor pure enough for this ! "

The ear educated to Tennyson's or Swinburne's verse would be jarred by the heavy aggregation of consonants here and there in the passage. But as a presentment of country, cliff, and ocean, it is alike so broad and delicate in colour and movement that it rises visibly before us, till the echo of the sea is in our ears, and we breathe and smell its keen savours. Then the human note with which it closes is inexpressibly touching.

It is not, however, implied that Ferguson is wanting in the musical ear or the appreciation of fine poetical crafts-manship, but rather suggested that, unlike Tennyson and other writers, he is not *sectus ad unguem* in everything he attempts, because he is not careful to be so. Moreover, like Wordsworth, he did not always write when his best mood was upon him. And hence like Wordsworth and, I may add, Browning, he will live in selections, though large selections, from his works, rather than in their entirety. Yet, *The Forging of the Anchor* is a remarkably finished achievement for a young man of one-and-twenty, and *The Fairy Thorn*, another early poem, is exquisite wizardry itself. True, it appears to have been conceived and executed with a rapidity which was inspiration, and is indeed one of Ferguson's gems without flaw.

Next come Ferguson's Translations from the Irish which arose from his study of his country's language along with O'Hagan, afterwards Lord Chancellor, and above all George Fox, a young Belfast man, of whom he writes in after life :

His discourse possessed a fascination equal to all that I have heard ascribed to that of Coleridge, and under his influence my poetic faculty, which had already shown itself in the ballad of Willy Gilliland, acquired strength for the production of *The Forging of the Anchor*, published in *Blackwood* in May 1832. We had formed a private class for the study of Irish. The early history of Ulster had already seized on my imagination, and the *Return of Claneboy*, a prose romance which I contributed about that time to *Blackwood*, may be regarded as the first indication of my ambition to raise the native elements of Irish History to a dignified level ; and this ambition, I think, may be taken as the key to almost all the literary work of my subsequent life.

George Fox probably died young. " He left Belfast to push his fortunes in British Guiana," writes Lady Ferguson in her memoirs of her husband, and no doubt succumbed to its unhealthy climate. His youthful friends heard no more of him. They spared no efforts, through a long period of years, to learn his fate.

When Ferguson, in 1864, published in his *Lays of the Western Gael* his *Versions from the Irish*, which had appeared first in the *Dublin University Magazine* of 1834 in the form of translations with a Commentary from Hardiman's Irish Minstrelsy, he would not include one of the best among them, as he considered George Fox entitled to share in the authorship of *The County Mayo*, and when almost fifty years had passed since his early friend had been heard of, and he, in 1880, published his Poems, the volume bore this brief and touching dedication—*Georgio, Amico, Condiscipulo, Instauratori.*

Ferguson's translations from the Irish differ from Miss Brooke's and Miss Balfour's versions and those of other translators preceding him, by their assimilation of Irish idioms and the Irish spirit into English verse without violence—indeed, with a happy judgment which lends a delightful effect to these lyrics. Edward Walsh has scarcely excelled Ferguson in this field; and Dr. Sigerson and Dr. Hyde, though they come much closer to the original metres, rarely go past him in poetical feeling and passion.

For the very character of the originals calls for simple treatment, and high polish would have spoilt Ferguson's verse translations from the Irish.

Ferguson was now casting round for nobler themes to work upon, whilst keeping his hand in at these translations from the Irish. Patriotic to the core, he was above all things eager to achieve something lofty in literature for

Ireland's sake—something that might help to lift her from the intellectual flats upon which she had fallen.

Moreover, another Belfast friend and mentor, Dr. Robert Gordon, was keeping him up to his highest poetical self by a series of memorable letters, extracts from which Lady Ferguson gives in her Biography of Sir Samuel, as thus :

"You rejoice me, I speak seriously, by saying you are 'doing.' To be and to do. O Ferguson, those little words contain the sum of all man's destiny. You are strong, and I would have you strike some note that will reverberate down the vista of time. Will you, Ferguson ?"

In the course of his delightful New Year's Epistle to Robert Gordon, M.D., dated 1st of January, 1845, Ferguson thus responds to his friends' appeal :

> For ilka day I'm growin' stranger
> To speak my mind in love or anger ;
> And, hech ! ere it be muckle langer,
> You'll see appearin'
> Some offerin's o' nae cauld haranguer,
> Put out for Erin.
>
> Lord, for ane day o' service done her !
> Lord, for ane hour's sunlight upon her !
> Here, Fortune, tak' warld's wealth and honour,
> You're no' my debtor,
> Let me but rive ae link asunder
> O' Erin's fetter !
>
> Let me but help to shape the sentence
> Will put the pith o' independence,
> O' self-respect in self-acquaintance,
> And manly pride
> Intil auld Eber-Scot's descendants—
> Take a' beside !
>
> Let me but help to get the truth
> Set fast in ilka brother's mouth,
> Whatever accents, north or south,
> His tongue may use,
> And there's ambition, riches, youth ;
> Tak' which you choose !

But before he had ripened for the full outcome of his

genius Ferguson anticipated it by one of the noblest laments in our language, *Thomas Davis: an Elegy*, 1845, a poignant expression of his grief at the death of his friend, the famous young National leader.

Sir Charles Gavan Duffy tells us that " Ferguson, who lay on a bed of sickness when Davis died, impatient that for the moment he could not declare it in public, asked me to come to him, that he might ease his heart by expressing in private his sense of what he had lost. He read me fragments of a poem written under these circumstances, the most Celtic in structure and spirit of all the elegies laid on the tomb of Davis. The last verse sounded like a prophecy ; it was, at any rate, a powerful incentive to take up our task anew."

This poem, which has not been as yet included in Ferguson's published works, and is in many respects especially typical of his genius, now follows at length. The modern Irish Celt has indeed inherited a wonderful gift for the elegy, as Moore's lines on the death of Sheridan, Dr. Sigerson's to the memory of Isaac Butt and Thomas Davis's own immortal lament for Owen Roe O'Neill abundantly demonstrate.

LAMENT FOR THOMAS DAVIS.

I walked through Ballinderry in the spring-time,
  When the bud was on the tree ;
And I said, in every fresh-ploughed field beholding
  The sowers striding free,
Scattering broadside forth the corn in golden plenty
  On the quick seed-clasping soil,
" Even such, this day, among the fresh-stirred hearts of Erin,
  Thomas Davis, is thy toil ! "

I sat by Ballyshannon in the summer,
  And saw the salmon leap ;
And I said, as I beheld the gallant creatures
  Spring glittering from the deep,
Through the spray, and through the prone heaps striving onward
  To the calm clear streams above,
" So seekest thou thy native founts of freedom, Thomas Davis,
  In thy brightness of strength and love ! "

I stood on Derrybawn in the autumn,
  And I heard the eagle call,
With a clangorous cry of wrath and lamentation
  That filled the wide mountain hall,
O'er the bare deserted place of his plundered eyrie ;
  And I said, as he screamed and soared,
" So callest thou, thou wrathful soaring Thomas Davis,
  For a nation's rights restored ! "

And, alas ! to think but now, and thou art lying,
  Dear Davis, dead at thy mother's knee ;
And I, no mother near, on my own sick-bed,
  That face on earth shall never see ;
I may lie and try to feel that I am dreaming,
  I may lie and try to say, " Thy will be done "—
But a hundred such as I will never comfort Erin
  For the loss of the noble son !

Young husbandman of Erin's fruitful seed-time,
  In the fresh track of danger's plough !
Who will walk the heavy, toilsome, perilous furrow
  Girt with freedom's seed-sheets now ?
Who will banish with the wholesome crop of knowledge
  The daunting weed and the bitter thorn,
Now that thou thyself art but a seed for hopeful planting
  Against the Resurrection morn ?

Young salmon of the flood-tide of freedom
  That swells round Erin's shore !
Thou wilt leap against their loud oppressive torrent
  Of bigotry and hate no more ;
Drawn downward by their prone material instinct,
  Let them thunder on their rocks and foam—
Thou hast leapt, aspiring soul, to founts beyond their raging,
  Where troubled waters never come !

But I grieve not, Eagle of the empty eyrie,
  That thy wrathful cry is still ;
And that the songs alone of peaceful mourners
  Are heard to-day on Erin's hill ;
Better far, if brothers' war be destined for us,
  (God avert that horrid day, I pray),
That ere our hands be stained with slaughter fratricidal
  Thy warm heart should be cold in clay.

But my trust is strong in God, Who made us brothers,
   That He will not suffer their right hands
Which thou hast joined in holier rites than wedlock
   To draw opposing brands.
Oh, many a tuneful tongue that thou mad'st vocal
   Would lie cold and silent then ;
And songless long once more, should often-widowed Erin
   Mourn the loss of her brave young men.

Oh, brave young men, my love, my pride, my promise,
   'Tis on you my hopes are set,
In manliness, in kindliness, in justice,
   To make Erin a nation yet ;
Self-respecting, self-relying, self-advancing,
   In union or in severance, free and strong—
And if God grant this, then, under God, to Thomas Davis
   Let the greater praise belong.

The Irish potato famine now intervened, and drove
Ferguson into the *sæva indignatio* of Juvenal at the Government mismanagement, which had multiplied its horrors a
hundredfold.

No one knew this better than himself, for he was
secretary to the Irish Council, whose wise advice, tendered
to the English Parliament, was rejected in favour of futile
experimental legislation in the way of relief-road making
and so forth.   Convinced that a Parliament after Grattan's
model would have saved the country, he became a Repealer
and one of the poets of Repeal.

   Deem not, O generous English hearts, who gave
   Your noble aid our sinking Isle to save,
   This breast, though heated in its Country's feud,
   Owns aught towards *you* but perfect gratitude.

   *   *   *   *   *

   But, frankly, while we thank you all who sent
   Your alms, so thank we not your Parliament,
   Who, what they gave, from treasures of our own
   Gave, if you call it giving, this half loan,
   Half gift from the recipients to themselves
   Of their own millions, be they tens or twelves ;

Our own as well as yours : our Irish brows
Had sweated for them ; though your Commons' House,
Forgetting your four hundred millions debt,
When first in partnership our nations met,
Against our twenty-four (you then two-fold
The poorer people), call them British Gold.
No ; for these drafts on our United Banks
We owe no gratitude, and give no thanks !
More than you'd give to us, if Dorsetshire
Or York a like assistance should require ;
Or than you gave us when, to compensate
Your slave-owners, you charged our common state
Twice the amount : no, but we rather give
Our curses, and will give them while we live,
To that pernicious blind conceit and pride,
Wherewith the aids we asked you misapplied.

*   *   *   *   *

Sure, for our wretched Country's various ills
We've got, a man would think, enough of bills—
Bills to make paupers, bills to feed them made ;
Bills to make sure that paupers' bills are paid ;
Bills in each phrase of economic slang ;
Bills to transport the men they dare not hang.
(I mean no want of courage physical,
'Tis Conscience doth make cowards of us all !)

Allowance must be made for the passionate bitterness of
this invective from the circumstances that Ferguson had
seen the Irish peasantry he loved dying of starvation before
his very eyes and because of the neglect of the British
Government of ordinary precautions for " more than a third
of the potato crop throughout the island was gone, in some
districts more than half, and at the same time the bulk of
the remaining supplies, cattle and corn, butter, beef and
pork, which would have fed all the inhabitants, continued
to be exported to England to pay the rent of farms which
would no longer yield the cultivators their ordinary food."

Ferguson, however, lived to turn this fine power of
literary invective against the successors of the Young Ireland poets and patriots with whom he had sympathised

when he found them descending from the high aspirations
and manly action of Davis and Duffy to what he
characterised as "a sordid social war of classes carried on
by the vilest methods."

In his satiric poems *The Curse of the Joyces* and
At the Polo Ground—an analysis in Browning's manner
of Carey's frame of mind before giving the fatal signal to
the assassins of Mr. Burke and Lord Frederick Cavendish
—and in his Dublin eclogue *In Carey's Footsteps*, he
exposes the cruelties of the boycotting system of political
agitation with unsparing severity.

In 1864 appeared Ferguson's *Lays of the Western
Gael*, a gratifying surprise even to many of his friends,
owing to the inclusion in it of fresh and finer work than
he had yet achieved. Their point of departure is thus
well described by Mr. A. M. Williams, the American
critic :

The *Lays of the Western Gael* are a series of ballads founded on
events in Celtic history, and derived from the Early Chronicles and
poems. They are original in form and substance, the ballad form and
measure being unknown to the early Celtic poets of Ireland ; but they
preserve in a wonderful degree the ancient spirit, and give a picture of
the ancient times with all the art of verity. They have a solemnity of
measure like the voice of one of the ancient bards chanting ot

> Old forgotten far-off things
> And battles long ago,

and they are clothed with the mists of a melancholy age. They
include such subjects as *The a Tin Quest*, the search of the bard for the
lost lay of the great cattle-raid of Queen Maeve of Connaught, and its
recovery, by invocation, from the voice of its dead author, who rises in
misty form above his grave ; *The Healing of Conall Carnach*, a story of
violated sanctuary and its punishment ; *The Welshman of Tirawley*, one
of the most spirited and original, and which has been pronounced by
Mr. Swinburne as amongst the finest of modern ballads, telling of a
cruel mulct inflicted upon the members of a Welsh Colony and its
vengeance ; and other incidents in early Irish history. In his poems,
rather than in Macpherson's *Ossian* or in the literal translations, will
the modern reader find the voice of the ancient Celtic bards speaking

to the intelligence of to-day in their own tones, without false change and dilution, or the confusion and dimness of an ancient language.

Of the longer lays thus far published, *The Tain Quest* found the greatest acceptance with his poetic compeers, and the most notable criticism of it was that of Thomas Aird, the fine Scottish poet, author of *The Devil's Dream on Mount Aksbeck*:

In all respects *The Tain Quest* is one of the most striking poems of our day. Specially do I admire the artistic skill with which you have doubled the interest of the Quest itself by introducing in the most natural and unencumbering way so many of the best points of the *Great Cattle Foray*, the subject-matter of the *Tain*. The shield has long been grand in poetry ; you have made it grander. The refusal of Fergus to stir to the force of private sympathy, but his instantaneous recognition of the patriotic necessity of song, is a just and noble conception

The power of the Bard over the rude men of Gort ; the filial piety of the sons of Sanchan, and their brotherly love ; that mysterious Vapour, and that terrible blast of entrance, and the closing malediction by the Maiden, are all very notable towards the consummation of effect. As for the kissing of the champions in the pauses of the fight, I know of nothing in the reaches of our human blood so marvellously striking and sweet ; you have now made it immortal in song. However admirably expressed, the last stanza is an error in art. Surely you spoil the grand close, and the whole piece, by appending your own personality of interference as a commentator on the malediction. Might I not further say (with a peculiar smile) you make the preordained fulfilment of Malison a sublime apology for Irish Grub Street ?

The sting in the tail of Aird's fine judgment is deserved, and it is curious to observe that Ferguson has been similarly unlucky in *The Welshmen of Tirawley* in this attempt to tag a comment on to the end of a tale which he has so nobly adorned. That magnificently savage lay should end with the anti-penultimate stanza.

This tendency to act at times as a commentator on his own work and to present it at others in a too ponderously Latinised form, as well as the careless, not to say bluff, disregard for verbal delicacies into which he now and again lapses, are the only proclivities to which exception can be taken in Ferguson's technique. For his method is uniformly manly, and his occasional periods of majestic inspiration sweep our minor critical objections before them, as the blast from his Mananan's mantle swept the chieftain and his hound into the valley like leaves before the wind.

We have taken Ferguson to our hearts as we take our best brother, loving his very ponderosities and carelessnesses as part and parcel of his greatness, as we love the kindred qualities in Samuel Johnson—for the sake of the man and the gentleman.

In 1872 appeared *Congal*, which Ferguson describes in a letter to Father Russell as an epic poem of greater length and higher literary pretension than his *Lays of the Western Gael*.

An epic requires a great subject, and he who writes it must have vision and manliness closely allied to his nature, else how can he realise the heroic ideal? These are Ferguson's pre-eminent qualities. He is manly. His heroes proclaim it in their every action, their every utterance; and his tender portrait of Lafinda could only have been drawn by a gallant gentleman. He has vision. The terrible shapes and Celtic superstitions—the Giant Walker, the Washer of the Ford—loom monstrously before us as he sings; and he marshals the contending hosts at Moyra with a magnificent realism to which we know no modern parallel.

His subject is a great old-world tale of love and hate, and ambition and jealousy, and craft and courage—a splendid story of the last heroic stand made by Celtic Paganism against the Irish Champions of the Cross.

But great though much of *Congal* undoubtedly is, Ferguson's genius was to break into finest flower at the last.

The volume of 1880 contains some striking verse of a

religious, philosophical and personal kind, including the searching *Two Voices*, the trenchant and yet more touching *Three Thoughts*, the noble lines entitled *The Morning's Hinges*, and the lofty *Hymn of the Fishermen*—a poem written after a surmounted danger of shipwreck. But in *Deirdre* and *Conary* he reaches his fullest height as a poet, and the best that has been said or could well be said about them comes from William Allingham and Aubrey de Vere— the two Irishmen of his time whose opinion should interest, if not influence, us most.

Allingham wrote on receipt of the volume: "Many thoughts of my own swarmed about the pages as I turned them, like bees in a lime-tree. In your style high culture is reconciled with simplicity, directness, and originality; and nothing can be happier than your enrichment of English speech with Irish forms without the least violence. All the Irish poems are very remarkable, but *Deirdre* I count the chief triumph. Its peculiar form of unity is perfectly managed, while in general effect it recalls nothing so much as a Greek play."

Mr. Aubrey de Vere and Mr. Yeats, and perhaps the larger proportion of the other leading Irish critics, prefer *Conary* to *Deirdre*.

"It would be difficult," writes De Vere, "to find, amid our recent literature, a poem which at once aims as high as *Conary* and as adequately fulfils its aim . . . Novel to English readers as is such a poetic theme, and embarrassing as are a few of the Gaelic names, the work belongs to the 'great' style of poetry—that style which is characterised by simplicity, breadth of effect, a careless strength full of movement, but with nothing of the merely sensational about it, and an entire absence of those unclassic tricks that belong to meaner verse. It has caught thoroughly that epic character so remarkable in those Bardic Legends which were transmitted orally through ages when Homer must have been a name unknown in Ireland."

To sum up : though at times over-scholarly and nodding
now and again—as all the great unconscious poets, from
Homer down, will occasionally nod, as opposed to the little
self-conscious ones who are never caught napping—Ferguson
is always human, always simple, always strong. Sense ever
goes before sound with him. He is no mere reed for
blowing music through. He takes you into no gorgeous
jungle of colour and scent, and stealing serpent and raven-
ing beast, where perspective is lost and will paralysed, and
passion riots unrestrained. No! What Mr. W. B. Yeats
finely wrote of him in 1886 is still true to-day :

" The author of these poems is the greatest poet Ireland
has produced, because the most central and most Celtic.
Whatever the future may bring forth in the way of a truly
great and national literature—and now that the race is so
large, so widely spread, and so conscious of its unity, the
years are ripe—will find its morning in these three volumes
of one who was made by the purifying flame of national
sentiment the one man of his time who wrote heroic
poetry—one who, among the somewhat sybaritic singers of
his day, was like some aged sea-king sitting among the
inland wheat and poppies—the savour of the sea about him
and its strength."

JOSEPH SHERIDAN LE FANU

WHEN in the year 1880 I wrote a memoir of Joseph
Sheridan Le Fanu, as a Preface to his *Purcell Papers*,
published by Bentley and Son, I was not aware that,
besides being the author of the Irish poems contained in
that collection of Irish stories and of the celebrated
Shamus O'Brien, Le Fanu had anonymously contributed
half-a-dozen other poems to the *Dublin University Magazine*
between the years 1863 and 1866 ; two of which, *The Legend
of the Glaive* and *Beatrice*, exhibit Le Fanu's genius in a
new and unexpected light. They show him to have been
capable of dramatic and lyrical creation on a distinctly
higher plane than he had hitherto reached, although the
forms in which the drama and the legend are cast are
clearly experimental and not always successful. The same
magnetic attributes of superhuman mystery, grim or ghastly
humour and diabolic horror which characterise the finest
of his prose fictions meet us again. But these qualities are
often conveyed with a finer touch, and at times with a
directness of suggestion that is overwhelming. Again, the
lurid terror of these narratives is happily relieved by inter-
ludes of such haunting beauty of colour and sound, that we
cannot but lament the lateness of this discovery of his
highest artistic self. Indeed, our literature can ill afford
to lose lyrical drama with such a stamp of appalling power
as is impressed on *Beatrice*, or old-world idylls so full of
Gaelic glamour as *The Legend of the Glaive*, and such a
terrible confession by a drunkard of how he had fallen
irrevocably into the toils of the Enchantress Drink.

Let this criticism be judged by the subjoined extracts:

CHORUS FROM "BEATRICE."

Sad night is o'er the city of the Isles
And o'er a palace that amid her glooming
With a radiant halo smiles,
While music from its windows booming
Floats the voice of masque and measure
Through distant domes and marble piles,
And hymns the jubilee of youth and pleasure.

Between the ripple dimly plashing,
And the dark roof looming high,
Lost in the funereal sky,
Like many-coloured jewels flashing,
Small lamps in loops and rosaries of fire,
Verdant and blood-red, trembling, turning—
Yellow and blue—in the deep water burning,
From dark till dawning
Illumine all the wide concave,
And plash and stain the marble and the wave

From balconies in air
Th' emblazoned silken awning
Flows like a lazy sail ;
And gondoliers down there,
And masks upon the stair,
Hear music swelling o'er them like a gale.
Italian grace and gaiety,
And silver-bearded policy,
Princes and soldiers, sage and great,
The craft and splendour of the State,
Proud dames and Adria's fair daughters,
The sirens of Venetian waters,
Beautiful as summer dreams
Dreamed in haunted forest glade,
By silvery streams in leafy gleams,
Floating through the shade.

The noble palace peopled was right meetly,
And in its wide saloons the dance went featly,
And high above the hum
Swelled the thunder and the hoot
Of theorbo and viol, of the hautboy and the flute,
And the roaring of the drum.

SCENE FROM "BEATRICE."

BEATRICE.

They lifted me down from the giddy plank
Into the boat that rose and sank ;
The eager sails that rattle and slap
With thundering flap,
At a turn of the tiller filled at last,
And stooped the mast.
As the wet rope raced through the mooring ring,
On the mad waves their boat was free ;
And like a wild bird on the wing,
With sudden dive and soaring swing,
Still bending with the breeze away,
Away she swept on the laughing sea
Among waves and romping sea and spray.

Away the dancing island goes,
The sleeping headland dipt and rose,
The billows, that wild creatures be
Of the hearty and wondrous sea,
In sport and power
Welcome the boat with snort and plash
And riotous dash,
And hail of foamy shower.
High, spring high,
Surge, in your roaring glee ;
Fly, foam, fly !
And whirling mist of the sea !

CHORUS FROM "BEATRICE."

Man upon his journey hies—
A chequered course and variable,
Walking through life as he is shown
By gleams through yawning darkness thrown—
By lights that fall from Paradise
And hues that cross from hell.

Can we read his words or ways ?
Whence he acts, or whereto thinks ?
A vapour changing as we gaze,
An utterance of the Sphinx.

Still the man our judgment baulks ;
Good is he ? or, is he evil ?
At his right an Angel walks,
At his left a Devil.

PART OF A SCENE FROM " BEATRICE.'

Who enters ? Lo !
Passing phantom-like the door,
A silent monk stands on the floor.
Is he anchorite or devil ?
High and gaunt this form of evil
Gliding noiselessly has sought her,
As a shadow on the water.
Marble-like beneath his cowl
Gleams the curve of his anguine scowl,
The broad cold eyes—that greenly stare
And ever seem to search and smile,
And find in all things something vile.

    *   *   *   *   *

She did not mean to greet him here ;
She rose as people rise in fear ;
He stood there in his garment sooty,
She stood gleaming in her glory,
Face to face, like Death and Beauty,
In a painted allegory.

FROM "THE LEGEND OF THE GLAIVE."

Through the woods of Morrua and over its root-knotted flooring
The hero speeds onward, alone, on his terrible message ;
When faint and far-off, like the gathering gallop of battle,
The hoofs of the hurricane louder and louder come leaping.
Dizzy lightnings split this way and that in the blind void above him ;
For a moment long passages reeling and wild with the tempest,
In the blue mass and dazzle of lightning, throb vivid and vanish ;
And white glare the wrinkles and knots of the oak-trees beside him,
While close overhead clap the quick mocking palms of the Storm-
    Fiend.

    *   *   *   *   *

The forest opens as he goes,
And smitten trees in groups and rows
Beneath the tempest's tune,
Stand in the mists of midnight drooping,
By moss-grown rocks fantastic stooping,
In the blue shadows of the yellow moon.

THE CROMLECH.

And in the moonlight, bleached as bones,
Uprose the monumental stones,
Meeting the hero suddenly
        With a blind stare
        Dull as despair.
The formless boulder that blocked the door
Like a robed monster, broad and hoar,
        He twice essayed to earth to throw
With quivering sinew, bursting vein,
        With grinding teeth and scowling brow.
From his dark forehead with the strain,
Beads start and drop like thunder-rain ;
And in the breathless tug and reek,
All his lithe body seems to creak.
        The mighty stone to earth is hurled,
Black gapes the violated door,
Through which he rushes, to rise no more
Into this fair, sad world.

THORGIL AND HIS GLAIVE.

Where high the vaults of midnight gape
In the black waste, a blacker shape—
And near against a distant dark,
He could the giant Norseman mark,
A black tarn's waters sitting by ;
Beneath a brazen, stormy sky,
That never moves but dead doth lie,
And on the rock could darkly see
The mighty glaive beside his knee.
The hero's front and upreared form
Loomed dim as headlands in a storm.
No more will flicker passion's meteors
O'er the dead shadow of his features,

Fixed in the apathy eternal
That lulls him in repose infernal.
The cornice of his knotted brows
A direful shadow downward throws
Upon his eyeballs, dull and stark,
Like white stones glimmering in the dark ;
And, carved in their forlorn despair,
His glooming features changeless wear
Gigantic sorrow and disdain,
The iron sneer of endless pain.
From the lips of the awful phantom woke
A voice ; and thus, by the tarn, it spoke :—

" Son of Malmorra, what canst thou gather here ? "
The spell was broke that struck him dumb,
And held his soul aghast and numb,
    With a wild throb,
      A laugh, and sob,
The frenzied courage came again
Of Cathair, the Prince of men.
With planted foot, with arm extended,
And his ferine gaze distended,
Back flowed the cataract of his hair
From the gleaming face of the great Cathair ;
And he shouted, lion-voiced,
Like one defying who rejoiced :—
" Thorgil, king of the wintry sea,
Of the nine-gapped sword and minstrel glee,
Of mountains dark and craggy valleys,
Of the golden cup and the hundred galleys,
Malmorra's son, myself, have sworn
To take thy sword or ne'er return ! "
The Norseman's phantom, black and dread,
Turned not, lifted not his head.
Mute, without anger or alarm
As shadow stretches, stretched his arm ;
Upon the hilt his hand he laid,
The metal dull one bell-note made—
One cold flash from the awakened blade
Flecked the waste sky with flying glare,
    Like northern lights
      That sport o' nights
Shuddering across the empty air.

High overhead, where died the light
Through the wide caverns of the night,
The imprisoned echoes, whispering first,
Afar in moaning thunders burst.
Mortal armour nought avails—
Shearing the air, the enchanted blade
Of Thorgil a strange music made ;
The brazen concave of the sky
Returns its shrilly sigh,
Above—around—along—
With the roaring shiver of a gong.
Black night around him floating, and booming of the sea
Have borne away the hero on the spirit-maelstrom free ;
The shadows round him deepen in his soft and dreamless
        flight—
    The pause of a new birth,
    A forgetting of the earth,
    Its action and its thinking,
    A mighty whirl and sinking,
A lapsing into Lethe, and the ocean caves of night.

A DRUNKARD'S ADDRESS TO A BOTTLE OF WHISKEY.

From what dripping cell, through what fairy glen,
Where 'mid old rocks and ruins the fox makes his den ;
Over what lonesome mountain,
        Acushla machree !
      Where gauger never has trod,
      Sweet as the flowery sod,
      Wild as the breath
      Of the breeze on the heath,
And sparklin' all o'er like the moon-lighted fountain,
      Are you come to me—
      Sorrowful me ?

      Dancing—inspirin'—
      My wild blood firin' ;
      Oh ! terrible glory—
      Oh ! beautiful siren—
      Come, tell the old story—
Come, light up my fancy, and open my heart.

Oh ! beautiful ruin—
My life—my undoin'—
Soft and fierce as a pantheress,
Dream of my longing, and wreck of my soul,
I never knew love till I loved you, enchantheress !

At first, when I knew you, 'twas only flirtation,
The touch of a lip and the flash of an eye ;
But 'tis different now—'tis desperation !
I worship before you,
I curse and adore you,
And without you I'd die.

Wirrasthrue !
I wish 'twas again
The happy time when
I cared little about you,
Could do well without you,
But would just laugh and view you ;
'Tis little I knew you !

Oh ! terrible darlin',
How have you sought me,
Enchanted, and caught me ?
See, now, where you've brought me—
To sleep by the road-side, and dress out in rags.
Think how you found me ;
Dreams come around me—
The dew of my childhood, and life's morning beam ;
Now I sleep by the road-side, a wretch all in rags.
My heart that sang merrily when I was young,
Swells up like a billow and bursts in despair ;
And the wreck of my hopes on sweet memory flung,
And cries on the air,
Are all that is left of the dream.

Wirrasthrue !
My father and mother,
The priest, and my brother—
Not a one has a good word for you.
But I can't part you, darling, their preachin's all vain ;
You'll burn in my heart till these thin pulses stop ;
And the wild cup of life in your fragrance I'll drain
To the last brilliant drop.

Then oblivion will cover
The shame that is over,
The brain that was mad, and the heart that was sore.
Then, beautiful witch,
I'll be found—in a ditch,
With your kiss on my cold lips, and never rise more.

Le Fanu, as Mr. T. W. Rolleston writes in *A Treasury of Irish Poetry*, edited by Dr. Stopford Brooke and himself, " was certainly one of the most remarkable of Irish writers.

In Uncle Silas, in his wonderful tales of the supernatural, such as *The Watcher*, and in a short and less known but most masterly story *The Room in the Dragon Volant*, he touched the springs of terror and suspense as perhaps no other writer of fiction in the language has been able to do. His fine scholarship, poetic sense, and strong yet delicate handling of language and of incident give these tales a place quite apart among works of sensational fiction. But perhaps the most interesting of all his novels is *The House by the Churchyard*, a wonderful mixture of sentimentalism, humour, tragedy and romance.

His *Legend of the Glaive* shows the weird and romantic touch which he had at command, and *The Address to the Bottle* has much of the almost savage energy which he showed more in certain scenes of *The House by the Churchyard* than anywhere else."

Le Fanu, as the readers of the *Purcell Papers*, and more recently of *Seventy Years of Irish Life* by his brother William, will know, showed unusual talent for verse as a boy of fifteen years of age, as witness these lines, in which, although the thought is evidently as secondhand as that pervading Tennyson's boyish lyrics, the medium of its expression is distinctly poetical.

There is an hour of sadness all have known,
That weighs upon the heart we scarce know why ;
We feel unfriended, cheerless and alone,
We ask no other pleasure but to sigh,
And muse on days of happiness gone by :

> *A painful, lonely pleasure* which imparts
> A calm regret, a deep serenity,
> That soothes the rankling of misfortune's darts,
> And kindly lends a solace even to broken hearts.

Young Le Fanu was naturally a student, and made good use of his father's excellent library. But though of a dreamy and evidently unmethodical disposition, he had his wits about him when they were wanted, as the following anecdote chronicled by his brother will show:

"One thing that much depressed the Dean was his habitually being late for prayers. One morning, breakfast was nearly over, and he had not appeared. My father, holding his watch in his hand, said in his severest tones, ' I ask you, Joseph, I ask you seriously, is this right?' ' No, sir,' said Joe, glancing at the watch, ' I'm sure it must be fast.' "

This was an instance of precocious wit further exemplified by the brilliant piece of doggerel sent as a valentine to a pretty Miss K—— a few years later, from which we may quote the following:

> Your frown or your smile make me Savage or Gay
> In action as well as in song;
> And if 'tis decreed I at length become Gray,
> Express but the word, and I'm Young.
> And if in the Church I should ever aspire
> With friars and abbots to cope,
> By a nod, if you please, you can make me a Prior,
> By a word you can render me Pope.
> If you'd eat, I'm a Crabbe; if you'd cut, I'm your Steele,
> As sharp as you'd get from the cutler;
> I'm your Cotton whene'er you're in want of a reel,
> And your livery carry, as Butler.

He had also an early eye for a humorous situation, for on another occasion an elderly woman, whom he had never seen before and never saw after, looked at him as if she recognised him.

WOMAN.—" O then, Masther Richard, is that yerself ? "

JOSEPH.—" Of course it is myself. Who else should I be ? "

WOMAN.—" Ah, then, Masther Richard, it's proud I am to see you. I hardly knew you at first, you're grown so much. And how is the mistress and all the family ? "

JOSEPH.—" All quite well, thank you. But why can't you ever come to see us ? "

WOMAN.—" Ah, Masther Richard, don't you know I daren't face the house since that affair of the spoons ? "

JOSEPH.—" Don't you know that is all forgotten and forgiven ? "

WOMAN.—" If I knew that, I'd have been up at the house long ago."

JOSEPH.—" I'll tell you what to do ; come up to dinner with the servants. You know the hour, and you will be surprised at the welcome you will get."

WOMAN.—" Well, please God, I will, Masther Richard."

The tone of *O'Donoghue,* an unfinished poem written at fifteen, and of his later *Irish National Ballads,* was due to his mother, who, as a girl, had been in her heart more or less a rebel, and she, not the Dean, was the critic of his boyish verse. She told him of the hard fate which in '98 befell many of those she knew and admired, including the brothers Sheares, and bequeathed to William Le Fanu a very interesting letter written, just before his execution, by John Sheares to her father, Dr. Dobbin, in which he defends himself from the charge of connivance at assassination for which he was about to suffer death. The character of Sheares makes it impossible to doubt the truth of these his dying words. She told him much of Lord Edward Fitz-Gerald and the fight he made for his life, and showed him the dagger with which he defended it. This dagger she possessed herself of, taking it surreptitiously from its owner, Major Swan, because, in her own words,—

" When I saw the dagger in the hands with which Lord

Edward had striven in the last fatal struggle for life or death,
I felt that it was not rightfully his who held it. I knew
the spot in the front drawing-room where it was laid, and
one evening I seized it, unobserved, and thrust it into
my bosom; I returned to the company, where I had to
sit for an hour. As soon as we got home I rushed up to
the room which my sister and I occupied, and plunged it
among the feathers of my bed, and for upwards of twelve
years I lay every night upon the bed which contained my
treasure.

" When I left home I took it with me and it has been my
companion in all the vicissitudes of life. When he missed
it, Major Swan was greatly incensed, and not without
apprehension that it had been taken to inflict a deadly
revenge upon him, but after a time his anger and uneasiness
subsided."

At the age of twenty-five Le Fanu wrote a vigorous
imitation of a street ballad bearing upon this subject.

From the year 1826 to 1831 the Le Fanu family were
on the most friendly terms with the peasantry in the
neighbourhood of Abington, in the county of Limerick, the
Dean of Emly being also Rector of Abington. To quote
William Le Fanu's account :—" They appeared to be devoted to us. If we had been away for a month or two, on
our return they met us in numbers some way from our home,
took the horses from the carriage, and drew it to our house
amid deafening cheers of welcome, and at night bonfires
blazed on all the neighbouring hills. In all their troubles
and difficulties the people came to my father for assistance.
There was then no dispensary nor doctor near us, and
many sick folk or their friends came daily to my mother
for medicine and advice ; I have often seen more than
twenty with her of a morning. Our parish priest also was a
special friend of ours, a constant visitor to our home. In
the neighbouring parishes the same kindly relations existed
between the priest and the flock and the Protestant clergy-

man. But in 1831 all this was suddenly and sadly changed, when the Tithe War came upon us."

A cousin of the Le Fanus, the Rev. Charles Coote, the Rector of the neighbouring parish of Doon, gave offence at the very commencement of the agitation by taking active measures to enforce the payment of his tithes. Wherever he or any of his family went they were received with opprobrium, and as frequent visitors to the Rectory at Doon, the Le Fanus soon came to be treated in a similar way.

Returning to Abingdon after a few years' absence, the young Le Fanus met on a steamboat, the *Garry Owen*, plying between Limerick and Kilrush, a famous character, one Paddy O'Neill, whose music and song, fiddling and playing on the bagpipes cheered the passengers on the trip. He was, moreover, a poet, and sang his own songs to his own accompaniments.

As showing the friendly feeling again existing between Joseph and the peasants, his brother relates the following :

" One summer's evening my brother, who was a prime favourite of his, persuaded Paddy to drive across with him from Kilrush to Kilkee, and there they got up a dance in Mrs. Reade's lodge, where some of our family were sojourning at the time ; I am sorry to say I was away at the time and missed the fun. The dance music was supplied by Paddy's pipes and fiddle, and between the dances he sang some of his favourite songs. Next day my brother wrote some doggerel verses celebrating the dance . . . ." A copy was presented to the highly delighted Paddy, who, for years after, sang them with much applause to the passengers on the *Garry Owen*.

But as Le Fanu had seen the best side of Irish peasant life, he had also seen its worst. His feelings as his mother's son prompted him to write *Shamus O'Brien ;* his personal experiences during the Tithe War, drew him away from the people's side in politics. He was none the less a " good

Irishman" in the National, not Nationalist, sense of that title.

Besides the poetical powers with which he was endowed, in common with his connections, the great Sheridan, the Dufferins, and the Hon. Mrs. Norton, Sheridan Le Fanu also possessed an irresistible humour and oratorical gift that, as a student of Old Trinity, made him a formidable rival of the best of the young debaters of his time at the " College Historical," not a few of whom eventually reached the highest eminence at the Irish Bar, after having long enlivened and charmed St. Stephen's by their wit and oratory.

Amongst his compeers he was remarkable for his sudden fiery eloquence of attack, and ready and rapid powers of repartee when on his defence.   But Le Fanu, whose under-standing was elevated by a deep love of the classics, in which he took University honours, and further heightened by an admirable knowledge of our own great authors, was not to be tempted away by oratory from literature, his first and, as it proved, his last love.

Very soon after leaving college, and just when he was called to the Bar, about the year 1841, he bought the *Warder*, a Dublin newspaper, of which he was editor, and took, what many of his best friends and admirers, looking to his high prospects as a barrister, regarded at the time as a fatal step to his career to fame.

Just before this period, Le Fanu had taken to writing humorous Irish stories, afterwards published in the *Dublin University Magazine*, such as the *Quare Gander*, *Jim Sullivan's Adventure*, *The Ghost and the Bone-setter*, etc.

These stories his brother, William Le Fanu, was in the habit of repeating for his friends' amusement, and about the year 1837, when he was about twenty-three years of age, Joseph Le Fanu said to him that he thought an Irish story in verse would tell well, and that if he would choose him a subject suitable. for recitation, he would write him one.

" Write me an Irish *Young Lochinvar*," said his brother, and in a few days he handed him *Phaudhrig Croohore—anglice, Patrick Crohore.*

Of course this poem has the disadvantage, not only of being written after *Young Lochinvar*, but also that of having been directly inspired by it, and yet, although wanting in the rare and graceful finish of the original, the Irish copy has, we feel, so much fire and feeling, that it at least tempts us to regret that Scott's poem was not written in that heart-stirring Northern dialect, without which many of the noblest of our British ballads would lose half their spirit.

To return to the year 1837, Mr. William Le Fanu, the suggester of this ballad, who was from home at the time, now received daily instalments of the second and more remarkable of his brother's Irish poems—*Shamus O'Brien* (James O'Brien)—learning them by heart as they reached him, and, fortunately, never forgetting them, for his brother Joseph kept no copy of the ballad, and he had himself to write it out from memory ten years after, when the poem was to appear in the *Dublin University Magazine.*

Few will deny that this poem contains passages most faithfully, if fearfully, picturesque, and that it is characterised throughout by a profound pathos and an abundant humour. Can we wonder then at the immense popularity with which Samuel Lover recited it in the United States? For to Lover's admiration of the poem, and his addition of it to his entertainment, *Shamus O'Brien* owes its introduction into America, where it is now so popular. Lover added some lines of his own to the poem, making Shamus emigrate to the States, and set up a public-house. These added lines appeared in most of the published versions of the ballad, but they are indifferent as verse, and certainly injure the dramatic effect of the poem.

Shamus O'Brien is so generally attributed to Lover (indeed, we remember seeing it advertised for recitation on

the occasion of a benefit at a leading London theatre as
" by Samuel Lover ") that it is a satisfaction to be able to
reproduce the following letter upon the subject from Lover
to William Le Fanu :—

ASTOR HOUSE,
NEW YORK, U.S. AMERICA.
September 30th, 1846.

MY DEAR LE FANU,—

In reading over your brother's poem while I crossed the
Atlantic, I became more and more impressed with its great beauty and
dramatic effect, so much so that I determined to test its effect in public,
and have done so here, on my first appearance, with the greatest
success. Now, I have no doubt there will be great praises of the poem,
and people will suppose most likely that the composition is mine, and
as you know (I take for granted) that I would not wish to wear a
borrowed feather, I should be glad to give your brother's name as the
author, should he not object to have it known ; but as his writings are
often in so different a tone, I would not speak without permission to do
so. It is true that in my programme my name is attached to other
pieces, and no name appended to the recitation. So far, you will see,
I have done all I could to avoid "appropriating"—the spirit of which
I might have caught here with Irish aptitude ; but I would like to have
the means of telling all whom it may concern the name of the author,
to whose head and heart it does so much honour. Pray, my dear Le
Fanu, inquire, and answer me here by next packet, or as soon as
convenient. My success here has been quite triumphant.

Yours very truly,

SAMUEL LOVER.

The outlaw Kirby, who was " on his keeping " (*i.e.*,
hiding from the police) at the time of his family's residence
in County Limerick, evidently suggested much of the devil-
may-care character of *Shamus O'Brien* to Le Fanu.
With a price upon his head, owing to his connection with
agrarian outrages, Kirby could not resist the temptation of
going to a hunt or a coursing match, narrowly escaping
capture on some of these occasions.

An informer, learning that Kirby would be at his
mother's house one Sunday night, communicated the fact
to Major Vokes, of Limerick, the most active magistrate in

the south of Ireland, who had more than once been baffled in his efforts to capture the outlaw.

Old Mrs. Kirby was in bed when the Major and two constables drew up to the door, but, fortunately, her daughter, Mary, had gone to a wake in the neighbourhood, and stayed out all night. Kirby, who was sitting by the fire, his pistols on a table beside him, sprang to his feet, and seizing them, cried, "At any rate, I'll have the life of one of them before I'm taken." "Whisht! you fool," said his mother. "Here, be quick! put on Mary's cap, take your pistols with you, jump into bed, turn your face to the wall, and lave the rest to me."

He was scarcely in bed when there was a loud knocking at the door, which his mother, having lit a rush, opened as quickly as possible. In came Major Vokes and the constables. "Where is your son?" said Vokes. "Plaze God, he's far enough from ye. It's welcome yez are this night," she said. "And thanks to the Lord it wasn't yesterday ye came, for it's me and Mary *there* that strove to make him stop the night wid us; but, thank God, he was afraid." They searched the house, but did not like to disturb the young girl in bed, and finding nothing, went, sadly disappointed, back to Limerick. The news of Kirby's escape soon spread through the country. Vokes was much chaffed, but Kirby never slept another night in his mother's house.

This incident, which is summarised from his brother's book, does not occur in Le Fanu's *Shamus*, but Mr. Jessop has seized the situation, and indeed improved upon it for his libretto of the opera of *Shamus O'Brien* by Sir Charles V. Stanford, which has been received with such pronounced popularity.

It is not as easy to see how the song, *I'm a young man that never yet was daunted*, quoted by Mr. W. Le Fanu in his *Irish Recollections*, suggested to his brother the plot of *Shamus O'Brien* beyond that it describes, though incoherently enough, the doings of an outlaw, who breaks gaol at Nenagh, and gets off scot-free after knocking down the sentry.

Le Fanu's literary life may be divided into three distinct periods. During the first of these, and till his thirtieth year, he was an Irish ballad, song, and story writer, his first published story being the *Adventures of Sir Robert Ardagh*, which appeared in the *Dublin University Magazine* in 1838.

In 1844 he was united to Miss Susan Bennett, the beautiful daughter of the late George Bennett, Q.C. From this time until her decease in 1858, he devoted his energies almost entirely to Press work, making, however, his first essays in novel writing during that period. The *Cock and Anchor*, a chronicle of old Dublin city, his first and, in the opinion of competent critics, one of the best of his novels, seeing the light about the year 1850. *Torlogh O'Brien* was its immediate successor. Their comparative want of success when first published, seems to have deterred Le Fanu from using his pen, except as a Press writer, until 1863, when the *House by the Churchyard* was published, and was soon followed by *Uncle Silas*, and other well-known novels. Finally, Le Fanu published in the pages of the *Dublin University Magazine*, *Beatrice* and *The Legend of the Glaive*, revised editions of which form the specially notable feature in the volume of his poems edited by me.

Those who possessed the rare privilege of Le Fanu's friendship, and only they, can form any idea of the true character of the man; for after the death of his wife, to whom he was most deeply devoted, he quite forsook general society, in which his fine features, distinguished bearing, and charm of conversation marked him out as the beau-ideal of an Irish wit and scholar of the old school.

From this society he vanished so entirely, that Dublin, always ready with a nickname, dubbed him "The Invisible Prince," and, indeed, he was for long almost invisible, except to his family and most familiar friends, unless at odd hours of the evening, when he might occasionally be seen stealing, like the ghost of his former self, between his newspaper office and his home in Merrion Square. Sometimes, too, he was to be encountered in an old, out-of-the-way bookshop, poring over some rare black letter Astrology or Demonology.

To one of these old bookshops he was at one time a pretty frequent visitor, and the bookseller relates how he used to come in and ask with his peculiarly pleasant voice and smile, " Any more ghost stories for me, Mr. ——? " and how, on a fresh one being handed to him, he would seldom leave the shop until he had looked it through. This taste for the supernatural seems to have grown upon him after his wife's death, and influenced him so deeply that, had he not been possessed of a deal of shrewd common sense, there might have been danger of his embracing some of the visionary doctrines in which he was so learned. But no ! even Spiritualism, to which not a few of his brother novelists succumbed, whilst affording congenial material for our artist of the superhuman to work upon, did not escape his severest satire.

Shortly after completing his last novel, strange to say, bearing the title *Willing to Die*, Le Fanu breathed his last at his home, No. 18, Merrion Square South, at the age of fifty-nine.

" He was a man," writes the author of a brief memoir of him in the *Dublin University Magazine*, " who thought deeply, especially on religious subjects. To those who knew him he was very dear ; they admired him for his learning, his sparkling wit and pleasant conversation, and loved him for his manly virtues, for his noble and generous qualities, his gentleness, and his loving, affectionate nature." And all who knew the man must feel how deeply deserved are these simple words of sincere regard for Joseph Sheridan Le Fanu.

WILLIAM ALLINGHAM

DESCENDED from English forbears, the son of a banker of substance and ability and of a capable and charming mother of the well-know Crawford family, William Allingham was born on March 19th, 1824, at Ballyshannon.   At an early age he was sent to Mr. Ray's school in his native town, and from his class-fellow and cousin, John Crawford, I have received these hitherto unpublished particulars of those school-days.

Mr. Ray taught Latin, nothing more, and the general curriculum was evidently unattractive.   For though the boy was a particularly bright and clever one and mastered his most difficult lessons with ease, the routine was so dull and irksome to him that while devoting just sufficient time to it to hold his own in class, he read widely and diligently on his own account.   As a result he often caused surprise to his elders by the fixed opinions he held on subjects supposed to be above his years and the remarkably clear expression of them.   Mentally much ahead of his compeers he did not associate much with them, but was never so happy as when surrounded by a crowd of boys younger than himself.   For these he had a great attraction, and his power of amusing them was inexhaustible.   Games of "follow the leader," including all sorts of difficult jumps and feats of bodily prowess, were led by young Allingham.

But perhaps the sport to which he was most attached was skating, which he has so well described in his poem

Frost in the Holidays. Yet whilst keenly enjoying the tricks played by one boy on another—and some of these were rough enough—he always kept the peace. He was a great lover of nature and particularly humane towards dumb animals, being always ready to defend them or rescue them from the hands of cruel or thoughtless boys. But for one of his adventurous spirit he was strangely indifferent to field sports. He did not fish or shoot like his fellows, or follow the hounds, abstaining from such pursuits on principle.

From Ray's he was sent to a boarding school at Killeshandra, but for a short time only. Yet distasteful as Ray's had been, this school was doubly so to him. By his own request he left it and was put into his father's bank in Ballyshannon in his fourteenth year. College life he had none, a circumstance over which he long repined, but which in the end he regarded as having been a benefit to him. For he was an indefatigable student of English literature and natural science and taught himself French, German, Latin and Greek, till he was able to enjoy the classics and the works of Continental writers in the original, and few University students can claim to have covered so wide a field of reading. Allingham passed from his father's bank into the Excise in the year 1846. A few years later his cousin Robert Crawford had this experience of him :

"On my return from the University I was engaged in making a geological survey around Ballyshannon, when William became my constant companion. Nor could there have been a pleasanter one ; he was so full of general information, and looked at everything from such an interesting and original point of view. Surgeon Tighe of the 12th Lancers attached himself to us in these rambles. My cousin and he were for the most part engaged in constant controversies on almost every conceivable topic, from the formation of gneiss to the political questions of the day. It was most amusing to hear the younger philosopher deftly conducting his attacks upon fortresses of opinion which the elder considered impregnable. Indeed, he was altogether lacking in veneration for old-established opinions the reasonableness of which was not apparent to him. One comic case of the kind I rememher. He was taking lessons on the violin, but the universally adopted shape of the instrument shocked his sense of the fitness of things, as he argued that a rectangular body would admit the sounds quite as well as one of the normal type with its fantastic curves, and he carried his theory into practice, for he got Higgins, the violin maker, to make him one on this pattern. What is more he had the courage of his opinions, insisting that the tone of his instrument surpassed that of any other he had heard, notwithstanding that there were a couple of Cremonas in the neighbourhood."

But his father, proud though he was of his son's intelligence, had little sympathy with his constant craving for knowledge. In the bank manager's eyes it was not the scholar, but the thorough business man who ranked highest. From the counting-house the young poet at last succeeded in escaping.

" Heart-sick of more than seven years of bank-clerking," he writes, " I found a door suddenly opened, not into an ideal region, or anything like one, but at least into a roadway of life somewhat less narrow and tedious than that in which I was plodding." A place had been found for him in the Customs, as it was found for another and a greater dreamer on the other side of the Atlantic.

" In the spring of 1846 I gladly took leave for ever of discount ledgers and current accounts, and went to Belfast for two months' instruction in the duties of Principal Coast Officer of Customs, a tolerably well-sounding title, but which carried with it a salary of but £80 a year. I trudged daily about the docks and timber-yards, learning to measure logs, piles of planks, and, more troublesome, ships of tonnage; indoors, part of the time practised customs book-keeping, and talked to the clerks about literature and poetry in a way that excited some astonishment, but on the whole, as I found at parting, a certain degree of curiosity and respect. I preached Tennyson to them. My spare time was mostly spent in reading and haunting book-sellers' shops, where, I venture to say, I laid out a good deal more than most people, in proportion to my income, and manged to get glimpses of many books which I could not afford or did not care to buy. I enjoyed my new position, on the whole, without analysis, as a great improve-ment on the bank; and for the rest, my inner mind was brimful of love and poetry, and usually all external things appeared trivial save in their relation to them. Yet I am reminded, by old memoranda, that there were sometimes overclouding anxieties: sometimes, but not very frequently, from lack of money; more often from longing for culture, conversation, opportunity; oftenest from fear of a sudden development of some form of lung disease, the seeds of which I supposed to be sown in my bodily constitution." This weakness he outgrew.

During his banking days Allingham had begun to write poetry, Leigh Hunt's journal being the first to print his lyrics. Leigh Hunt himself he met for the first time in Edwardes Square in 1847. In 1849 Henry Sutton, a poet now too little known, gave him a letter of introduction to Coventry Patmore, who later introduced him to Tennyson, with whom he afterwards became intimate. He also was made acquainted with Mr. and Mrs. Browning, Emerson, Arthur Hugh Clough, George Eliot, Thackeray, and Dickens. Moreover, Patmore brought him into the artist group, which comprised Rossetti, Millais, and other members of the Pre-Raphaelite Brotherhood.

Allingham's acquaintance with Rossetti ripened into friendship, and the letters of Dante Gabriel Rossetti to William Allingham, edited by Dr. Birkbeck Hill, record the chief facts of his life and literary friendships. Much supple-

mentary detail, however, is to be found in a set of reminiscences chiefly relating to Tennyson and Carlyle, which
Mrs. Allingham has edited. For it should be added that
Leigh Hunt introduced our poet to Carlyle in early days,
and that later on they became close companions. In the
year 1862 Allingham came over to London, still engaged in
the Customs, but he disliked the noise and the confinement
of city life near the docks, and was very glad of a transfer
to Lymington, where for seven years he saw much of
Tennyson.

He retired from the Government service in 1870, when
he became sub-editor, under Mr. Froude, of *Fraser's
Magazine*, succeeding him as editor in 1874. It was during
this period that I became personally acquainted with the poet.
He was then a well preserved man of middle age, and I
agree in Nathaniel Hawthorne's description of his looks as
" intelligent, dark, pleasing, and not at all John Bullish."
His voice was musical, touched with the Donegal accent,
but his pronunciation of English was finely correct and he
was a most fascinating conversationalist, who, if he did not
set the table in a roar, always started it smiling and
thinking.

Much my senior, he was singularly courteous to my
young opinions, and I well remember that when I sent my
first long poem to *Fraser*, calling it *Vox Veris*, and on
getting no reply, perhaps too impatiently suggested that
spring was passing and my verses would soon be out of
date, he replied in choice Latin, " Spring is ever with us,"
at the same time accepting the poem. We became engaged
to be married at about the same time, and I had the pleasure
of meeting him and his then *fiancée*, Miss Helen Paterson,
the well-known water-colour artist and book illustrator, at the
house of Tom Taylor, the dramatist, whose wife arranged
the Irish airs collected by Allingham and enriched by his
lyrics.

Of Carlyle he saw much more than most of that great

man's friends, for during some years scarcely a week went by in which they did not walk together. "Strange to say," writes Dr. Hill, "this intimacy has been passed over in total silence by Mr. Froude. In the four volumes of his hero's life there are sins of omission as well as of commission."

Allingham used to recount how Carlyle would sometimes begin by flatly contradicting him, and end by tacitly adopting what he had said. One day the old man was describing his interview with the Queen at the Dean of Westminster's. "She came sliding into the room," he said—"as if on wheels," exclaimed Allingham, interrupting him. "Not at all, Allingham," he gruffly replied. A few days later his friend overheard him telling the story to Mr. Lecky. "The Queen," he said, "came sliding into the room as if on wheels," and in that form he ever afterwards told it. He used to add that he saw that he was expected to stand during the interview, but that he took hold of a chair, and saying that he hoped Her Majesty would allow an old man to sit down, down he sat.

During his connection with *Fraser's Magazine*, Allingham lived near Carlyle, in Chelsea, and walked out regularly with him on several afternoons of each week. It was at his suggestion that Allingham started a series of chapters on Irish history in *Fraser*.

But Allingham's walks were not all strolls with brother men of letters. A large proportion of his prose work and much of his best poetical description had their origin in solitary rambles undertaken from his boyhood upwards, and which he kept up all through his life. In this way as "Patricius Walker" he tramped through Ireland, England, Wales, and Scotland, collecting his "harvest of the quiet eye," studying the country folk as he went, musing over the great cathedrals and abbeys, and reviving recollections of Swift and Prior, Herbert and Dickens, Burns and Scott, on the very ground where they had walked and talked, written and sung. These rambles awakened many an interesting train of thought, and his records of them crystallise into charming essays, amongst which we can trace the germs of subsequent poems.

His later poems give a delightful picture of his home life in Surrey, and during this period Allingham saw Tennyson several times each summer, when the Laureate and his wife came to Blackdown. *Fraser's Magazine* had by this time ceased to be, and Allingham occupied his time with prose and verse composition entirely, including the preparation of his various works for the Press, as well as a complete edition of them.

He had a fall from his horse in the year 1888, from which serious consequences ensued. He removed to Hampstead in bad health, and died on November 18th, 1889.

In the preface to *The Music Master*, published in 1855, Allingham states that five of the songs or ballads, namely, *The Milkmaid, The Girl's Lamentation, Lovely Mary Donnelly, Nanny's Sailor Lad,* and *The Nobleman's Wedding,* have already had an Irish circulation as halfpenny ballads, and the first three were written for this purpose.

This statement is explained in Dr. Birkbeck Hill's letters of Dante Gabriel Rossetti to William Allingham. In evening walks at Ballyshannon he would hear the Irish girls at their cottage doors singing old ballads which he would pick up. If they were broken or incomplete he would add to them or finish them ; if they were improper he would refine them. He could not get them sung till he got the Dublin Catnach of that day to print them on long strips of blue paper, like old songs ; and if about the sea, with the old rough woodcut of a ship at the top. He either gave them away or they were sold in the neighbour-hood. Then, in his evening walks, he had at last the pleasure of hearing some of his own ballads sung at the cottage doors by the crooning lasses, who were quite unaware that it was the author who was passing by. This is exactly what Oliver Goldsmith had done a century before, when a student of Trinity College, Dublin, though the lanes in which he listened to his ballads were very other from those at beautiful Ballyshannon.

In this connection Allingham raises a very interesting literary question. He states he did not find it easy in ballad writing to employ a diction that might hope to come home to the English-speaking Irish peasant using his customary phraseology, and also keep within the laws of poetic taste and the rules of grammar; "for that phraseology, being as regards its structural peculiarities but an imperfect or distorted expression, not an ancient dialect like that of Scotland, is generally too corrupt, though often forcible, to bear transplantation into poetry. Only familiar experience, too, and constant attention can enable one to use words in the exact significance which the popular custom has assigned. For instance, among the Irish peasantry 'distress,' as far as I know, always means bodily want, 'trouble' affliction of mind, 'misery' penuriousness, 'care' responsibility, and 'sorrow' commonly means ill-luck or misfortune, while 'sorry' has the usual dictionary meaning. From these conditions it comes that the choice of words for poetry in Irish-English is narrowly limited, instead of there being both that variety and raciness which is sometimes in the gift of a genuine peculiar dialect."

But after fifteen years' experience, Allingham qualifies the strong term "imperfect or distorted expression," as applied to the structural peculiarities of the Irish peasants' phraseology, to mean unusual forms, some of them old-fashioned English, some translated or adapted from Gaelic forms. This is a very important modification of view, and surely such forms, derived as they are from Shakespearean English and classical Gaelic, are as ancient and respectable in their historic and literary associations as the idioms of the modern Scotch dialect.

Allingham's final concession that some not unimportant poetical results might flow from a judicious treatment of Irish dialect has been more than justified by the event. The water has been flowing for thirty-three years under Essex—now the O'Connell—Bridge since then, and we have half-a-dozen writers of successful Irish-English dialect poetry, amongst whom may be mentioned Moira O'Neill, Francis Fahy, P. J. McCall, George Savage Armstrong, John Stephenson, and others, whilst quite as much interest attaches to "Gaelic English," now familiar in the prose and poetry of Douglas Hyde and the plays of Synge, Yeats, Boyle, Lady Gregory, and other dramatists of the Irish Literary Theatre. Allingham has, however, very justly pointed out that during his time Irish-English has never been properly examined, though quite recently this deficiency has been atoned for by Dr. Joyce in his admirable little volume, *The English we speak in Ireland* published by Longmans for only half-a-crown.

Allingham, in spite of his preface to his 1855 edition, returned to Irish ballad writing, and may be said to have achieved his masterpiece in the *Winding Banks of Erne* or the *Emigrant's Adieu to Ballyshannon,* a ballad which has gone round the world, in spite of Mr. Stephen Gwynn's statement that it is too little known. To readers of the class to whom Mr. Gwynn has addressed his delightful *Highways and Byways in Donegal and Antrim* this is doubtless true, but the beautiful ballad has reached the hearts of the Irish people, wedded to the haunting old air to which it is set.

It is still difficult to fix Allingham's position in the poetical hierarchy. This is undoubtedly due to his remarkable open-mindedness to the influences of both nature and art. A lover of nature before he could read, Allingham, almost as soon as he could do so, saturated himself with Tennyson's poems. Then, as has been pointed out, he was brought into touch with the Pre-Raphaelite Brotherhood, and caught some of their inspiration, but he was none the less an "open-air poet," which Rossetti certainly was not, and wholly original in all his best work. But with Irish nature and Irish human nature he had most affinity, though his Anglo-Irish race and creed kept him, like Ferguson, apart from, though not without warm sympathy for, his Celtic compatriots, literary and political. He lamented the destruction of early Irish civilisation and the internecine feud, political and religious, between Saxon and Celt. If Home Rule could make Ireland as "homely," as he puts it, "as Devonshire," which delighted him by its happy union of Celtic and Saxon characteristics, he would have given his vote for Home Rule, but he dreaded leaving the dissident elements in Ireland to take care of themselves. Yet he was proud to call himself an Irishman, and Carlyle got little change out of him when he insisted that Allingham was an Anglian name, meaning the "hame" or "home" of one of the Ellings.

His earliest volume contains five Irish ballads. *Lawrence Bloomfield* is an entirely Irish theme, and his last collection of Irish songs and poems consists of thirty-two pieces written round "Ballyshanny." But this is not all, as Lionel Johnson finely puts it in his estimate of Allingham in *The Treasury of Irish Poetry*, edited by Stopford Brooke and Rolleston. "Song upon song makes no mention, direct or indirect, of Ireland, yet reveals an Irish atmosphere and temperament. As the outward aspect of the man so is his characteristic work, the work of a poet who is many things but always essentially an Irishman of the secluded west, with ancient visions and ponderings in his heart, and the gift of tears and smiles. He passed along his way alone, with a heart responding, a soul vibrating to the voices of nature and of tranquil lives, and to him came those voices in Irish. He wrote much ambitious work which may not live, but his lyric voice of singular sweetness, his muse of passionate and pensive meditation, his poetic consecration of common things, his mingled aloofness and homeliness assured him a secure place among the poets of his land and the Irish voices which never will fall silent; and though the Irish cause receives from him but little direct encouragement or help, let it be remembered that Allingham wrote this great and treasurable truth :

> We're one at heart if you be Ireland's friend,
> Though leagues asunder our opinions tend,
> There are but two great parties in the end."

Lionel Johnson has not done him justice in the matter of his assistance to the Irish cause if, as seems almost certain, *Lawrence Bloomfield* first fired Gladstone's imagination upon the Irish Land Question.

For a highly eulogistic review of this poem in *The Athenæum*, in which statesmen were besought to read it, was followed by an invitation to the poet to breakfast with the famous Irish land-law reformer. Let me press my point that Allingham was a good Irishman on Irish questions by a few passages from this poem, which both Stopford Brooke and Lionel Johnson fitly describe as combining the descriptive grace of Goldsmith and the ironic force of Crabbe. Very justly indeed *Lawrence Bloomfield* has been called the epic of the Irish Land Question.

SIR ULICK HARVEY.

> You find in old Sir Ulick Harvey's face
> The looks of long command and comely race ;
> No small man sees a brother in those eyes
> Of calm and frosty blue, like winter skies ;
> Courteous his voice, yet all the pride is there,
> Pride like a halo crowns the silvery hair ;
> 'Tis unmisgiving pride that makes him frank
> With humble folk, and dress beneath his rank.

Born in the purple, he could hardly know
Less of the tides of life that round him flow.
The Laws were for the Higher Classes made ;
But while the Lower gratefully obey'd,
To patronise them you had his consent,
Promote their comfort, to a safe extent,
And teach them—just enough, and not too much ;
Most careful lest with impious hand you touch
Order and grade as planned by Providence.

    *   *   *   *   *

He sometimes took a well-meant scheme in hand,
Which must be done exactly as he plann'd ;
His judgment feeble, and his self-will strong,
He had his way, and that was mostly wrong.
The whim was such, that seized his mind of late,
To "square" the farms on all his wide estate ;
Tim's mountain grazing, Peter's lough-side patch,
This onion-field of Ted's that few could match,
Phil's earliest ridges, Bartly's bog, worse hap !
By mere new lines across his Honour's map
From ancient holdings have been clipt away,
Despite the loud complaints, or dumb dismay.

LORD CRASHTON—THE ABSENTEE LANDLORD.

Joining Sir Ulick's at the river's bend,
Lord Crashton's acres east and west extend ;
Great owner here, in England greater still.
As poor folk say, " The world's divided ill."
On every pleasure men can buy with gold
He surfeited, and now, diseased and old,
He lives abroad ; a firm in Molesworth Street
Doing what their attorneyship thinks meet.

    *   *   *   *   *

Twice only in the memory of mankind
Lord Crashton's proud and noble self appear'd ;
Up-river, last time, in his yacht he steer'd,
With Maltese valet and Parisian cook,
And one on whom askance the gentry look,
Altho' a pretty, well-dress'd demoiselle—
Not Lady Crashton, who, as gossips tell,
Goes her own wicked way. They stopped a week ;

Then, with gay ribbons fluttering from the peak,
And snowy skirts wide spread, on either hand,
The *Aphrodite* curtsied to the land,
And glided off. My Lord, with gouty legs,
Drinks Baden-Baden water, and life's dregs ;
With cynic jest inlays his black despair,
And curses all things from his easy chair.

FINLAY.

Finlay, next landlord (I'll abridge the tale),
Prince of Glenawn, a low and fertile vale,
No fool by birth, but hard, and praised for wise,
The more he learn'd all softness to despise,
Married a shrew for money, louts begot,
Debased his wishes to a vulgar lot,
To pence and pounds coin'd all his mother-wit,
And ossified his nature bit by bit.
A dull, cold home, devoid of every grace,
Distrust and dread in each dependent's face,
Bullocks and turnips, mighty stacks of grain,
Plethoric purse, impoverished heart and brain—
Such Finlay's life ; and when that life shall end,
He'll die as no man's debtor, no man's friend.

TOM DYSART.

Unlike this careful management (between
The two, Sir Ulick's townlands intervene)
Is that of Termon on the river-side,
Domain and mansion of insolvent pride,
Where Dysart, drawing from ancestral ground
One sterling shilling for each phantom pound
Of rent-roll lives, when all the truth is known,
Mere factor in the place he calls his own ;
Through mortgages and bonds, one wide-spread maze,
Steps, dances, doubles round by devious ways,
While creditor, to creditor a foe,
Hangs dubious o'er the vast imbroglio.
And thus, minute in bargain where he can,
There, closing quick with ready-money man,

Despised for cunning, and for malice fear'd,
Yet still by custom and old name endear'd,
To Keltic minds, who also better like
A rule of thumb than Gough's arithmetic,
Tom Dysart shuffles on, to this good day,
Let creditors and courts do what they may.

ISAAC BROWN.

Pass on to Isaac Brown, a man elect,
Wesleyan stout, our wealthiest of his sect ;
Who bought and still buys land, none quite sees how,
Whilst all his shrewdness and success allow.
On Crashton's mortgage he has money lent,
He takes a quiet bill at ten per cent.,
The local public business much he sways,
He's learn'd in every neighbour's means and ways,
For comfort cares, for fashion not a whit,
Nor if the gentry to their ranks admit.
All preachers love him ; he can best afford
The unctuous converse and the unctuous board ;
Ev'n the poor nag, slow-rattling up the road
In ancient rusty gig a pious load,
Wags his weak tail, and strikes a brisker trot,
Approaching Brownstown, Isaac's pleasant lot.
For though at Poor-House Board was never known
A flintier Guardian-angel than good Brown,
As each old hag and shivering child can tell,—
Go dine with Isaac, and he feeds you well.

And hear him pray, with fiercely close-shut eyes !
Gentle at first the measured accents rise,
But soon he waxes loud, and storms the skies.
Deep is the chest and powerful bass the voice,
The language of a true celestial choice ;
Handorgan-wise the holy phrases ground
Go turning and returning round and round ;
The sing-song duly runs from low to high ;
The chorus'd groans at intervals reply ;
Till after forty minutes' sweat and din,
Leaving perhaps too little prayer within,
Dear Brother Brown, athletic babe of grace,
Resumes his bench, and wipes his reeking face.

JACK DORAN.

Jack was a plodding man, who deem'd it best
To hide away the wisdom he possess'd ;
Of scanty words, avoiding all dispute ;
But much experience in his mind had root ;
Most deferential, yet you might surprise
A secret scanning in the small grey eyes ;
Short, active, tho' with labour's trudge, his legs ;
His knotted fingers, like rude wooden pegs,
Still firm of grip ; his breath was slow and deep ;
His hair unbleach'd with time, a rough black heap.
Fond, of a night, to calmly sit and smoke,
While neighbours plied their argument or joke,
To each he listen'd, seldom praised or blamed,
All party-spirit prudently disclaim'd,
Repeating, in his wise old wrinkled face,
" I never knew it help a poor man's case " ;
And when they talked of " tyrants " Doran said
Nothing, but suck'd his pipe and shook his head.

THE EVICTION.

The Sheriff's painful duty must be done ;
He begs for quiet—and the work's begun.
The strong stand ready ; now appear the rest,
Girl, matron, grandsire, baby on the breast,
And Rosy's thin face on a pallet borne ;
A motley concourse, feeble and forlorn.
One old man, tears upon his wrinkled cheek,
Stands trembling on a threshold, tries to speak,
But, in defect of any word for this,
Mutely upon the doorpost prints a kiss,
Then passes out for ever.

               Through the crowd
The children run bewilder'd, wailing loud ;
Where needed most, the men combine their aid ;
And, last of all, is Oona forth convey'd,
Reclined in her accustom'd strawen chair,
Her agèd eyelids closed, her thick white hair
Escaping from her cap ; she feels a chill,
Looks round and murmurs, then again is still.

Poor consumptive Rosy has shared in the Eviction, but her poor friends come to her rescue.

> Those, too, with less to spare, and those with nought,
> To this poor girl their friendly succour brought.
> Here in a neighbouring house, but whence no noise
> Can reach her, some well-wishing girls and boys
> Have clubb'd their moneys, raffling for a shawl ;
> Of Rose's other shreds the pawn has all.
> Three simple pence entitle to a throw ;
> Down on a slate the names and numbers go ;
> The wooden cubes mark'd with a red-hot wire
> (No better dice or dice-box they require)
> In old tin porringer flung rattling fast.
> A warmer interest watches every cast ;
> "Follie' your han' !" "You're lucky, throw for me !"
> "More power !" "Tim Ryan has it—fifty-three !"
> Then silver, copper, mix'd, a bulky pound
> Makes haste to Rosy, feebly turning round
> With grateful smile ; and back the shawl comes too,
> The winner swearing 'twas for her he threw.

THE UNHAPPY COUNTRY.

> Derided in her torture and her tears,
> In sullen slavery dragging hopeless years ;
> Of social ties mere cruel scourges made ;
> A ban upon her learning and her trade ;
> Possessions, rights, religion, language, torn
> And crushed by Law—a word to hate and scorn
> For those taught English in oppression's school,
> And reading good words by the witches' rule ;
> A name for powerful wrong, with no appeal ;
> Since law at every moment made them feel
> To live an Irishman on Irish ground
> The sole unpardonable crime was found.
>
> Island of bitter memories, thickly sown
> From winding Boyne to Limerick's treaty-stone,
> Bare Connaught Hills to Dublin Castle wall,
> Green Wexford to the glens of Donegal,
> Through sad six hundred years of hostile sway,
> From Strongbow fierce to cunning Castlereagh !
> These will not melt and vanish in a day.
> These can yet sting the patriot thoughts which turn
> To Erin's past, and bid them weep and burn.

In another respect Allingham has not been done justice
to by Lionel Johnson.   He is spoken of as no Irish scholar
and therefore unable to draw inspiration from Gaelic literature.   Allingham's essays distinctly show that he was a
student of Gaelic literature, even to the extent of wading
through *The Four Masters*, and though unfortunately he did
not, until rather late in life, try his hand at a subject inspired
by Gaelic literature, the one piece of work of the kind that
he attempted only makes us regret that he had not turned
his thoughts in that direction long before.   I refer to his
Lady of the Sea.   He is also taxed with not seeking a centre
of Irish Literary Society.   But what centre of Irish Literary
Society existed in England or Ireland until the Irish
Literary Society of London and the National Literary
Society of Dublin were founded in the year 1892, three
years after Allingham's death?   In the bibliography of
Allingham's works in *The Treasury of Irish Poetry*, no men-
tion is made of his prose writings, but had Johnson studied
Allingham's *Varieties in Prose* he would have given him
credit for even greater versatility than he allows him.   I
give a few brief selections from his *Rambles by Patricius
Walker* as evidence of his powers as a prose writer.

Here is his new-style description of the river Erne :

> After running swiftly half a mile between bare slopes, the Erne
> finds its channel suddenly contracted to a narrow passage between two
> ledges of limestone, and down into this gully it sweeps, racing in long
> black ridges, leaping in amber curves, dashed into foam against
> hidden rocks in its bed, sending up from the boiling depths great
> gulching bubbles, and whirling into crannies and corners, raging
> continually, with a commingled roaring and hissing as of lions and
> serpents.   After this tumultuous rush at " Kathleen's Fall," the
> Erne, spreading wide, runs at a steadier pace, but still rapidly, by
> the walls of Ballyshannon and under the arches of the old long bridge,
> and 300 yards lower down makes its final plunge into the tidal waters
> of the harbour, over the Fall of Assaroe, otherwise called the Salmon
> Leap.

How curiously this contrasts with the old style prose

description of the same fall, in an ancient Irish tale, *The Banquet of Dunagay and the Battle of Moira*, translated by John O'Donovan (Irish Archæological Society, 1842), which Allingham himself calls attention to:

The clear-watered, snowy-foamed, ever-roaring, parti-coloured, bellowing, in-salmon-abounding, beautiful old torrent, whose celebrated well-known name is the lofty-great, clear-landed, contentious, precipitate, loud-roaring, headstrong, rapid, salmon-ful, sea-monster-ful, varying, in-large-fish-abounding, rapid-flooded, furious-streamed, whirling, in-seal-abounding, royal and prosperous cataract of Eas Ruaidh.

Here is a very different specimen of Allingham's prose:

Was it while he was staying at Broadstairs (it was certainly in Kent) that I Patricius met Charles Dickens one day in Regent Street? With one sharp glance, and a quiver of the wide flexible nostrils, "O, lord!" he exclaimed, "how are you?" and taking my arm walked off at five miles an hour towards a railway station. But great as his hurry was, he suddenly stopped short as quickly, and pressed with me into the edge of a crowd in the street to see what was happening. It was only a horse down, and Dickens hurried me along again, saying, "I'm a country cousin now, and stare at everything when I come up." A trivial anecdote, but it recalls the man. Nor was it a trivial incident to the worshipping youth; it was almost as though his arm were taken by an angel dropping from the sky!

But much more valuable specimens of his prose style, and specially interesting as exhibiting his own intellectual points of view, are the following sketches, criticisms, and recollections of his great compeers, Tennyson, Browning, Rossetti, and Jowett, extracted from Allingham's Diary, edited by Mrs. Allingham and Mrs. Ernest Radford, and published by Macmillan and Co., in 1907.

The first extract has to me a special interest, because Allingham once told me himself how Tennyson had abandoned the theme of King Arthur when "his mind was in flower with it" owing to a want of warmth in the reception by the critics of his *Morte d'Arthur*, due, in part, he himself afterwards felt, to his own somewhat apologetic verse preface to that incomparable poem, of which Froude once said to me, "Alfred will not live except in selection, but the *Morte d'Arthur* is immortal."

Sunday, October 16th, 1881. T. told me that he had planned out his *Arthuriad*, and could have written it all off without any trouble. But in 1842 he published, with other poems, the *Morte d'Arthur*, which was one book of his Epic (though not really the eleventh), and the review in the *Quarterly* disheartened him, so that he put the scheme aside. He afterwards took it up again, but not as with the first inspiration. This unlucky article in the *Quarterly* was written by John Sterling, who was then thirty-six years old, just three years older than Tennyson. It may be interesting now to read what it said of the *Morte d'Arthur*: "The first poem in the second volume seems to us less costly jewel work, with fewer of the broad flashes of passionate imagery, than some others, and not compensating for this inferiority by any stronger human interest. The miraculous legend of Excalibur does not come very near to us, and as reproduced by any modern writer must be a mere ingenious exercise of fancy. The poem, however, is full of distinct and striking description, perfectly expressed, and a tone of mild dignified sweetness attracts, though it hardly avails to enchant us."

This, it will be observed, chimes in with the doubts expressed by the poet himself in the lines written by way of prologue. Blame or doubt in regard to his own writings always weighed more with Tennyson than praise. He often said that he forgot praise and remembered all censure.

Sterling's review, meant to be friendly, was a thin, pretentious piece, and of no value whatever; a pity it should have chanced to prove so miseffectual !

Tuesday, February 18th, 1868. Browning's "Sludge," etc. Mem.—There is too often a want of solid basis for Robert Browning's brilliant and astounding cleverness. *A Blot in the 'Scutcheon* is solid. How try to account for Browning's twists and turns? I cannot. He has been and still is very dear to me. But I can no longer commit myself to his hands in faith and trust. Neither can I allow the faintest shadow of a suspicion to dwell in my mind that his genius may have a leaven of quackery. Yet, alas ! he is not solid— which is a very different thing from prosaic. *A Midsummer Night's Dream* is as solid as anything in literature ; has imaginative coherency and consistency in perfection. Looking at forms of poetic expression, there is not a single utterance in Shakespeare, or of Dante as far as I know, enigmatic in the same sense as so many of Browning's are. If you suspect, and sometimes find out, that riddles presented to you with Sphinxian solemnity have *no* answers that really fit them, your curiosity is apt to fall towards freezing point, if not below it. Yet I always end by striking my breast in penitential mood and crying out, "O rich mind ! wonderful Poet ! strange great man ! "

I recall an interesting talk with Professor Jowett at Freshwater, one night that I walked with him from Tennyson's to his lodging at the Terrace. The conversation turned to the subject of conventionalities, and I urged how lamentable it was to see men, and especially distinguished men, accepting in public, or even actively supporting ideas which they abjured in their own minds. This was my hobby, and I rode it at a pace that the Professor was probably little accustomed to, yet he listened and answered not only with patience but apparent interest, and when we arrived at his door invited me, somewhat to my surprise, to come in and continue the conversation, I remember, in a room dimly lighted with one candle. He seemed to agree with me in the main, but argued to the effect that by an open and unguarded nonconformity a man might ruin his career and lose all influence and authority. I said in my usual impulsive style : "Oh, he would find the apparent obstacles to be only shadows on his road." To which J—— replied gently, but with a tone of conviction, " I fear he would find them very real."

He is a soft, smooth, round man, with fat soft hands and a very gentle voice and manner, but with no weakness of will or lack of perseverance. He is extremely cautious, but not in the least cowardly, can quietly make his way, doubtless, into very hard substances, as some very soft creatures do (speaking without disparagement). J. indeed has publicly shown great frankness, *for an Oxford Don*, and will be a reformer *ab intra*.

I know full well how too impatient I always am, how too lacking in *savoir faire*. Yet I don't think I was wrong to speak freely to him, for once. Nay, I don't see how any thinking man can be at perfect peace with himself while his public conduct and private belief are not in agreement. I do not know one English writer now living who is consistent. Emerson is : but supposing he were an Englishman ?—an absurd supposition, for Emerson is entirely an American product.

Thursday, September 19th, 1867. Rossetti and I look round the furniture brokers ; he buys an old mirror and several other things "for a song," but they will have to be done up "otherwise you fill your house with dinginess." Then a walk. R. walks very characteristically, with a peculiar lounging gait, often trailing the point of his umbrella on the ground, but still obstinately pushing on and making way, he humming the while with closed teeth, in the intervals of talk, not a tune or anything like one, but what sounds like a *sotto voce* note of defiance to the universe. Then suddenly he will fling himself down somewhere and refuse to stir an inch further. His favourite attitude—on his back, one knee raised, hands behind head. On a sofa he often, too, curls himself up like a cat. He very seldom takes particular notice of anything as he goes, and cares nothing about natural history or science in any form or degree. It is plain that the simple, the natural, the naive are merely insipid in his mouth ; he must have strong savours, in art, in literature, and in life. Colours, forms, sensations are required to be pungent, mordant. In poetry he desires spasmodic passion, and emphatic, partly archaic, diction. He cannot endure Wordsworth any more than I can S. He sees nothing in Lovelace's " Tell me not, Sweet, I am Unkind." In foreign poetry he is drawn to Dante by inheritance (Milton, by the way, he dislikes) ; in France he is interested by Villon and some others of the old lyric writers ; in Germany by nobody. To Greek literature he seems to owe nothing, nor to Greek art directly. In Latin poetry he has turned to one or two things of Catullus for sake of the subjects. English imaginative literature—poems and tales, here lies his pabulum : Shakespeare, the old ballads, Blake, Keats, Shelley, Browning, Mrs. Browning, Tennyson, Poe being first favourites, and now Swinburne. *Wuthering Heights* is a Koh-i-noor among novels, *Sidonia the Sorceress* "a stunner." *Any* writing that with the least competency assumes an imaginative form, or any criticism on the like, attracts his attention more or less ; and he has discovered in obscurity, and in some cases helped to rescue from it, at least in his own circle, various unlucky books ; those, for example, of Ebenezer Jones and Wells, authors of *Joseph and His Brethren* and *Stories after Nature*. About these and other matters Rossetti is chivalrously bold in announcing and defending his opinions, and he has the valuable quality of knowing what he likes and sticking to it. In painting, the early Italians with their quaintness and strong rich colouring have magnetised him. In sculpture, he only cares for picturesque and grotesque qualities ; and of architecture, as such, takes, I think, no notice at all.

The two *Aeolian Harps*, one of which Tennyson read aloud with deep appreciation to its author, *Would I knew*, *St. Margaret's Eve, The Girl's Lamentation, The Sailor—*the last two described as " most admirable "—and *The Dream* were Rossetti's favourites in Allingham's first volume. His opinion of the one long poem in it, *The Music Master*, is mixed, his adverse criticism being that it is not a strong enough narrative poem to form the *pièce de résistance* in a first volume of poems, and that it chiefly awakens contemplation like a walk on a fine day with a churchyard in it, instead of rousing one like part of one's own life and leaving one to walk it off as one might live it off; but he praises the poem for its many artistic merits.

I have studied the poem at three times of my life—five and twenty years ago, fifteen years ago, and in preparation for this study.   First I read it with unmixed pleasure, then with considerable disappointment, lastly with mixed feelings, my artistic and dramatic instincts somewhat pitted against each other.   For the dramatic interest drags at Gerald's irresolute attitude and inarticulate farewell to Mollie, and it is hard to forgive him for the unexplained silence that consumed her very life.   "The only part," writes Rossetti, "where I remember being much affected was at the old woman's narrative of Mollie's gradual decline."   The interest certainly revives here, but not convincingly, and there is a lack of the romantically passionate which, as Rossetti points out, Keats satisfies us with in his dramatic narratives.   But the poem so abounds with artistic beauties, both of personal and natural description, that we accept it thankfully on these grounds alone, *pace* Coventry Patmore, who thought it perfect from every point of view.   It has, moreover, the note of distinction.   It was the first serious poem upon a musical theme, as its author claims.

Tacitly Allingham has taken Rossetti's advice, and made *The Music Master* second in a series of four stories of Irish life, old world and modern, in his final collection of Irish poems, where its tranquil, calm and poignant restraint contrasts happily with the mystery and romance of *The Lady of the Sea* and the *Abbot of Inisfallen*, and the uncanny power and gloom of the *Goblin Child* and a *Stormy Night*.

Throughout his letters to Allingham we find Rossetti seeking and generally accepting his friends' opinions of his

poems, and glorifying, by recitation amongst his friends,
and approving or criticising, Allingham's, with a combined
delicacy and frankness which it does one good to dwell
upon.   This was the period of Allingham's *Day and Night
Songs*, and *Lawrence Bloomfield* and *Nightingale Valley*, an
anthology of lyrics and short poems.   But alas! while
Allingham preserved Rossetti's critical letters, his own to
Rossetti perished, for it is chronicled that the great painter
was in the habit from time to time of clearing out his
drawers by the simple method of destroying all their
accumulations.

The ballad of *Elfin Mere*, "one of the very few really
fine things of the kind written in our day," as Rossetti
characterised it, was illustrated by that painter in the *Day
and Night Songs*.

Here is, in brief, the story of *The Lady of the Sea*.

Brother of Diarmid, king of West Ierne, Dalchamar
becomes the apt pupil of the Arch poet Conn :

> Who taught the Prince of Fairy folk
> Who dwell within the hollow hills,
> In founts of rivers and of rills,
> In caves and woods and some that be
> Underneath the cold green sea ;
> The spells they cast on mortal men,
> And spells to master them again.

Therefore Dalchamar, to his brother's dread, turns his
mind to some love the wide earth cannot give and lives
absorbed in dreams thereof.   Till, as with the return of
spring, he paddles his coracle in a rocky cove and up a
lonely little strand :

> What spies he on the tawny sand ?
> A cold sea-jelly, cast away
> By fling of ebbing water ? nay !
> A little Cap of changeful sheen,
> A seamless Cap of rippled green,
> Mingling with purple, like the hue
> Of ocean weeds.

He stoop'd ; its touch
Like thinnest lightning ran him through
With blissful shiver, sharp and new !
What might it mean ?   For never such
A chance had come to Dalchamar ;
He felt as when, in dream, a star
Flew to him, bird-like from the sky.

But then he heard a sad low cry,
And, turning, saw five steps away—
Was it a woman ?—strange and bright,
With long loose hair, and her body fair,
Shimmering as with watery light ;
For nothing save a luminous mist
Of tender beryl and amethyst
Over the living smoothness lay,
Statue-firm from head to feet,—
A breathing Woman, soft and sweet,
And yet not earthly.

So she stood
One marvellous moment in his sight ;
Then, lapsing to another mood,
Her mouth's infantine loveliness
Trembling pleaded in sore distress ;
Her wide blue eyes with great affright
Were fill'd ; two slender hands she press'd
Against the roundlings of her breast,
Then with a fond face full of fears
She held them forth, and heavy tears
Brimm'd in silence and overflow'd.

He, doubting much what this might be,
Watched her.
Swiftly pointed she ;
Utter'd some sound of foreign speech ;
But Dalchamar held out of reach
The Cap, behind-back,—and so each
Regarded other.
Then she flung
Her arms aloft,—stood straight,—her wide
Eyes gazed on his, and into him ;
And she began a solemn song,
Of words uncouth, slow up and down ;

A song that deepen'd as she sung,
That soon was loud and swift and strong
Like the rising of a tide,
With power to seize and drench and drown
The senses,—till his sight grew dim,
A torpor crept on every limb.
What could he do?—an ocean-spell
Was on him.

But old wisdom rush'd
Into his mind, and with a start,
One gasp of breath, one leap of heart,
He pluck'd his dagger from its sheath,
Held forth the little Cap beneath
Its glittering point.   The song was hushed,
Prone on the yellow sand she fell.

He kneels, he takes her hands, with gentle,
Tender, passionate words—in vain ;
Then with a heart of love and pain
Wraps her in his crimson mantle,
Lifts her, lays her down with care,
As she a one-year infant were,
Within his woven coracle,
And o'er the smooth sea guides it well,
And bears her up the rocky path,
And through the circle of the rath,
To Banva's bower, his sister dear.
There, half in pity, half in fear,
The women tend her, till she sighs
And opens wide her wondrous eyes.

She is a Sea Maid, Moruach (Merrow) of Irish tradition and wears a *Connleen Druith*—a magical little cap on which depends her power of living under water.   The Sea Maid becomes Dalchamar's bride, but in the end leaves her mortal lover and children to return to the ocean depths, just as Matthew Arnold's Margaret is constrained to forsake the Neckan and her children of the sea.

Allingham has written two remarkable poems on the supernatural, one upon an Irish, the other upon an English subject, namely, *The Goblin Child of Belashanny* and *Squire*

Curtis. This is the legend of *The Goblin Child of Bela-shanny.* "In the large old house by the bridge, once a barrack, the room is still shown in which Robert Stewart, afterwards Lord Castlereagh, is said to have seen a ghost, which made a lasting impression on his mind. From early childhood Allingham heard as one of the local traditions that Castlereagh, after marching in with his regiment into Ballyshannon, saw a ghost in the barracks, and there is no reason to doubt that this is the ghost described in Lock-hart's *Life of Scott*, chapter lvi. Thomas Moore sets down in his diary (Abbotsford, October 20th, 1835): 'Scott said the only two men who had ever told him that they had actually seen a ghost afterwards put an end to themselves; one was Lord Castlereagh, who had himself mentioned to Scott his seeing The Radiant Boy. It was one night when he was in barracks and the face brightened gradually out of the fire-place and approached him. Lord Castlereagh stepped forward to it, and it receded again, and faded into the same place. It was the Duke of Wellington made Lord Castlereagh tell the story to Sir Walter, and Lord Castle-reagh told it without hesitation and as if believing in it implicitly.'"

But whilst Allingham had the warm suffrages of famous men and women of letters—the elect of various schools—Dickens and Thackeray, Patmore and Rossetti, Ruskin and George Eliot, Leigh Hunt, Tennyson and Browning—it is impossible to avoid the conclusion that his poems did not meet with the general recognitiont that hey deserved, while such obviously unfinished work as *The Songs of Two Worlds* and such charming but comparatively slight performances as the lyrics of the author of *Songs of Seven* were widely read. No doubt Allingham was clever enough to have tickled the taste of the English middle-class tens of thousands by oleo-graphs of the order of *The Light of Asia* or sham antiques of the type of *The Epic of Hades*. But he was above such a prostitution of his powers, even though he had by his

independence to suffer "fools" sadly—young lions, I should
say, or rather young jackasses in critical lions' skins who
brayed out of *The Saturday Review*—" New Poems by William
Allingham, and who is William Allingham ? " William
Allingham ! over whose *Day and Night* songs Ruskin went
into raptures, whom Rossetti and Tennyson recited and
Emerson quoted at length in the course of a famous oration.

But, if discouraged, the poet was in no sense daunted.
With the doggedness that ran in his northern blood he
thought and wrote on.

In *Flower Pieces* he exercised his fancy upon the lovely
nurslings of garden and field, while in *Thought and Word* he
attempts, as he says in his dedication to his children, " to
put into words some faint hint of the highest truths." Here
he tilts against Sacerdotalism and Un-Christian Science with
equal ardour, and in *An Evil May Day* shows the horror of
the loss of belief and the joy of its recovery, released from
the letter which kills, and full of the spirit which gives life;
whilst in his *News from Pannonia* he conducts a noble
dialogue on the death and motive philosophy of the great
Emperor Marcus Aurelius.

Allingham's penultimate volume, *Life and Phantasy*, is
prefaced by an interesting note of his plan of poetical work:
" There are various modes of producing what a man is able
to produce, and in my case I have, as it were, gone on
knitting, in the midst of other occupations, a little web of
poetry for myself and those near me out of designs suggested by the influences of the passing hours, have looked
back at these from time to time, reconsidered, retouched,
omitted, added new things to old."

By this process his "six volumes have taken substance
and shape," and thus they should " show something of the
quality of homogeneity, so far as this may belong to a man's
progress through successive stages of life and their various
moods."

His attitude to his art is to expound the miracle of

universal beauty, which, though linked with evil, is subject to a divine law.

I have marked *Prince Brightkin* as a delightful fairy pastoral for children's theatricals, and *George and the School-fellows* as one of the most striking poems in this volume, and was not surprised to find in a note at the end of it this letter:

TAVISTOCK HOUSE,
Monday, Ninth November, 1857.

My dear Sir,—I am happy to retain the poem, which is mournfully true and has moved me very much. You shall have a proof without fail.

Faithfully yours,
CHARLES DICKENS.

His new *Bona Dea* is an address to Mother Nature— the Bride of God—his childhood's rapture, his manhood's guard against a despair, which, however, for a time broke through her embrace and his ultimate consoler and spirit-ualiser.

In both *Thought and Word* and *Life and Phantasy* begins that series of epitaphs, aphorisms and *obiter dicta* of all kinds of which his final volume, *Blackberries*, is compounded:

These berries swell with autumn's power:
Some are red and green and sour,
Some are black and juicy to bite,
Some have a maggot, some a blight.

Here a new quality of our versatile author is apparent —satire, quizzical, ironical, sarcastic, sardonic, the possession of which is traditionally attributed to the Irish Bard, and whose exercise owing to its supposed maleficent effects he kept like a rod in pickle for his detractors.

We do not now believe in this power of rhyming human rats to death, however we might rejoice at such a form of euthanasia. But are there not still certain letter-boxes into which the dropping of such epigrams as follow, upon their owners' well-advertised birthdays, might not have a searching effect? I will leave my readers to address the envelopes.

> "Man's a machine?" Well, if we ever can
> Construct one, bit by bit, on some new plan,
> Be sure 'twill be, a *scientific* man.

> *I* believe without bother in This, That and T'other;
>   Whatever is current, no matter.
> *I* believe in success, and in comfort no less;
>   *I* believe all the rest is but patter.

> Dorr through his life has been content to wait
> In lazy hopes of doing something great;
> In practice null, in theory surprising,
> Dorr sleeps till noon to dream of early rising.

> Arr *does* write books, and, to exalt his own,
> On principle runs every other's down.

> Scratch also writes; and if you can and do
> Praise Scratch, then Scratch will honestly praise *you*.

> MAXIMILIAN GUSHER.

> A torrent of abuse, or praise,
>   What matters which? I'll pour,
> Let folk but on the sparkle gaze,
>   And listen to the roar.

> With wrappings and knottings your meaning you hide;
> Good sooth, *is* there always a meaning inside?

> I dreamt I went to hell one night.
> The little devils were impolite;
> But Satan with the sweetest air
> Bowed me into a red-hot chair.

Finally, here is Allingham's—

> ADVICE TO A YOUNG POET.

> You're a true Poet: but, my dear,
> If you would hold the public ear,
> Remember to be, NOT TOO CLEAR.
> Be strange, be verbally intense;

WORDS matter ten times more than *sense:*
In *clear* streams, under *sunny* skies,
The fish *you* angle for won't rise ;
In *turbid* water, *cloudy* weather,
They'll rush to you by shoals together.
"Ignotum pro mirifico " ;
The *least part* of your meaning show ;
Your readers must not understand
Too well ; the mist-wrapt hill looks grand,
The placid noonday mountain small.
Speak *plainly* and folk say—"Is that all?"
Speak *riddles*—"What is here ?"   They read
And re-read, many times indeed ;
"How fine ! how strange ! how deep ! how new !
Here's *my* opinion ; what say you ?
It may be this, it might be that ;
Who can be certain what he's at,
This *necromancer?* "   While they talk
You swing your solemn cloak and stalk
Or else look on with smile urbane,
"Well done, my children,—guess again !"
O let me not advise in vain,
Be what you will, but don't be plain !

Thus writing, gardening, and musing afield with good friends from the highest to the humblest, with many interests in a life of high thinking and plain living, and above all, the happiest of homes through the devoted companionship of his wife and children, Allingham's days went by.

He wrote *Ashby Manor*, a telling poetical drama of Puritan and Royalist times (as Allingham tells us), which a London manager highly praised, regretting, however, that it was not *exactly* suited to his company, but asking for another drama from the same hand. Some months later the manager produced a play which was without doubt a clumsy parody of *Ashby Manor*, in time, story, incidents and characters, with senseless melodramatic additions and an entirely irrelevant fifth act.

The manager, on this being pointed out to him, asserted that he had never read a page of *Ashby Manor*, and scarcely recollected anything about it. His bold enterprise, adds Allingham, deservedly proved a failure. He received similar treatment when his one-act prose comedy, *Hopwood & Co.*, was shown to another stage shark, who swallowed his ideas whole but returned the play. This piece might well be undertaken by the Irish Literary Society with some modification of the part of the Irish *Dea ex machina*. Mrs. Allingham illustrated *Ashby Manor* and other of her husband's works with the rarest charm.

When next we have to think of Christmas presents, I cannot conceive of a more enjoyable one for children, young and growing up, than *Allingham's Rhymes for the Young Folk*, with delightful pictures by Mrs. Allingham, Kate Greenaway, Caroline Paterson and Harry Furniss. Another Allingham souvenir is a selection from his poems, which, by the consent of Mrs. Allingham, Mr. W. B. Yeats has made, and which has been issued from his sister's beautiful Cuala Press. To these Allingham souvenirs may now be added the new volume of Messrs. Macmillan's *Golden Treasury*, i.e., the selections from William Allingham's poetry, by his wife, Helen Allingham.

EARLY IRISH RELIGIOUS POETRY

(*With original translations*)

DR. DOUGLAS HYDE, who has done much to preserve the Gaelic religious poetry of Connaught, and who has turned so much of it into beautiful English verse, first drew my serious attention to the study of sacred poetry in the Irish language.

I then read, with much pleasure, Dr. Alexander Carmichael's fine prose versions of Hebridean prayer poems and charms in his delightful *Carmina Gadelica;* and, of course, I had been happily familiar, from the time of their publication, with Dr. Sigerson's verse renderings of Irish Gaelic poems in his *Bards of the Gael and Gall.*

A German historian's opinion, quoted by Dr. Sigerson, is that the civilisation of Europe belonged to Ireland for three centuries, from the fifth to the ninth, and that an Irish influence upon Latin verse first made itself manifest in the works of Sedulius (Shiel) and especially in his *Carmen Paschale*, the earliest Christian epic of importance. True, the poet's Irish nationality has been questioned by the German critic Huemer, but Dr. Sigerson applies Gaelic verse tests which afford the strongest internal evidence that he was an Irish writer.

Zeuss calls attention to Irish rhymes in the verses in praise of St. Patrick by his nephew, St. Secundinus, also a fifth century writer, and Dr. Sigerson enforces this view by even more distinct proofs of the influence of the Bardic schools upon these verses and upon his " Sancti, Venite," the celebrated post-communion hymn, sung, according to tradition, by angels in the Saint's church at Bangor.

Then, in the sixth century, we have, in St. Columkille himself, an author of both Gaelic and Latin sacred verse, one who moreover Gaelicised Latin verse, as in his *Altus Prosator*, composed in trochaic tetrameters. But, as a writer in the ancient *Lebor Breac* points out—distinguishing between artificial rhythm, or that of quantity, and that of accent in the syllables of the quatrain and half-quatrain— this hymn is composed in the latter and popular Irish rhythm. St. Columkille also uses trisyllabic and even four-syllabled, as well as internal rhymes and assonances in his Latin verse—all Gaelic verse peculiarities.

Columbanus, twenty years later, whilst composing in classical metres and pure Latin, also introduced Irish alliteration and rhyme; and St. Ultan's seventh century Latin hymn in honour of St. Brigit abounds in Irish-Gaelic verse characteristics, as do the Latin hymns of the seventh century poet saints, Cummain and Colman.

In the eighth century, according to Dr. Sigerson, St. Cucuimne, who died A.D. 742, "employed both vowel and consonant rhyme, with alliteration, in a manner most dear to the Gaelic bards of Munster a thousand years ago. His contemporary, St. Œngus, son of Tipraite, makes use of woven rhyme with like liberality in his hymn to St. Martin. As written, the lines are :

> Martinus mirus ore laudavit deum,
> Puro corde cantavit atque amavit eum.

Here we see the rhymes, but not the system, until we arrange the lines as a Gaelic quatrain :

> Martinus Mirus *more*
> *Ore laudavit* deum,
> Puro Corde *Cantavit*
> Atque *amavit* eum."

The old Spanish *redondellas* are so obviously akin in their imperfect rhyming to the Irish quatrains that it is amusing to find Ticknor claiming them as an original con-

tribution to Spanish poetical culture, as Dr. Sigerson points
out.   Of course they came into Spain out of Ireland.   For
the fact was that Ireland was at this time not only " The
Island of the Saints," but that of the scholars and students
as well—an International University, in fine, where all
foreigners, Continental and British, were not only received
with the warmest of welcomes, but actually given a free
education in all the learning of the time, free living and
free lodging, as The Venerable Bede expressly tells us.
What a comment this upon the tardiness with which Ireland
has secured a latter day National University of her own
from her Anglo-Saxon rulers, and in how different a spirit
from that of Prince, afterwards King, Aeldfrid of Northum-
bria, who, in those good old days, praised, in a Gaelic
poem of his own, the beauty and hospitality and learning
and wisdom of Ancient Erin.

Then the foreign students learnt Irish from their Irish
teachers, and carried Gaelic poetry abroad with them into
France, Spain, Germany and Scandinavia, there infusing
their native verse with such Irish elements as are found, as
pointed out, in the Spanish *redondellas*.

It will thus be seen that Gaelic verse, written side by
side with Latin, had not only influenced that language in
rhyme and accent, but had begun to emerge as a separate
vehicle for the expression of religious thought as early as
the fifth century.

I propose here to place before the readers of the
Dublin Review a few translations of some of the Gaelic
religious poems in early Irish, collected by Professor Kuno
Meyer, and the editors of *The Irish Liber Hymnorum*.

Let me preface my own translations with one by Dr.
Sigerson, published in his work already referred to.   He
prefixes to this translation the following observations :

In Gaelic, many hymns and poems relating to religious subjects
made their appearance subsequent to St. Patrick's *Guardsman's Cry*.
They show originality and independence of thought and expression.

Perhaps the earliest is the Hymn of St. Ita (who was born A.D. 480) ; it is classic in form and bold in conception.

The absolute faith of the ancient Irish inspired them with the love which casts out fear, and their poems show no trace of servile dread.

They prefixed the pronoun "mo," "my," to the names of their saints, which they modified by fond diminutives.

Saint Ita, in this way, uses an endearing diminutive with the name of the Redeemer. "Isa," the ancient Irish form of Jesus (which is now "Iosa") became "Isucan"—Jesukin—in her poem. It was applied to the infant Saviour who, it was believed, abode with her at night, in her lonely cell in the desert. The following translation is in the metre of the original :

JESUKIN.

St. Ita (B. 480—D. 570.)

Jesukin
Lives my little cell within ;
What were wealth of cleric high—
All is lie but Jesukin.

Nursling nurtured, as 'tis right—
Harbours here no servile spright—
Jesu of the skies, who art
Next my heart thro' every night !

Jesukin, my good for aye,
Calling and will not have nay,
King of all things, ever true,
He shall rue who will away.

Jesu, more than angels' aid,
Fosterling not formed to fade,
Nursed by me in desert wild,
Jesu, child of Judah's Maid.

Sons of Kings and kingly kin
To my land may enter in ;
Guest of none I hope to be,
Save of Thee, my Jesukin !

Unto heaven's High King confest,
Sing a chorus, maidens blest !
He is o'er us, though within
Jesukin is on my breast!

The legendary story of the famous hymn known as *The Lorica of St. Patrick*, or *The Guardsman's Cry*, or *The Deer's Cry*, is, according to the Tripartite Life of St. Patrick, as follows :

" Patrick and King Loegaire (Leary) met at Tara Hill, when that monarch was presiding at a heathen festival, which was to begin with the extinction of all fires throughout the country.   But Patrick disregarded the regulation, and defiantly lighted his Paschal fire on the Hill of Slane, in full view of the King and his Druids.   Then followed contested arguments between the Saint and the Druids, in which Patrick triumphed, as Moses of old triumphed over the magicians of Egypt.   The King thereupon purposed to kill Patrick by a treacherous assault ; but he and his companions escaped, being miraculously transformed into deer, but the hymn or chant which he recited in his flight was the ' Lorica S. Patricii,' commonly called ' Faeth Fiada,' or ' The Deer's Cry '—the chanting of the Saint and his monks appearing to those lying in ambush against them to be the cry of deer."

In his *Essay on Tara Hill*, published in 1839, in which this piece was first printed, Petrie stated that some portions of the hymn were then in use amongst the peasantry, and repeated at bed-time as a protection against evil.   But Dr. O'Donovan translates " fath fia " to mean magical darkness, and Professor O'Curry explains that " fath fiadha " was a spell, peculiar to druids and poets, who, by pronouncing certain verses, made themselves invisible.   " Thus *The Lorica* may have gained its title, not from any tradition about St. Patrick and the deer at Tara," writes Dr. Bernard, " but from its use as a charm or incantation to ensure invisibility." That the hymn is of early date there can be no doubt, and it may be identified with the " Canticum Scoticum," ordered to be sung in all Irish monasteries in honour of St. Patrick. " The original," writes Dr. Sigerson, " is a ' Rosg,' a poem of short sentences, with irregular rhythm and rime."

THE BREASTPLATE OF ST. PATRICK.

I invoke, upon my path
To the King of Ireland's rath,
  The Almighty power of the Trinity ;
Through belief in the Threeness,
Through confession of the Oneness
  Of the Maker's Eternal Divinity.

I invoke, on my journey arising,
The power of Christ's Birth and Baptizing,
The powers of the hours of His dread Crucifixion,
  Of His Death and Abode in the Tomb,
The power of the hour of His glorious Resurrection
  From out the Gehenna of gloom,
The power of the hour when to Heaven He ascended,
And the power of the hour when by Angels attended
  He returns for the Judgment of Doom !
      On my perilous way
      To Tara to-day,
     I, Patrick, God's servant,
       Invoke from above
       The Cherubim's love !
Yea ! I summon the might of the Company fervent
Of Angel obedient, ministrant Archangel
To speed and to prosper my Irish Evangel.
I go forth on my path in the trust
Of the gathering to God of the Just ;
In the power of the Patriarchs' prayers ;
The foreknowledge of Prophets and Seers ;
The Apostles' pure preaching ;
The Confessors' sure teaching ;
The virginity blest of God's Dedicate Daughters,
And the lives and the deaths of His Saints and His Martyrs !

    I arise to-day in the strength of the heaven,
      The glory of the sun,
      The radiance of the moon,
    The splendour of fire and the swiftness of the levin,
      The wind's flying force,
      The depth of the sea,
     The earth's steadfast course,
      The rock's austerity.

I arise on my way,
With God's Strength for my stay,
God's Might to protect me,
God's Wisdom to direct me,
God's Eye to be my providence,
God's Ear to take my evidence,
God's Word my words to order,
God's Hand to be my warder,
God's Way to lie before me,
God's Shield and Buckler o'er me,
God's Host Unseen to save me,
   From each ambush of the Devil,
      From each vice that would enslave me,
   And from all who wish me evil,
      Whether far I fare or near,
      Alone or in a multitude.

All these Hierarchies and Powers
   I invoke to intervene,
When the adversary lowers
   On my path, with purpose keen
      Of vengeance black and bloody
      On my soul and on my body ;
I bind these Powers to come
   Against Druid counsel dark,
The black craft of Pagandom,
   And the false heresiarch,
The spells of wicked women,
And the wizard's arts inhuman,
And every knowledge, old and fresh,
Corruptive of man's soul and flesh.

May Christ, on my way
To Tara to-day,
Shield me from poison,
   Shield me from fire,
Drowning or wounding
   By enemy's ire,
So that mighty fruition
May follow my mission.
Christ behind and before me,
Christ beneath me and o'er me,
Christ within and without me,
Christ with and about me,

Christ on my left and Christ on my right,
Christ with me at morn and Christ with me at night ;
Christ in each heart that shall ever take thought of me,
Christ in each mouth that shall ever speak aught of me ;
Christ in each eye that shall ever on me fasten,
Christ in each ear that shall ever to me listen.

I invoke, upon my path
To the King of Ireland's rath,
    The Almighty Power of the Trinity ;
Through belief in the Threeness,
Through confession of the Oneness
    Of the Maker's Eternal Divinity.

The originals of these early religious poems are as remarkable for their style as Matthew Arnold leads us to expect in a fine passage on the study of Celtic literature.

" The Celts certainly have style in a wonderful measure. Style is the most striking quality of their poetry. Celtic poetry seems to make up to itself for being unable to master the world and give an adequate interpretation of it, by throwing all its force into style, by bending language, at any rate, to its will, and expressing the ideas it has with unsurpassable intensity, elevation, and effect. It has all through it a sort of intoxication of style—a *Pindarism*, to use a word formed from the name of the poet, on whom, above all other poets, the power of style seems to have exercised an inspiring and intoxicating effect ; and not in its great poets only, in Taliesin, or Llywarch Hen, or Ossian, does the Celtic genius show this Pindarism, but in all its productions :

The grave of March is this, and this the grave of Gwythyr ;
Here is the grave of Gwgawn Gleddyfreidd ;
But unknown is the grave of Arthur.

That comes from the Welsh *Memorials of the Graves of the Warriors*, and if we compare it with the familiar memorial inscriptions of an English churchyard (for we English have so much Germanism in us that our productions offer abundant examples of German want of style as well as of its opposite) :

Afflictions sore long time I bore,
Physicians were in vain,
Till God did please Death should me seize,
And ease me of my pain—

If, I say, we compare the Welsh memorial lines with the English, which, in their *Gemeinheit* of style are truly Germanic, we shall get a clear sense of what that Celtic talent for style I have been speaking of is.

Or take this epitaph of an Irish Celt, Ængus the Culdee, whose ' felire,' or festology, I have already mentioned ; a festology in which, at the end of the eighth or beginning of the ninth century, he collected from ' the countless hosts of the illuminated books of Erin ' (to use his own words) the festivals of the Irish saints, his poem having a stanza for every day in the year.   The epitaph on Ængus, who died at Cluain Eidhnech, in Queen's County, is by no eminent hand, and yet a Greek epitaph could not show a finer perception of what constitutes propriety and felicity of style in compositions of this nature."

ON ÆNGUS THE CULDEE.

Delightful here at Disert Bethel,
  By cold, pure Nore at peace to rest,
Where noisy raids have never sullied
  The beechen forest's virgin vest.

For here the Angel Host would visit
  Of yore with Ængus, Oivlen's son,
As in his cross-ringed cell he lauded
  The One in Three, the Three in One.

To death he passed upon a Friday,
  The day they slew our Blessed Lord.
Here stands his tomb ; unto the Assembly
  Of Holy Heaven his soul has soared.

'Twas in Cloneagh he had his rearing ;
'Tis in Cloneagh he now lies dead,
'Twas in Cloneagh of many crosses
That first his psalms he read.*

" Irish religious poetry," writes Professor Kuno Meyer,
" ranges from single quatrains to lengthy compositions
dealing with all the varied aspects of religious life. Many
of them give us a fascinating insight into the peculiar character of the early Irish Church, which differed in so many
ways from the Christian world. We see the hermit in his
lonely cell, the monk at his devotions or at his work of
copying in the scriptorium or under the open sky ; or we
hear the ascetic who, alone or with twelve chosen companions, has left one of the great monasteries in order to
live in greater solitude among the woods or mountains, or
on a lonely island. The fact that so many of these poems
are fathered upon well-known saints emphasises the friendly
attitude of the native clergy towards vernacular poetry."

With these words before me, which summarise the contents of the Professor's section of Religious Poetry in his
beautiful prose translations from Ancient Irish Poetry in
his book of that name, published a year ago by Messrs.
Constable, let me express my deep indebtedness to him for
the pleasure these consummate versions from the Gaelic
have given me.

They beguiled the tedium of a troublesome illness last
spring, and if the verse translations that follow have been
successful, it is largely because they have caught, through
Professor Kuno Meyer's prose, some of the inspiration of
their Gaelic originals.

* Matthew Arnold only quotes the last two quatrains of this epitaph
in the following prose version :

" Angus is in the assembly of Heaven, here are his tomb and his
bed ; it is from hence he went to death in the Friday, to holy Heaven.
It was in Cluain Eidhnech he was rear'd ; in was in Cluain Eidhnech
he was buried; in Cluain Eidhnech, of many crosses, he first read his
psalms." The verse rendering of the whole poem is my own. A. P. G.

CRINOG.

A.D. 900—1,000.

[This poem relates, on the authority of Professor Kuno Meyer, by whom the Irish text was first published, " to one who lived like a sister or spiritual wife with a priest, monk, or hermit, a practice which, while early suppressed and abandoned everywhere else, seems to have survived in the Irish Church till the tenth century."]

Crinog of melodious song,
  No longer young, but bashful-eyed,
As when we roved Niall's Northern Land,
  Hand in hand, or side by side.

Peerless maid, whose looks ran o'er
  With the lovely lore of Heaven,
By whom I slept in dreamless joy,
  A gentle boy of summers seven.

We dwelt in Banva's broad domain,
  Without one stain of soul or sense ;
While still mine eye flashed forth on thee
  Affection free of all offence.

To meet thy counsel quick and just,
  Our faithful trust responsive springs ;
Better thy wisdom's searching force
  Than any smooth discourse with kings.

In sinless sisterhood with men,
  Four times since then, hast thou been bound,
Yet not one rumour of ill-fame
  Against thy name has travelled round.

At last, their weary wanderings o'er,
  To me once more thy footsteps tend ;
The gloom of age makes dark thy face,
  Thy life of grace draws near its end.

Oh, faultless one and very dear,
  Unstinted welcome here is thine.
Hell's haunting dread I ne'er shall feel,
  So thou be kneeling at my side

Thy blessed fame shall ever bide,
    For far and wide thy feet have trod.
Could we their saintly track pursue,
    We yet should view the Living God.

You leave a pattern and bequest
    To all who rest upon the earth—
A life-long lesson to declare
    Of earnest prayer the precious worth.

God grant us peace and joyful love !
    And may the countenance of Heaven's King
Beam on us, when we leave behind
    Our bodies blind and withering.

THE DEVIL'S TRIBUTE TO MOLING.

(Once, when St. Moling was praying in his church, the Devil visited him in purple raiment and distinguished form. On being challenged by the saint, he declared himself to be the Christ, but on Moling's raising the Gospel to disprove his claim, the Evil One confessed that he was Satan. "Wherefore hast thou come?" asked Moling. "For a blessing," the Devil replied. "Thou shalt not have it," said Moling, "for thou deservest it not." "Well, then," said the Devil, "bestow the full of a curse on me." "What good were that to thee?" asked Moling. "The venom and the hurt of the curse will be on the lips from which it will come." After further parley, the Devil paid this tribute to Moling.)

He is pure gold, the sky around the sun,
    A silver chalice brimmed with blessed wine,
    An Angel shape, a book of lore divine,
Whoso obeys in all the Eternal One.

He is a foolish bird that fowlers lime,
    A leaking ship in utmost jeopardy,
    An empty vessel and a withered tree,
Who disobeys the Sovereign Sublime.

A fragrant branch with blossoms overrun,
    A bounteous bowl with honey overflowing,
    A precious stone, of virtue past all knowing
Is he who doth the will of God's dear Son.

A nut that only emptiness doth fill,
    A sink of foulness, a crookt branch is he
    Upon a blossomless crab-apple tree,
Who doeth not his Heavenly Master's will.

Whoso obeys the Son of God and Mary—
    He is a sunflash lighting up the moor,
    He is a daïs on the Heavenly Floor,
A pure and very precious reliquary.

A sun heaven-cheering he, in whose warm beam
    The King of Kings takes ever fresh delight,
    He is a temple, noble, blessed, bright,
A saintly shrine with gems and gold a-gleam.

The altar he, whence bread and wine are told,
    Where countless melodies around are hymned,
    A chalice cleansed, from God's own grapes upbrimmed,
Upon Christ's garment's hem the joyful gold.

MAELISU'S HYMN TO THE ARCHANGEL MICHAEL.

By Maelisu ua Brocháin, a writer of religious poetry both in Irish
and Latin, who died in 1051.

Mael-Isu means "the tonsured of Jesus." He is the author of the
beautiful "Hymn to the Holy Spirit."

Angel and Saint,
    O Michael of the oracles,
    O Michael of great miracles,
Bear to the Lord my plaint !

Hear my request !
    Ask of the great, forgiving God,
    To lift this vast and grievous load
Of sin from off my breast.

Why, Michael, tarry,
    My fervent prayer with upward wing
    Unto the King, the great High King
Of Heaven and Earth to carry ?

Upon my soul
    Bring help, bring comfort, yea, bring power
    To win release, in death's black hour,
From sin, distress and dole.

Till, as devoutly
  My fading eyes seek Heaven's dim height ;
  To meet me, with thy myriads bright,
Do thou adventure stoutly.

Captain of hosts,
  Against earth's wicked, crooked clan
  To aid me lead thy battle van,
And quell their cruel boasts.

Archangel glorious,
  Disdain not now thy suppliant urgent,
  But over every sin insurgent
Set me at last victorious.

Thou art my choosing !
  That with my body, soul and spirit
  Eternal life I may inherit,
Thine aid be not refusing !

In my sore need
  O thou of Anti-Christ the slayer,
  Triumphant victor, to my prayer
Give heed, O now give heed !

THE HERMIT'S SONG.

See *Eriu*, vol. I, p. 39, where the Irish text will be found.
According to Professor Kuno Meyer it dates from the ninth century.

I long, O Son of the living God,
  Ancient, eternal King,
For a hidden hut on the wilds untrod,
  Where Thy praises I might sing ;
A little, lithe lark of plumage grey
  To be singing still beside it,
Pure waters to wash my sin away,
  When Thy Spirit has sanctified it.
Hard by it a beautiful, whispering wood
  Should stretch, upon either hand,
To nurse the many-voiced fluttering brood
  In its shelter green and bland.
Southward, for warmth, should my hermitage face,
  With a runnel across its floor,
In a choice land gifted with every grace,
  And good for all manner of store.

A few true comrades I next would seek
   To mingle with me in prayer,
Men of wisdom, submissive, meek ;
   Their number I now declare,
Four times three and three times four,
   For every want expedient,
Sixes two within God's Church door,
   To north and south obedient ;
Twelve to mingle their voices with mine
   At prayer, whate'er the weather,
To Him Who bids His dear sun shine
   On the good and ill together.
Pleasant the Church with fair Mass cloth—
   No dwelling for Christ's declining—
To its crystal candles, of bees-wax both,
   On the pure, white Scriptures shining.
Beside it a hostel for all to frequent,
   Warm with a welcome for each,
Where mouths, free of boasting and ribaldry, vent
   But modest and innocent speech.
These aids to support us my husbandry secks,
   I name them now without hiding—
Salmon and trout and hens and leeks,
   And the honey-bees' sweet providing.
Raiment and food enow will be mine
   From the King of all gifts and all graces ;
And I to be kneeling, through rain or shine,
   Praying to God in all places.

A PRAYER TO THE VIRGIN.

Edited by Strachan in *Eriu*, vol. I, p. 122. Tenth or perhaps
ninth century.

   Gentle Mary, Noble Maiden,
      Hearken to our suppliant pleas !
   Shrine God's only Son was laid in !
      Casket of the Mysteries !

   Holy Maid, pure Queen of Heaven,
      Intercession for us make,
   That each hardened heart's transgression
      May be pardoned for Thy sake.

Bent in loving pity o'er us,
  Through the Holy Spirit's power,
Pray the King of Angels for us
  In Thy Visitation hour.

Branch of Jesse's tree whose blossoms
  Scent the heavenly hazel wood,
Pray for me for full purgation
  Of my bosom's turpitude.

Mary, crown of splendour glowing,
  Dear destroyer of Eve's ill,
Noble torch of Love far-showing,
  Fruitful Stock of God's good will ;

Heavenly Virgin, Maid transcendent,
  Yea ! He willed that Thou should'st be
His fair Ark of Life Resplendent,
  His pure Queen of Chastity.

Mother of all good, to free me,
  Interceding at my side,
Pray Thy First-Born to redeem me,
  When the Judgment books are wide ;

Star of knowledge, rare and noble,
  Tree of many-blossoming sprays,
Lamp to light our night of trouble,
  Sun to cheer our weary days ;

Ladder to the Heavenly Highway,
  Whither every Saint ascends,
Be a safeguard still, till my way
  In Thy glorious Kingdom ends !

Covert fair of sweet protection,
  Chosen for a Monarch's rest,
Hostel for nine months' refection
  Of a Noble Infant Guest ;

Glorious Heavenly Porch, whereunder,
  So the day star sinks his head,
God's Own Son—O saving wonder !
  Jesus was incarnated ;

For the fair Babe's sake conceivèd
   In Thy womb and brought to birth,
For the Blest Child's sake, receivèd
   Now as King of Heaven and Earth ;

For His Rood's sake ! starker, steeper
   Hath no other Cross been set,
For His Tomb's sake ! darker, deeper
   There hath been no burial yet ;

By His Blessed Resurrection,
   When He triumphed o'er the tomb,
By The Church of His affection
   During till the Day of Doom,

Safeguard our unblest behaviour,
   Till behind Death's blinding veil,
Face to face, we see our Saviour.
   This our prayer is : Hail ! All Hail !

ON THE FLIGHTINESS OF THOUGHT.

A tenth century poem.   See *Eriu*, vol. III, p. 13.

Shame upon my thoughts, O shame !
   How they fly in order broken,
Much therefore I fear the blame
   When the Trump of Doom has spoken.

At my psalms, they oft are set
   On a path the Fiend must pave them ;
Evermore, with fash and fret,
   In God's sight they misbehave them.

Through contending crowds they fleet,
   Companies of wanton women,
Silent wood or strident street,
   Swifter than the breezes skimming.

Now through paths of loveliness,
   Now through ranks of shameful riot,
Onward evermore they press,
   Fledged with folly and disquiet.

O'er the Ocean's sounding deep
  Now they flash like fiery levin ;
Now at one vast bound they leap
  Up from earth into the heaven.

Thus afar and near they roam
  On their race of idle folly ;
Till at last to reason's home
  They return right melancholy.

Would you bind them wrist to wrist —
  Foot to foot the truants shackle,
From your toils away they twist
  Into air with giddy cackle.

Crack of whip or edge of steel
  Cannot hold them in your keeping ;
With the wriggle of an eel
  From your grasp they still go leaping.

Never yet was fetter found,
  Never lock contrived, to hold them ;
Never dungeon underground,
  Moor or mountain keep controlled them.

Thou Whose glance alone makes pure,
  Searcher of all hearts and Saviour,
With Thy Sevenfold Spirit cure
  My stray thoughts' unblessed behaviour.

God of earth, air, fire and flood,
  Rule me, rule me in such measure,
That, to my eternal good,
  I may live to love Thy pleasure.

Christ's own flock thus may I reach,
  At the flash of Death's sharp sickle,
Just in deed, of steadfast speech,
  Not, as now, infirm and fickle.

THE MOTHERS' LAMENT AT THE SLAUGHTER OF THE INNOCENTS.

Probably a poem of the eleventh century.   It is written in Rosg metre, and was first published by Professor Kuno Meyer, in *The Gaelic Journal*, May, 1891.

Then, as the executioner plucked her son from her breast, one of the women said:

    " Why are you tearing
        Away to his doom,
    The child of my caring,
        The fruit of my womb.
    Till nine months were o'er,
    His burthen I bore,
    Then his pretty lips pressed
    The glad milk from my breast,
    And my whole heart he filled,
    And my whole life he thrilled.

    All my strength dies,
    My tongue speechless lies,
    Darkened are my eyes !
    His breath was the breath of me ;
    His death is the death of me !"

Then another woman said:

    " Tis my own son that from me you wring,
        I deceived not the King.
    But slay me, even me,
    And let my boy be.
    A mother most hapless,
    My bosom is sapless,
    Mine eyes one tearful river,
    My frame one fearful shiver,
    My husband sonless ever,
    And I a sonless wife,
    To live a death in life.

    Oh, my son !   Oh, God of Truth !
    Oh, my unrewarded youth !
    Oh, my birthless sicknesses,
    Until doom without redress !
    Oh, my bosom's silent nest !
    Oh, the heart broke in my breast !"

Then said another woman :

    " Murderers, obeying
      Herod's wicked willing,
    One ye would be slaying,
      Many are ye killing.
    Infants would ye smother ?
      Ruffians ye have rather
      Wounded many a father,
    Slaughtered many a mother.
    Hell's black jaws your horrid deed is glutting,
    Heaven's white gate against your black souls shutting.

    Ye are guilty of the Great Offence !
    Ye have spilt the blood of Innocence."

And yet another woman said :

    " O Lord Christ come to me !
      Nay, no longer tarry !
    With my son, home to Thee
      My soul quickly carry.
    O Mary great, O Mary mild,
      Of God's One Son the Mother,
    What shall I do without my child,
      For I have now no other.
    For Thy Son's sake my son they slew,
      Those murderers inhuman ;
    My sense and soul they slaughtered too.
      I am but a crazy woman.
    Yea ! after that most piteous slaughter,
    When my babe's life ran out like water,
    The heart within my bosom hath become
    A clot of blood from this day till the Doom ! "

THE MONK AND HIS WHITE CAT.

After an eighth or early ninth century Irish poem. Text and
translation in *Thesaurus Palæohibernicus.*

    Pangar, my white cat, and I
      Silent ply our special crafts ;
    Hunting mice his one pursuit,
      Mine to shoot keen spirit shafts.

Rest I love, all fame beyond,
   In the bond of some rare book ;
Yet white Pangar from his play
   Casts, my way, no jealous look.

Thus alone within one cell
   Safe we dwell—not dull the tale—
Since his ever favourite sport
   Each to court will never fail.

Now a mouse, to swell his spoils,
   In his toils he spears with skill ;
Now a meaning deeply thought
   I have caught with startled thrill.

Now his green full-shining gaze
   Darts its rays against the wall ;
Now my feebler glances mark
   Through the dark bright knowledge fall.

Leaping up with joyful purr,
   In mouse fur his sharp claw sticks,
Problems difficult and dear
   With my spear I, too, transfix.

Crossing not each other's will,
   Diverse still, yet still allied,
Following each his own lone ends,
   Constant friends we here abide.

Pangar, master of his art,
   Plays his part in pranksome youth :
While, in age sedate, I clear
   Shadows from the sphere of Truth.

THE RELIGIOUS SONGS OF CONNACHT

For vigour and versatility Dr. Douglas Hyde occupies a unique position amongst Irishmen of letters. A fine classical and modern languages scholar, he can yet translate into racy Hiberno-English prose and verse his own Gaelic description and collection of the religious songs of Connacht. He dedicates them, moreover—he, a Bachelor of Divinity of Dublin University—in graceful Latin, to the memory of Father Eugene O'Growney, his intimate associate in the Irish language revival. Could literary catholicity go much further?

An extract from his interesting preface will show the scope and purpose of the work :

While collecting the poetry of the province of Connacht—a work which I began some twenty years ago—I found that those poems which touched upon piety or religion were very numerous. I found, moreover, that prayers put in a setting of poetry, melodious "paidirs" and short petitions composed in metre, were very numerous also. I found at the same time charms or "orthas" or "amhras," I found pieces concerning the Church, I found pieces praising or dispraising people for their religion, I found stories about the Church or about the persecution of the Church, or about some saint or other, I found blessings, I found curses, and I put all these things down here with the rest. These things are all mixed together in this book. There is no special order or arrangement in them, and it is now in my reader's power to form his own judgment—a thing which he could not have done if I had concealed from him anything that was coarse, bitter, foolish, half Pagan or otherwise unpleasing. . . . Very few indeed of these things have ever been put upon paper until now, and they will be becoming more scarce from day to day. If the " National Schools " ruined the indigenous literature (the love songs, the drinking songs, the keenes), they have torn these religious songs up out of the roots altogether. . . . "In my youth," says Father Walter Conway of Glenaddy, "there was no house in which the 'paidirin' or rosary used not to be said throughout all the year. When I came to this parish some eight or nine years ago, this custom had been given up by the majority of people. I frequently inquired the cause and never heard any answer except the one from everybody : 'We cannot say it in English, and the young people will not repeat it with us in Irish.'" And another priest, Father O'Concannon, also gives evidence of the neglect of the ancient Irish prayers and the old religious poems, adding : "It is upon the flagstone of the hearth that the foundations of piety and nationality are laid, and alas ! that the foreign schools should be destroying them !"

Dr. Hyde will certainly have the sympathy he asks from his readers for having preserved for the history of his country this leaf plucked out of the book of pre-Reformation Christendom. But to an historian's and folk-lorist's zeal to contribute a chapter to his country's records, Dr. Hyde also adds the desire of a good Irishman to preserve the evidences of her piety through the ages. For, as he points out, "the Irish Gael is pious by nature, there is not an Irishman in a hundred in whom is the making of an unbeliever. God is for him assured, true, intelligible. When he meets a neighbour, instead of saying 'Bon jour' or 'Good morning,' he says 'God salute you.'" Indeed, all the ordinary invocations and salutations of the Irish language are governed by this religious feeling. "When he takes snuff from you he will say : 'The blessing of God be with the souls of your dead.' If a sudden wonderment surprise him, he will cry : 'A thousand laudations to God'; and if he be shown a young child or anything else for the first time, he will say : 'Prosperity from God on it.'"

Dr. Hyde adduces two reasons for the persistence of the Irishman in the Roman Catholic faith. The old Church gave him more to believe than did the new Churches, and he was ready to believe more than they did, even in the face of bitter persecution. Again, the Irish Roman Catholic was

never " insular."   Much traffic prevailed between Ireland and
the Continent.   Her clergy were trained in its great Colleges,
and brought home with them the thoughts, the spirit, and the
literature of Roman Catholic Europe during the seventeenth
and eighteenth centuries.   This is shown by the numbers of
books translated from the Italian, French, and Spanish into
Irish.   Yet Dr. Hyde maintains that, in spite of what they
suffered, the Irish Roman Catholics were not unreasonably
embittered against those of the old Gaelic families whom the
Penal Laws converted to the new faith, though the bards gave
many a blow to " Martin " or to " John," and to " the lot who
fatten on Friday,"—that is to say, the people of the Bearla
(the English language).   And no doubt many of the new
clergy were time-servers, and through the relaxation of a
stricter rule of life became lazy and self-indulgent, and justified
such gibes as this :

> If yon fat friar be a poor friar,
>   Then a fat desire is his life's rule ;
> But if man by fat to Heaven aspire,
>   Then the lean friar is a lean fool !

" Yet a change came at last.   There grew out of the new
clergy many true Irishmen who had the love and respect of
the entire people."   Donough O'Daly, said to have been
Abbot of Boyle in the beginning of the thirteenth century,
was, in Dr. Hyde's opinion, the finest religious poet of old
Ireland.   His poem, *My son, remember*, taken down by
Dr. Hyde from the lips of a travelling man near Belmullet,
appears to have been kept alive by oral tradition for six
hundred odd years.   It is composed in the measure called
Ranneeacht, the quatrains of which had seven syllables in
each line, and were end-rhymed and internally rhymed as in
these specimen stanzas :—

> My son, remember what I say,
>   That in the day of Judgment shock,
> When men go stumbling down the mount,
>   The sheep may count thee of their flock.

*   *   *   *   *

> Shun sloth, shun greed, shun sensual fires
>   (Eager desires of men enslaved),
> Anger and pride and hatred shun,
>   Till Heaven be won, till man be saved.

Here, too, is an excerpt from one of the many poems dealing with the vanity of this world :

> Sleek and unhealthy this world is,
>   Where "wealthy" means wise and good and free,
> Where if a man is only poor,
>   All men are sure a fool is he.

> *   *   *   *   *

> The men I saw they saw me not,
>   Or if they saw they would not see.
> They thought, I think, I was not I,
>   But something different from me.

The religious bards of the seventeenth and eighteenth centuries dropped the syllabic metrification, and only counted the stressed syllables of their lines. Their themes are largely spiritual dialogues, such as those between Death and a Sinner, or the Body and the Soul. In these life is treated as a pilgrimage, and Dr. Hyde points out that those of them of Munster origin are more Puritanical in spirit than the Connacht examples. For, according to him, " it is not to God's vengeance but to His mercy that the Connacht man most looks, and his religious poems are always advising good works as the true road to heaven," as in this version of the original :

> Sister to sister, brother to brother
> Speak truth, show ruth to one another ;
> This the one road to heavenly profit ;
> This Christ's own way ! Oh, stray not off it.

These religious songs were chiefly composed by the friars, regulars, and the people themselves, not by the parish priests.

Indeed, the latter had to suffer from the satire of the former, as in the following example :

> O priest of the hips that are strong and portly and fine,
> Bring in my soul safe in the shade of that corpus of thine !

But another bard thus makes amends to his parish priest :

> When you lifted your voice to plead in Christ's cause,
>   You made sinners to pause, you so looked through us,
>   You seemed in Kilcornin that Sunday morning
>   Like an angel of God sent to us.

Space does not permit of dealing with Dr. Hyde's religious folk tales : a Rip Van Winkle tale of a student who left college, the story of a friar driven mad by love, another of a mad priest who wrought miracles, the strange legend of the Stone of Truth, and above all, a unique version of St. Paul's Vision contained in a manuscript between two hundred and three hundred years old, picked up by Dr. Hyde in County Meath, and all written down by him in racy Irish vernacular.

The religious poems of blind Raftery, who also wrote satires on the Tithe War, the establishment of National Schools, and the Clare Election of 1828, closed the series of the genuine religious Irish poets ; and to Raftery Dr. Hyde gives the palm amongst later writers on the score of taste, sweetness, and simplicity.   This praise is borne out by extracts from several of his longer poems, including a very remarkable one on *The Cholera Morbus*, and another entitled *Raftery's Repentance*.   It is only right, in conclusion, to call attention to the interesting series of prayers and invocations, not only of duty and observance, but also concerning such special acts as the covering up of the hearth fire, and even the smoking of tobacco.   Dr. Hyde gives many charms against diseases and pains, such as whooping-cough, ague, and toothache.   A comparison of these Irish charms with those in Alexander Carmichael's delightful *Carmina Gadelica* shows that not a few of these are common to Ireland

and the Western Isles, but Mr. Carmichael's collection is
both stranger and more beautiful than Dr. Hyde's.   It may
be mentioned in conclusion that Dr. Hyde not only gives the
Irish text of his collection on the left-hand pages of his book,
and the English version on the right-hand pages, but also
adds literal translations of the religious poems in the footnotes
below his metrical translations, thus enabling the Sassenach
to compare the one with the other for critical purposes.

CELTIC NATURE POETRY

MATTHEW ARNOLD'S book on the study of Celtic Literature contains perhaps the first realisation by a keen and wise English critic of the Celtic feeling for Nature as distinguished from that of the Greek, the Roman or the Teuton. Matthew Arnold has, indeed, coined a phrase expressive of that Celtic feeling for Nature which has been a sentiment for centuries, and which, when combined with the feeling for style with which he also credits the Celt, produces in Celtic prose tales and verse those flashes of beautiful expression in description of Nature which he terms "natural magic." Byron, as he points out, is more of the Celt than the Saxon in his poetry ; and no wonder, for was he not a Gordon of Highland descent ? "All Byron's heroes," he writes, "are consumed with the Celtic passion of revolt, so warm-breathing, puissant and sincere." He might have added that Byron, like the great Irish and Welsh poets, nurses his melancholy and exalts his spirits in companionship with Nature, rejoicing in its sullen solitudes of frowning mountain top and moaning sea, and again exhilarated by the dancing wave or the leaping lightning.

Shakespeare, he considers full of Celtic magic in his handling of Nature. Where did he come by this superlative gift ? Was it at second hand through Edmund Spenser, or his friend Dowland the Lutenist, through whom he is said to have introduced our Irish Puca, as his Puck, and our Queen Meabh, as his Queen Mab, into his plays ? Or was his mother, Mary Arden, who came from the Welsh border and whose kin was connected with the Welsh Tudor court, of Cymric blood? However this may be, Matthew Arnold's fine discrimination between Shakespeare's Greek and Celtic Nature notes deserves careful weighing. Thus he writes :

> I know a bank whereon the wild thyme blows,
> Where oxlips and the nodding violet grows,

strikes a Greek note. Then again in his :

> Look how the floor of heaven
> Is thick inlaid with patines of bright gold,

we are at the very point of transition from the Greek note to the Celtic ; there is the Greek clearness and brightness, with the Celtic aerialness and magic coming in.

Then we have the sheer, inimitable Celtic note in passages like this :

> The moon shines bright. In such a night as this,
> When the sweet wind did gently kiss the trees,
> And they did make no noise, in such a night
> Troilus, methinks, mounted the Trojan walls.
>
> *   *   *   *
>
> . . . In such a night
> Stood Dido, with a willow in her hand,
> Upon the wild sea banks, and waved her love
> To come again to Carthage.

The earliest Celtic Nature poems have a mystical magic about them which indicate a Druidical influence, or at any rate reminiscences of Druidism, as will be seen from the following specimens which represent the ancient poetry of four of the Celtic peoples: the Irish, Welsh, Cornish and Breton. Of this strange Pantheistic fragment called *The Mystery of Amergin*, Dr. Douglas Hyde states it is his opinion that whilst it is credited to Amergin, one of the first Milesian princes who colonised Ireland many hundreds of years before Christ, no faith can be placed in the alleged date, or genuineness of this poem, but that it is of interest " because, as Irish tradition has always represented

Amergin's verses as being the first made in Ireland, so it may very well be that they actually do present the oldest surviving lines in any vernacular tongue in Europe except Greek."

THE MYSTERY OF AMERGIN.

I am the wind which breathes upon the sea,
I am the wave of the ocean,
I am the murmur of the billows,
I am the ox of the seven combats,
I am the vulture upon the rocks,
I am the beam of the sun,
I am the fairest of plants,
I am a wild boar in valour,
I am a salmon in the water,
I am a lake in the plain,
I am a word of science,
I am the point of the lance of battle,
I am the God who creates in the head (*i.e.*, of man) the
    fire (*i.e.*, of thought).
Who is it who throws light into the meeting on the mountain?
Who announces the ages of the moon (if not I)?
Who teaches the place where couches the sun (if not I)?

The early Cymric fragment which follows is of unknown antiquity, but it is stated to be as old as the sixth, or possibly the fifth century. It is from the *Black Book of Caemarthen* (1154–1189), "that remarkable depository of early Cymric Law," as Mr. William Sharp calls it in his note to the poem in his wife's *Lyra Celtica.*

THE SOUL.

It was with seven faculties that I was thus blessed,
With seven created beings I was placed for purification;
I was gleaming fire when I was caused to exist;
I was dust of the earth, and grief could not reach me;
I was a high wind, being less evil than good;
I was a mist on a mountain seeking supplies of stags;
I was blossoms of trees on the face of the earth.
If the Lord had blessed me, He would have placed me on matter.
    Soul, since I was made——

The third example of early Celtic Nature poetry of the mystical order is *Merlin the Diviner*, which, although it is to be found in the old Cornish dialect, is really an ancient Breton incantation. The translation is from a *Memoir* of Thomas Stevens, the author of the following version published by William Rees, Llandovery, 1849.

MERLIN THE DIVINER.

Merlin ! Merlin ! where art thou going
So early in the day with thy black dog ?
Oi ! oi ! oi ! oi ! oi ! oi ! oi ! oi ! oi ! oi !
Oi ! oi ! oi ! oi ! oi !

I have come here to search the way,
To find the red egg ;
The red egg of the marine serpent,
By the sea-side in the hollow of the stone.
I am going to seek in the valley
The green water-cress, and the golden grass,
And the top branch of the oak,
In the wood by the side of the fountain.

Merlin ! Merlin ! retrace your steps ;
Leave the branch on the oak,
And the green water-cress in the valley,
As well as the golden grass ;
And leave the red egg of the marine serpent,
In the foam by the hollow of the stone.
Merlin ! Merlin ! retrace thy steps,
There is no diviner but God.

The poetry of Nature may be applied in two senses ; it may first mean " the work of the poet," as Wordsworth puts it, " with his eye on the object," and using all his ability to draw and paint a lifelike and justly coloured picture of the scene before him. The power to do this does not imply more than accurate observation and artistic sensitiveness to the relation between what is presented to the eye and the language in which it is interpreted.

The second view, which latterly appears to have become

the paramount view of Nature poetry, is that of Wordsworth
and his school, namely, " The poetry of Nature for Nature's
sake," or as it has been well put by Professor Lewis Jones
(to whom in conjunction with Mr. Stopford Brooke belongs
the credit of a fuller development of Matthew Arnold's
theory), " the poetry which seeks to interpret Nature in
terms of mind and spirit, the attempt to divine its inner
meaning and its relation to the mind and soul of man."

The history of the poetry of Nature in the world's
literature, adds the Professor, " is the history of the development of the poetry of pure natural description as we find it
in Homer into the reflective, the emotional, the philosophical treatment of Nature of which Wordsworth and his
disciples are the recognised modern exponents."

With this second view of Nature poetry, the Words-
worthian, Mr. Ruskin joins issue. As he put it, " for one
who can see, thousands can think. To see clearly is poetry,
prophecy, and religion all in one." This introspective
influence, called by Ruskin " the pathetic fallacy," tends,
he thinks, to a withdrawal into self, arising from solitary
communion with Nature, which breaks that sympathy
between the poet and his fellow-men, which is a higher
poetic bond than that between him and Nature.

" Scott," according to Ruskin, " approaches nearest of
modern poets to the Greek attitude towards Nature. He
conquers all tendencies towards the pathetic fallacy and
instead of making Nature anywise subservient, does not
venture to bring his own cares and thoughts into her pure
and quiet presence, presents her in her simple and universal
truth, and appears, therefore, at first shallower than other
poets, being in reality wider and healthier."

Commenting upon these views of Ruskin contained in
his *Modern Painters*, Professor Lewis Jones points out that
" the history of the rise of the habit of regarding Nature as
a subject in itself fit and adequate for poetry " is paralleled
by that of the growth of landscape painting.

For Ruskin shows that mediæval landscape was made so subsidiary to human interest that "the workman who was first led to think *lightly* of natural beauty as being subservient to human, was next led to think *inaccurately* of natural beauty because he had continually to alter and simplify it for his practical purposes." He thus conventionalised Nature to such a degree that these mediæval landscapes became largely artificial.

Even Chaucer is affected by the same vice though in a limited degree. His interest in Nature is not as consistent as that of the early Celtic poets, or indeed the mediæval ones. He is the poet of April and May and their inspiration to man through the reawakening of the earth to life in its glory of new green and the voices of its singing birds, but he cannot paint an autumn or winter landscape with the sympathy of the Irish or the Welsh bard. Where amongst his tales can such a stark presentment of the rigours of winter be found as this song attributed to Finn MacCumhal, 200 B.C., though, of course, of much later date. My verse rendering could hardly be more literal in its reproduction of the Irish original :

> Take my tidings !
> Stags contend ;
> Snows descend—
> Summer's end !
>
> A chill wind raging ;
> The sun low keeping,
> Swift to set
> O'er seas high sweeping.
>
> Dull red the fern ;
> Shapes are shadows ;
> Wild geese mourn
> O'er misty meadows.
>
> Keen cold limes each weaker wing.
> Icy times—
> Such I sing !
> Take my tidings !

Though there is a great deal of truth in it I cannot quite agree with Professor Lewis Jones' statement that in Spenser "Nature is but the background to his splendid pictures of romantic life and action, and that the environment of the *Faerie Queen* is that of Fairyland"; a non-Celtic fairyland I presume he means—"the atmosphere vague, dreamy, ethereal, fading away into the verdurous gloom of forests or into the blue mists of pleasant glades and shadowy valleys." I regard much of the fairy poetry of Spenser to be touched just by the same Celtic fairy magic which suffuses many of the border ballads and takes us captive in *The Ancient Mariner*, whose author, as his grandson, Mr. Ernest Hartley Coleridge, has pointed out, had Celtic blood in his veins. No one who has, like myself, sat under Spenser's oak by the Blackwater where the poet composed much of the *Faerie Queen*, and who knows, therefore, the landscape that was then before his brooding eyes; and no one who is conversant with the fact that Spenser enjoyed, in translation, the poems of the Irish bards could avoid the conclusion that the spell of Celtic natural magic had fallen upon Spenser. May he not indeed have caught inspiration from some such verses as follow, in my close translation from an Irish original which, to use Spenser's own words in praise of Irish bardic poems, "savours of sweet wit and good invention . . . and is sprinkled with some pretty flowers of their natural device which give good grace and comeliness unto them."

MIDIR'S CALL TO EDAIN.

[This Midir (the Fairy King), like the rest of his race, was an accomplished magician; and, in a short time after the marriage of Edain, he appeared in disguise at the Palace of Tara. He asked to play a game of chess with the monarch, Eochy Fedleach, and won the Queen Edain as the stake. As he is about to carry her off he thus addressed her.]

Queen of women, oh come away !
 Come to my kingdom strange to see ;
 Where tresses flow with a golden glow,
 And white as snow is the fair bodie.

Under the arching of ebon brows,
　　Eyes of azure the soul enthral,
And a speech of songs to the mouth belongs,
　　And sorrowful sighing shall ne'er befall.

Bright are the blooms of Innisfail,
　　Green her forests wave in the west :
But brighter flowers and greener bowers
　　Shall all be ours in that country blest.

Can her streams compare to the runnels rare,
　　Of yellow honey and rosy wine,
That softly slip to the longing lip,
　　With magic flow, through that land of mine ?

We roam the earth in its grief and mirth,
　　But move unseen of all therein ;
For before their gaze there hangs a haze,
　　The heavy haze of their mortal sin.

But our age wastes not, our beauty tastes not
　　Evil's apple, nor droops nor dies ;
Death slays us never, but love for ever
　　With stainless ardour illumes our eyes.

Then, queen of women, oh come away !
　　Come and sit on my fairy throne,
In the realm of rest with spirits blest,
　　Where sin and sorrow are all unknown.

It is none the less true, as pointed out by the Professor, that pre-eighteenth and much of the eighteenth century poetry in the English language suffers from too strict an interpretation of the point of view pithily put by Pope that " The proper study of mankind is man."

The glory and wonder of mountain and forest are undescribed because unknown, but the petty pastoral aspects of "dawn" and "bower" and "grove," rhyming with "lawn" and "flower" and "love," are the Nature notes harped upon *ad nauseam* by the imitators of Theocritus and Virgil through the lips of their conventional shepherds and shepherdesses.

As ancient Ireland was covered with forest its invaders were of necessity oversea people and maintained their position from points of vantage upon the shores, and more especially upon islands or peninsulas in the great estuaries, still keeping in touch with the sea and its suggestions. This is true even of the later invaders of Ireland, the Danes, who never moved far inland, penetrating no further than the waters of the great rivers and lakes would allow them. The early Irish and Irish-Danish Sagas are therefore permeated with the joys and terrors of the ocean. Here is a portion of a fine early sea-chant (in translation by myself), the original of which is ascribed to the celebrated poet Rumann, who died in 748. It was first published and translated by Professor Kuno Meyer, whose version I have followed :

SONG OF THE SEA.

Huge, huge the tempest that disorders
    All the Pleasant Plain of Lir,
Hurling whirl-blasts o'er its borders ;
    At the winter's onset sheer,
    Piercing us, as with a spear.

*   *   *   *   *

Rude, tremendous waves are tumbled
    Round each mighty river mouth ;
Wild, white Winter has us humbled
    Past Cantire from Alba south ;
    Torrents quench Slieve Dremon's drouth.

*   *   *   *   *

Full the tide to overflowing ;
    Pleasant is the Home of Ships ;
Eddying airs the sands are strowing
    Round the Estuary's lips ;
    Smooth and free the rudder slips.

But when the early waves of oversea invasion had ceased to break upon the island, and the successive races of conquerors had been driven inland by one another and had become more or less united, the Irish visionary outlook

upon the sea ceased, and the joys of mountain and forest
and plain overtook the hearts and minds of the ancient
Irish people. The mystery of magic stored in their
imaginations was given forth again and united them
intimately with their new surroundings. The extraordinary
physical and mental vigour inherent in a race which had
not so long ago faced the dangers of an uncharted ocean
in primeval vessels, incited them to constant deeds of arms
and a not less constant activity in the chase of the boar
and elk and red deer and wolf, which were then indigenous
in Ireland.

The Celtic love of Nature, pre-eminent in Finn and his
companion, stamps the Fenian tales with a picturesque
beauty nearer to earth because out of sight of the sea; but
not nearer to heaven, because the other world of this
people was not imagined as contained in a sphere outside
their own, but intimately in touch with it, either within its
green hills or among the invisible islands which surrounded
its shores. As Mr. Brooke well puts it : "The great beauty
of the cloud-tragedies of storm, the gorgeous sunrises and
sunsets, so dramatic in Ireland, or the magnificence of the
starry heavens, are scarcely celebrated. But the Irish folk
have heard the sound of the wind in the tree-tops and marked
its cold swiftness over the moor, and watched with fear or
love the mists of ocean and the bewilderment of the storm-
driven snow and the sweet falling of the dew." These are
fully celebrated, as the following extracts from Irish Gaelic
poetry will show, proving, as Mr. Stopford Brooke points
out, "that the great and small aspects of Nature are so
near to the heart of the Celtic story-teller—as they are not
to the writers of the Teutonic and Norse Sagas—that, even
where there is no set description of scenery, an atmosphere
is created around the heroes and heroines of early Irish
heroic romance, that all other European early literatures
are without."

Thus the "Three Sorrows of Irish Story-Telling," as they

have been called, *The Fate of the Children of Lir*, *The Fate of the Sons of Usnach*, and *The Fate of the Sons of Turann*, tragedies all of them, are interwoven with beautiful descriptions of natural beauty which add greatly to their enchantment. And the same is true of the wonderful old tale of *The Pursuit of Dermid and Grania*. The episodes descriptive of the sufferings of the Swan children upon the three Irish Seas and of their return to their father's ruined palace are vivid to a degree in their realisation of the savage aspects of Nature, though the atmospheric gloom is now and again suffused by returning sunshine, and the close of the tragedy is a beautifully hopeful one.

Here is a fresh translation from *The Fate of the Sons of Usnach*, who carried off Deirdre, King Conor's bride, to Scotland, where she was wed to Naisi, the eldest brother, and where the four abode in great happiness till their fatal return to Erin. The joy in the life of Nature exhibited in this farewell to Scotland by Deirdre is very delightful in the original.

DEIRDRE'S FAREWELL TO SCOTLAND.

A land well-beloved is yon Easterly Land,
Alba of marvels, from mountain to strand,
   Thence unto Erin I had not been faring,
Were Naisi not leading me still by the hand.

Beloved is Don Fidga, beloved is Dun Finn,
To the Fortress above 'twas delightful to win ;
   Dear is the Isle where the thorn bushes smile,
Very dear is Dun Sweeny, without and within.

Caill Cuan, Caill Cuan, where Ainli was blest,
Caill Cuan, Caill Cuan, for you I'm distressed,
   May was in prime, when we fleeted the time,
Naisi and I, on your beautiful breast.

Glen Lay, O, Glen Lay, where we hunted all day,
Or crouched under cliffs in the summer moon's ray,
   Venison and fish, and badger on dish—
That was our portion in lovely Glen Lay.

Glen Massan, Glen Massan, of blossoming bowers,
Tall its wild garlic, white over with flowers,
 Joy-broken sleep upon beds grassy deep,
By thy River-mouth's murmur, Glen Massan was ours !

Glen Etive, Glen Etive—ah ! where art thou now,
And the bothy I built on thy verdurous brow ;
 When we rose with the dawn and looked into our bawn,
A cattle-fold sunny, Glen Etive wert thou !

Glen Urchain, Glen Urchain, now far from our ken,
O that was the straight and the fair-shouldered glen,
 There in the flower of his pride and his power,
Stood Naisi exulting, my monarch of men.

Glen da Ruadh, Glen da Ruadh, hail ! to the Chief
Who hath thee in heritage, lap of green leaf !
 Thy green peak behind, sweet to hear, hard to find,
The cuckoo enchanting goes banishing grief.

Belovèd is Draighen above a firm strand !
How soft its stream purls over silver-pure sand !
 Till death I'd be under its sky of blue wonder,
Were Naisi not leading me home by the hand.

But it is not only the warrior Irish bards who delight us
with such glimpses of the green countryside, of the heather-
clad hill ; the monks and hermits and some of the great
ecclesiastics, Columkille and the Bishop-King Cormac
MacCullenann, and indeed St. Patrick himself, give us
beautiful passages of Nature poetry in the midst of their
sacred verse. Here is Dr. Hyde's charming rendering of
St. Columkille's *Farewell to Erin*, which he was ordered
to quit for ever, by the judgment of St. Molaise, owing to
his responsibility for the battle of Cooldrevin. He returned
once, however, it is said, to save the Irish bards from
expulsion from their native land :

COLUMCILLE'S FAREWELL.

Alas for the voyage, O high King of Heaven,
 Enjoined upon me,
For that I on the red plain of bloody Cooldrevin
 Was present to see.

How happy the son is of Dima ; no sorrow
　　For him is designed,
He is having, this hour, round his own hill in Durrow
　　The wish of his mind.

The sounds of the winds in the elms, like the strings of
　　A harp being played,
The note of a blackbird that claps with the wings of
　　Delight in the glade.

With him in Ros-Grencha the cattle are lowing
　　At earliest dawn,
On the brink of the summer the pigeons are cooing
　　And doves in the lawn.

Three things am I leaving behind me, the very
　　Most dear that I know,
Tir-Leedach I'm leaving, and Durrow and Derry ;
　　Alas, I must go !

Yet my visit and feasting with Comgall have eased me
　　At Cainneach's right hand,
And all but thy government, Eire, has pleased me,
　　Thou waterfall land.

The sentiment contained in the last two lines has been
reiterated time out of mind since the Saint's day, and we
seem almost as far as ever from being able to vary it
satisfactorily.

The early Welsh poets, Aneurin, Taliesyn and Llywarch
Hen, were warrior bards, yet possessed with a love of
Nature so absorbing that they have left behind them entire
poems devoted to Nature, some of them running to con-
siderable length, such as Aneurin's *Months* and Llywarch
Hen's *Tercets* and poem on *Winter*, while Taliesyn's
Song of the Wind forms a considerable episode in one
of his longer poems.

Space does not permit of our quoting more than a few
fragments from these somewhat mystical and distinctly
gnomic odes.　This is from the *Tercets* of Llywarch
Hen, a sixth century Welsh bard, though the version of his

poem, from which the following is my translation, is in language of a much later date :

> Set is the snare ; the ash clusters glow,
> Ducks plash in the pools ; breakers whiten below ;
> More strong than a hundred is the heart's hidden woe.
>
> *   *   *   *   *
>
> The brambles with berries of purple are dressed ;
> In silence the brooding thrush clings to her nest,
> In silence the liar can never take rest.
>
> *   *   *   *   *
>
> Rain is without, but the shelter is near ;
> Yellow the furze, the cow-parsnip is sere,
> God in Heaven, how couldst Thou create cowards here !
>
> Rain and still rain, dank these tresses of mine !
> The feeble complain of the cliff's steep incline ;
> Wan is the main ; sharp the breath of the brine.
>
> Rain falls in a sheet ; the Ocean is drenched ;
> By the whistling sleet the reed-tops are wrenched ;
> Feat after feat ; but Genius lies quenched.

Much of the spirit of St. Francis animates these monkish and hermit poems. There is a tenderness for the sufferings, not only of the half-frozen wren during the snowstorm, but even of the prowling wolf or the hovering eagle.

> Not even in Cuan's forest deep,
> To-night the shaggy wolves can sleep,
> Nor can the little wren keep warm
> On Lon's wild side against the storm.
>
> The ancient eagle of Glen Rye
> Gets grief from out the storm-swept sky,
> Great her misery, dire her drouth,
> Famished, frozen, craw and mouth.

But if, as Matthew Arnold has pointed out, Nature poetry, in a sense between that of the Greeks and that of Wordsworth and his school, can thus be proved to be a Celtic endowment, from whence did the English school of

Nature poets derive its inspiration? Mr. Stopford Brooke and Mr. F. T. Palgrave give us the clue which I hope to follow out in a subsequent essay. The connection can be traced in the streams of Celtic verse which mingled themselves with English poetry : the first a legacy of the Celtic blood in the Lowlands and flowing in the veins of the mediæval Scottish poets, Douglas and Dunbar ; the second having its source in the Principality and represented in the writings of the Welsh poets, George Herbert and Henry Vaughan.

Indeed, in a paper read by Professor Palgrave before the Cymmrodorion Society, he goes so far as to write : " It is safe to affirm that of all our poets until we reach Wordsworth, including here Chaucer, Spenser, and Milton, Vaughan affords decidedly the most varied and the most delicate pictures of Nature; that he looked upon the landscape both in its fine details and its larger, and, as they might be called, its cosmic aspects, with an insight and an imaginative penetration not rivalled till we reach our own century (the nineteenth)."

But behind the Scotch Lowland Nature poets of the fifteenth and sixteenth centuries, and behind the Welsh Nature poets of the seventeenth century, lie the gardens of Irish and Welsh and Highland mediæval bardic poetry, tended by the O'Dalys, O'Carrolls, O'Higgins and O'Coffeys, joint Irish and Scotch bards, the O'Husseys, the Rhys Gochs, and beyond all, as the laureate of Celtic Nature poets, Davydd ap Gwilym—true descendants of Finn and Ossian, Aneurin and Llywarch Hen.

THE PRETERNATURAL IN EARLY IRISH POETRY

THE study of early Irish literature, whether professedly historical or romantic, is of that of a world possessed with preternatural beliefs. As it has been very well put by Miss Eleanor Hull in her work on Irish Literature : *

> Everywhere in the literature which the old Gael has produced we find the mingling of the actual and the purely imaginative ; in his serious annals and historical tracts he surprises us by the perpetual intrusion of fairy lore, or by the gravely historic importance which he attaches to the genealogies and wars and settlements of the gods ; his legal decisions and ancient lores have "a thread of poetry thrown round them," and his official verse contains the geography, the genealogies, and the historical traditions of Ireland. . . . The accounts of Brian Boru, early in the eleventh century, are tinged with fairy belief, just as are the tales of Conaire Mor at the beginning of the Christian era ; nor, when Dr. Geoffrey Keating comes to compile a connected history of Ireland in the seventeenth century, does he show much desire to sift the real from the unreal.

In the two great groups of Irish romantic tales, those of the Red Branch Knights and those of Finn Mac-Cumhal and his heroic companions, while there is, no doubt, an underlying historical basis of fact, kinship with the gods involving supernatural powers, and then companionship with the heroes and heroines of the De Danann race who had passed into fairy lands across the seas or under them and the earth, are treated as naturally as they are in

* *A Text-Book of Irish Literature.* By Eleanor Hull (M. H. Gill and Sons, Dublin).

associations of a similar kind in the *Iliad* and *Odyssey*.
The heroic warfare of the early Irish Gaelic warriors, their
martial equipment and their mode of life ring true to the
descriptions by Cæsar, Livy, and Tacitus of the Britons and
Gauls with whom the Irish chieftains were contemporary,
according to the traditional dates of these cycles of early
Irish romance.

Yet while the Red Branch heroes claimed descent from
the Tuatha De Danann gods, and the preternatural feats of
Cuchulain and his companions were said to be due to this
divine connection, their attitude towards these ancestral
deities was too intimate to admit of acts of worship towards
them.   The relations between these gods and heroes
resemble those that subsisted between the heroes of early
Greece and their gods in the Trojan war, and not only
do the gods take sides for or against Cuchulain, as the
Greek gods did for or against Achilles, but we even find the
De Danann divinities seeking the aid of the Irish heroes
when engaged in conflicts with one another.

As suggested, the relation between the defeated De
Danann gods, when they have passed into fairyland, and
the Fenian heroes is of a still more intimate kind.   These
gods, turned fairies, engage the Fenian heroes in their wars
with one another, spirit them off under a spell of magic
mist into underground palaces, from which they are released
by mortal brother warriors, befriend them when pursued by
their enemies, or by the glamour of their fairy women draw
them for a while into Tir n' an Oge, the land of perpetual
youth.

As Mr. Stopford Brooke writes in his fine introduction
to his son-in-law, Mr. T. W. Rolleston's *High Deeds of Finn* :

These were the invisible lands and peoples of the Irish imagination ;
and they live in and out of many of the stories.   Cuchulain is lured
into a fairy land, and lives for more than a year in love with Fand,
Manannan's wife.   Into another fairy land, through zones of mist,
Cormac, as is told here, was lured by Manannan, who now has left the sea

to play on the land.   Oisin flies with Niam over the sea to the Island of
Eternal Youth.   Etain, out of the immortal land, is born into an Irish
girl and reclaimed and carried back to her native shore by Midir, a
prince of the Fairy Host.   Ethne, whose story also is here, has lived for
all her youth in the court of Angus, deep in the hill beside the rushing
of the Boyne.

Observe the intimate description of this fairy cavalcade,
not of pigmy warriors, but of powerful, heroic fairy princes
as they pass before Laegaire (Laery) Mac Crimthainn when
he visits the Fairy Realm of Magh Mell.   They might be
the fiercest of Norse warriors devastating the Irish coasts,
but for the arts that endear them to the Gael, music and
poetry and their kindred skill at chess playing.   Clearly
they are of the stock of the De Dananns, who, upon the
Milesian invasion, descended into fairyland.   I here versify,
in old Irish measure, the prose rendering of the lyric in
the *Book of Leinster*, a MS. of the twelfth century, made by
Professor Kuno Meyer:

THE FAIRY HOST.

Pure white the shields their arms upbear,
    With silver emblems rare o'er-cast ;
Amid blue glittering blades they go,
    The horns they blow are loud of blast.

In well-instructed ranks of war
    Before their Chief they proudly pace ;
Cœrulean spears o'er every crest—
    A curly-tressed, pale-visaged race.

Beneath the flame of their attack,
    Bare and black turns every coast ;
With such a terror to the fight
    Flashes that mighty vengeful host.

Small wonder that their strength is great,
    Since royal in estate are all,
Each Hero's head a lion's fell—
    A golden yellow mane lets fall.

Comely and smooth their bodies are,
　Their eyes the starry blue eclipse ;
The pure white crystal of their teeth
　Laughs out beneath their thin red lips.

Good are they at man-slaying feats,
　Melodious over meats and ale ;
Of woven verse they wield the spell,
　At chess-craft they excel the Gael.

More, a Munster Princess, was carried off by the fairy host in her youth, but escaped from them and became the wife of Cathal, King of Cashel. Afterwards her sister was similarly abducted, but was rescued by More, who recognised her by her singing, and thus advises her how she may free herself from the spells of the Sidh (Shee) :

Little sister, whom the Fay
　Hides away within his Doon,*
Deep below yon tufted fern,
　Oh, list and learn my magic tune !

Long ago, when snared like thee
　By the Shee, my harp and I
O'er them wove the slumber spell,
　Warbling well its lullaby.

Till with dreamy smiles they sank,
　Rank on rank before the strain ;
Then I rose from out the rath
　And found my path to earth again.

Little sister, to my woe
　Hid below among the Shee,
List, and learn my magic tune,
　That it full soon may succour thee.

The beautiful old air to which *More of Cloyne* is sung is of the sleep-disposing kind, under which lullabies and fairy music are classed. It formed the third of the three Musical Feats, or three styles of playing, which gave

* A fortified residence.

the dignity of Ollamh, or Doctor of Music, to the ancient professors of the harp, and whose origin is given in this weird old Folk Tale.

Lugh, the king of the Tuatha de Danann and the Daghda, their great chief and Druid, and Ogma, their bravest champion, followed the Formorians and their leader from the battle-field of Moyturah, because they had carried off the Daghda's harper, Uaithne by name.

The pursuers reached the banquet house of the Fomorian chiefs and there found Breas, the son of Elathan, and Elathan, the son of Delbath, and also the Daghda's harp hanging upon the wall. This was the harp in which its music was spellbound so that it would not answer when summoned until the Daghda evoked it, when he said, "Come Durdabla, come Coircethaircuir (the two names of the harp) . . ." The harp came forth from the wall then and killed nine persons in its passage. And it came to the Daghda, and he played for them the three musical feats which give distinction to a harper, namely, the *Goltree* which, from its melting plaintiveness, caused crying, the *Gentree*, which, from its merriment, caused laughter, and the *Soontree*, which, from its deep murmuring, caused sleep.

He played them the *Goltree*, till their women cried tears ; he played them the *Gentree* until their women and youths burst into laughter; he played them the *Soontree* until the entire host fell asleep. It was through that sleep that they, the three champions, escaped from those Fomorians who were desirous to slay them

Observe the dignified bearing of the Fomorian champions who held back their tears and laughter when their women and young folk gave way to them, and could only be won from their fell purpose by the fairy music of the De Danann harp.

Dr. George Petrie, in his *Ancient Music of Ireland*, prints a wonderful old fairy lullaby, sung to a Gaelic poem, of which Eugene O'Curry writes : " This rare and remarkable

poem contains . . . more of authentic fairy fact and
doctrine than, with some few exceptions, has been ever
before published in Ireland."

Here is a prose rendering of the original.

O Woman below on the brink of the stream. Sho hoo lo !
Do you understand the cause of my wailing? Sho hoo lo !
A year and this day I was whipt off my palfrey. Sho hoo lo !
And was carried into Lios-an-Chnocain. Sho hoo lo ! Sho-heen,
    Sho hoo lo !

There is here my beautiful great house. Sho hoo lo !
Abundant is new ale there and old ale. Sho hoo lo !
Abundant is yellow honey and bee's wax there. Sho hoo lo !
Many is the old man tightly bound there. Sho hoo lo ! Sho heen,
    etc.

Many is the curling brown-haired boy there. Sho hoo lo !
Many is the yellow-haired comely girl there. Sho hoo lo !
There are twelve women bearing sons there. Sho hoo lo !
And as many more are there beside them. Sho hoo lo ! Sho-heen,
    etc.

Say to my husband to come to-morrow. Sho hoo lo !
With the wax candle in the centre of his palm. Sho hoo lo !
And in his hand to bring a black-hafted knife. Sho hoo lo !
And beat the first horse out of the gap. Sho hoo lo ! Sho-heen, etc.

To pluck the herb that's in the door of the *fort.* Sho hoo lo !
With trust in God that I would go home with him. Sho hoo lo !
Or if he does not come within that time. Sho hoo lo !
That I will be queen over all these women. Sho hoo lo ! Sho-
    heen, etc.

"The incident here clearly narrated," writes O'Curry, "was
believed at all times to be of frequent occurrence. It was for the last
sixteen hundred years, at least, and is still, as firmly believed in as any
fact in the history of this country—that the Tuatha de Danann, after
their overthrow by the Milesians, had gone to reside in their hills and
ancient forts, or in their dwellings on lakes and rivers—that they were
in possession of a mortal immortality—and that they had the power to
carry off from the visible world men and women in a living state, but
sometimes under the semblance of death.

" The persons taken off were generally beautiful infants, wanted for
those in the hill who had no children, fine young women, before
marriage and often on the day of marriage, for the young men of the
hills who had been invisibly feasting on their growing beauties—
perhaps from childhood ; young men, in the same way, for the
languishing damsels of fairyland ; fresh, well-looking nurses for their
nurseries. . . ."

This poem refers to all the classes of abducted persons
—abducted young men now grown old, comely young
men and maidens and married women, like the speaker,
needed for nurses. She describes a period before wine and
whiskey were in use, and therefore more than three hundred
years past, in Irish of, at any rate, the fifteenth century.
By her own account she was snatched from her palfrey, and
must, therefore, have been a woman of consequence. She
sees from within Lios-an-Chnocain, or the Fort of the
Hillock, a neighbour, perhaps, washing clothes by the brink
of the stream which runs past the fort, and, in the intervals
of her hush-cries to her fairy nursling, she gives instructions
to her friend how to secure her freedom.

The bit of wax candle which her husband was to carry
in the centre of his palm would be, no doubt, a candle
blessed on Candlemas Day, and the black-hafted knife was
the only mortal weapon feared by the fairies.

Its use, as called for in the poem, was to strike the
leading horse of the woman's fairy chariot when she left the
fort the following day, and thus render her visible to her
rescuing husband, who was then to possess himself of the
herb that grew at the fort door, whose magical properties
would guard her from recapture by the fairies.

The next early Irish poem which I present in English
verse, is taken from Professor Kuno Meyer's *Fianaigecht*, a
hitherto unedited collection of Fenian poems and tales, and
probably belongs to the ninth century. The original is a
very remarkable poem, both from the historical and
preternatural point of view.

THE TRYST AFTER DEATH.

Fothad Canann, the leader of a Connaught warrior band, had carried off the wife of King Alill, of Munster, with her consent. The outraged husband pursued them and a fierce battle was fought, in which Fothad and Alill fell by each other's hands. The lovers had engaged to meet in the evening after the battle. Faithful to his word, the spirit of the slain warrior kept the tryst and thus addressed his paramour :

Hush, woman ! Do not speak to me ;
   My thoughts are not with thee to-night.
They glance again and yet again
   Among the slain at Féic fight.

Who'd find my bloody corpse must grope
   Upon the slope of Double Brink ;
My head unwashed is in the hands
   Of bands who ne'er from slaughter shrink.

Dark Folly is that tryster's guide
   Who Death's black tryst aside would set ;
To keep the tryst at Claragh made
   The living and the dead are met.

Unhappy journey ! Evil doom
   Had marked my tomb on Féic field,
And pledged me in that fateful strife
   To foreign foes my life to yield.

Not I alone from Wisdom's way
   Have gone astray, by Passion led;
Yet though for thee to death I came,
   I put no blame on thy bright head.

Full wretched is our meeting here
   In grief and fear, O hapless one !
Yet had we known it should be thus,
   Not hard for us our sin to shun.

The proud-faced, grey-horsed warrior band
   At my command fought faithful on ;
Till all their wondrous wood of spears
   Beneath Death's shears to earth had gone.

Had they but lived, their valour bright
　　To-night had well avenged their lord.
And had not Death my purpose changed,
　　I had avenged them with my sword.

Theirs was a lithe and blithesome force,
　　Till man and horse lay on the mould.
The great, green forest hath received
　　And overleaved the champions bold.

The sword of Domnall drank red dew,
　　The Lugh of hosts,* accoutred well ;
Before him in the River Ford
　　By Death's award slim Comgal fell.

The three fierce Flanns, the Owens three,
　　From sea to sea six outlaws famed—
Each with his single hand slew four,
　　No coward's portion thus they claimed.

Swift charged Cu-Domna, singling out,
　　With gleesome shout, his name-sake dread.
Down the Hill of Conflict rolled,
　　Lies Flann, the Little, cold and dead.

Beside him in his bloody bed
　　Six foes death-sped by Flann are sleeping—
Though *we* esteemed them feeble ones—
　　The chaff of Mughirne's Son's red reaping.

Red Falvey, how your spear-strings' play
　　Amid the fray made manhood melt ;
Forchorb, the Radiant, on his foes
　　Seven murderous blows, outleaping, dealt.

Twelve warriors in the battle brunt
　　Front to front against me stood.
Yet now of all the twelve are left
　　But corses cleft and bathed in blood.

Then I and Alill, Owen's son,
　　To shun each other's arms were loath.
With drooping sword and lowered shield,
　　Still stood the field to view us both.

　　* A De Danann hero and God.

Oh, then we too exchanged our spears,
  Heroic peers, with such dread art,
I pierced him to the very brain,
  He me again unto the heart.

Abide not on the battle-plain
  Among the slain, in terror's toils ;
Shun ghostly converse ; home with speed
  Bear thou my meed of manly spoils.

All know that I was never seen,
  Oh, Queen, apparelled as a boor,
But crimson-cloaked, with tunic white,
  And belt of silver, bright and pure.

A five-edged spear, a lance of trust,
  Of many slaying thrust I bore ;
A shield five-circled, bronze its boss,—
  Firm oaths across its midst they swore.

My silver cup, a shining gem ;
  Its glittering stem will flash to thee ;
Gold ring and bracelets, famed afar,
  By Nia Nar brought over sea.

Then Cailte's brooch, a pin of luck,
  Though small, a buckle of price untold ;
Two little silver heads are bound
  Deftly around its head of gold.

My draught-board, no mere treasure-stake,
  Is thine to take without offence ;
Noble blood its bright rim dyes,
  Lady, it lies not far from hence.

While searching for that treasure prized,
  Be thou advised thy speech to spare.
Earth never knew beneath the sun
  A gift more wonderfully fair.

One half its pieces yellow gold,
  White bronze of mould are all the rest ;
Its woof of pearls a peerless frame
  By every smith of fame confessed.

The piece-bag—'tis a tale of tales—
  Its rim with golden scales enwrought.
Its maker left a lock on it
  Whose secret no want-wit hath caught.

Small is the casket and four-square,
  Of coils of rare red gold its face,
The hundredth ounce of white bronze fine
  Was weighed to line that matchless case.

O'ersea the red gold coil firm-wrought
  Dinoll brought, a goldsmith nice ;
Of its all-glittering clasps one even
  Is fixed at seven bondwomen's price.

Tradition tells the treasure is
  A masterpiece of Turvey's skill ;
In the rich reign of Art the Good,
  His cattle would a cantred * fill.

No goldsmith at his glittering trade
  A wonder made of brighter worth ;
No royal jewel that outdid
  Its glory hath been hid in earth.

If thou appraise its price with skill,
  Want shall thy children ne'er attack ;
If thou keep safe this gem of mine,
  No heir of thine shall ever lack.

There are around us everywhere
  Great spoils to share of famous luck ;
Yet horribly at entrails grim
  The Morrigan's dim fingers pluck.

Upon a spear-edge sharp alit,
  With savage wit she urged us on.
Many the spoils she washes ; dread
  The laughter of Red Morrigan.

Her horrid mane abroad is flung,
  The heart's well strung that shrinks not back.
Yet though to us she is so near,
  Let no weak fear thy heart attack.

    * A large acreage of land.

At dawn I part from all that's human,
    To join, O woman, the warrior band.
Delay not ! Homeward urge thy flight ;
    The end of night is nigh at hand.

Unto all time each ghostly rann
    Of Fothad Canann shall remain,
My speech with thee reach every breast,
    If my bequest I but obtain.

Since many to my grave will come,
    Raise thou for me a tomb far-seen.
Such trouble, for thy true love's sake,
    Wilt thou not undertake, O Queen?

My corse from thee must earthward pass,
    My soul, alas ! to torturing fire.
Save worship of Heaven's Lord of lords
    All earth affords but folly dire.

I hear the dusky ousel's song,
    To greet the faithful throng, outpour ;
My voice, my shape, turn spectral weak—
    Hush, woman, speak to me no more.

The relations between the phantom lover and his paramour are here very finely and delicately described. The
Queen does not appear to be terrified by his appearance in
the first instance, and is about to address him passionately,
but, like Protesilaus, when permitted to appear to Laodamia,
he gravely repels her affection, deplores the madness of
their passion, and yet forgives her for her share in it. He
proudly tells her of the details of the battle in which hero
after hero fell, until he and her husband, King Alill of
Munster, encountered one another and perished at each
other's hands. Again growing considerate for her, he warns
her of the dangers of the battlefield, and above all cautions
her against the haunting spirit of the Morrigan, one of the
Battle goddesses or demons of the Gael. Of these there
were three weird sisters, Anann or Ana, Bove or Bauv, and
Macha, all malignant beings. " In an ancient glossary

quoted by Stokes," writes Dr. Joyce in his *Social History of Ireland*, " Macha's mast-food is said to be the heads of men slain in battle."   The accounts of these battle furies are somewhat confused, but they were all called Morrigan and Bauv.   Morrigan means great queen ; Bauv did not appear, as a rule, in queenly shape, but as a carrion crow fluttering over the heads of the combatants.   Bauv was the war goddess among the ancient Gauls from whom her legend was brought to Ireland.   Strangely enough, not many years ago, a small pillar stone was found in France with an interesting votive inscription upon it, addressed to this goddess under the name of Cathu (Irish Cath = battle) bodvae (the Irish Bauv).

Fothad Canann goes on to tell the queen where his special accoutrements, weapons, and treasures of jewelry are to be found on the battlefield, and he enters into a curiously close description of his draught-board, a very masterpiece of art.   He ends his conversation by promising that she shall be famous to all time for these ghostly *ranns* or verses addressed to her, if she will raise him a worthy tomb—a far-seeing monument, for the sake of her love to him. There follows a final Christian touch, not improbably one of those Monkish interpolations, introduced at the close of Pagan poems in order to justify their circulation, but contradicted by the phantom's previous statement, that he was returning not to the fires of Purgatory, but to the companionship of the warrior band.

We have dealt with cases of reincarnation as described in the old Pagan Irish poems.   Here is an instance of a kindred character, but not one of transmigration of soul. This remarkable poem, of which a translation follows, refers to the rejuvenations of an old Irish princess, more fortunate than Tithonus, who received the fateful gift of immortality only to wither slowly in the arms of the Goddess Aurora. This princess, on the contrary, was dowered with seven periods of youth and so, during her Pagan period, was wedded to one prince of the Gael after another. The poem, uttered by her, expresses, however, in the language of the late tenth century her misery when she finds that her youth is to be renewed no more, and her final position is thus quaintly described in the prose introduction to this lament of the old woman of Beare, or Beara, from which *The O'Sullivan Bear* takes his title, and round whose shores the British fleet anchors in the great harbour of Berehaven.

THE LAMENT OF THE OLD WOMAN OF BEARE.*

The reason why she was called the Old Woman of Beare was that she had fifty foster children in Beare. She had seven periods of youth, one after another, so that every man who had lived with her came to die of old age, and her grandsons and great-grandsons were tribes and races. For a hundred years she wore the veil which Cummin had blessed upon her head. Thereupon old age and infirmity came upon her. 'Tis then she said :

> Ebb-tide to me as of the sea ;
>   Reproaches free old age o'ertake ;
> Full limbs and bosom favours follow,
>   The lean and hollow they forsake.
>
> The Beldame I of Beare confessed,
>   Who once went dressed in garments fine ;
> Ill Fortune's miserable mock,
>   Not even a cast-off smock is mine.
>
> At riches now girls' eyes grow bright,
>   Not at the sight of heroes bold ;
> But when *we* lived, ah then, ah then,
>   We gave our love to men, not gold.
>
> Swift chariots glancing in the sun,
>   Swift steeds that won the bright award—
> Their day of plenty hath gone by,
>   My blessings lie with their dead lord.

* Founded on Professor Kuno Meyer's prose version of this tenth century Irish poem. The introductory words are his translation from the early Irish.

My body bends its bitter load
  Towards the abode ordained for all,
And when He deems my days are done,
  Then let God's Son my soul recall.

My arms, if now their shape is seen,
  Are bony, lean, discoloured things;
Yet once they fondled soft and warm,
  Form after form of gallant kings.

To-day, alas, when they are seen,
  They are such lean, long skeletons,
'Twere folly now to cast their wrecks
  Around the necks of fair kings' sons.

When maidens hail the Beltane bright
  With footsteps light and laughter sweet,
Then unto me, a withered crone,
  The loud lament alone is meet.

No sheep are for my bridals slain,
  None now are fain for converse kind;
My locks of gold, turned leaden pale,
  Lie hid a wretched veil behind,

I do not deem it ill at all,
  A mean white veil should thrall them so;
With ribbons gay they once were dressed
  Above the good ale's festal flow.

The Stone of Kings on Femer fair,
  Great Ronan's Chair * in Bregon's bound—
'Tis long since storms upon them prey,
  Their masters' tombs decay around.

The Great Sea's waters talk aloud,
  Winter arises proud and grey;
Oh, Fermuid, mighty son of Mugh,†
  I shall not meet with you to-day.

---

* Inauguration stones, or stone chairs, on which the candidate king or prince stood to receive the wand of office, " a straight white wand, a symbol of authority and also an emblem of what his conduct and judicial decisions should be—straight and without a stain."—Dr. Joyce, *Social History of Ireland*, Book 1, p. 46.

† One of her princely lovers.

I know what they are doing now ;
   They row and row and row across
The rustling reeds of Alma's Ford—
   Death-cold each Lord, alas, my loss !

'Tis, " Oh my God ! and Ochonee ! "
   To-day to me, whate'er my fate,
Even in the sun my cloak I wear ;
   Time shall not now repair my state.

Youth's summer sweet in which we were
   And autumn fair I too have spent ;
But winter's overwhelming brow
   Is o'er me now in anger bent.

Amen ! So be it ! Woe is me !
   Each acorn from its tree takes flight ;
After the banquet's joyful gleam,
   Can I esteem a prayer-house bright ?

I had my day with kings indeed,
   Rich wine and mead would wet my lip,
But all among the shrivelled hags
   Whey-water now in rags I sip.

Upon my cloak my locks stream white,
   My head is light, my memory numb ;
Through cheek and chin grey bristles grow,
   A beldame lo ! I am become.

Seven flood-waves over me were cast,
   Six ebb-tides passed into my blood ;
Too well I know, too well indeed,
   The seventh ebb will lead no flood.

The flood-wave never more shall stir
   With laughing whirr my kitchen now
Many my comrades in the gloom,
   But Death's black doom is on each brow

Isles of the Sea to you 'tis sweet
   Again to greet the flooding brine ;
After my seventh ebb I know
   Time's joyous flow shall not be mine.

The smallest place that meets my eyes
I cannot recognise aright.
What was in flood with flowing store
Is all in ebb before my sight.

Miss Hull reminds us, when dealing with the literature of vision, of Cæsar's statement in Book IV, chapter 15, of the Gallic War, that "one of the chief convictions which the Druids of Gaul desired to instil, is that souls do not perish, but pass, after death, from one body to another; and they think this is the greatest incentive to valour, as it leads men to despise the fear of death."

Undoubtedly there is much evidence in early Irish mythology of transmigration from form to form: thus the De Danann hero-god, Lugh, was re-born in Cuchulain, and Diarmuid is a reincarnation in Ossianic times of Angus the De Danann love-god, whose "love spot" or beauty fascinated all women.

There is this difference, however, between the teaching of the Gaulish Druids as observed by Cæsar and that contained in early Irish Druidic influences. There was no belief in a life beyond the grave in ancient pagan Ireland. As Miss Hull puts it:

The mortals who went into Magh Mell, or the Irish pagan Elysium, did not go there by means of, or after death, they went as visitors, who could at will return again to earth. The distinction is essential. Until after the introduction of Christian teaching, the idea of a life after death seems to have been non-existent. It is quite different when we come to the late dialogues between Oisin and St. Patrick, which makes up a large portion of the Ossianic poetical literature. Though anti-Christian in tone, Oisin has so far adopted the standpoint of the Saint that he admits the continued existence of Fionn and his warriors after death, the point of contention between them being where and under what circumstances this existence is carried on. Such a line of argument would have been impossible in pre-Christian times, when the idea of a future existence had not yet been conceived of.

Manannan Mac Lir, himself the son of a Celtic sea deity, after whom the ocean is sometimes called the Plain of Lir—

and who probably is the shadowy origin of Shakespeare's King Lear—was the King of the Land of Promise of Sorcha (" clearness "), or Magh Mell the " Honey Plain." Thither Bran, who is connected with Manannan in the oversea voyage myths, sails under the influence of a beautiful princess who describes the marvellous land in the delightful strains of which an original verse translation is subjoined. This passage appears as a poem contained in the prose tale called *The Voyage of Bran Son of Febal to the Land of the Living.* The whole of the tale and interspersed poems have been published under the editorship of Professor Kuno Meyer, by David Nutt. It was probably first written down early in the eighth, perhaps late in the seventh century.

THE ISLES OF THE HAPPY.

Once when Bran, son of Feval, was with his warriors in his royal fort, they suddenly saw a woman in strange raiment upon the floor of the house. No one knew whence she had come or how she had entered, for the ramparts were closed. Then she sang these quatrains to Bran while all the host were listening :

A branch I bear from Evin's apple trees
　　Whose shape agrees with Erin's orchard spray ;
Yet never could her branches best belauded
　　Such crystal-gauded bud and bloom display.

There is a distant Isle, deep sunk in shadows,
　　Sea horses round its meadows flash and flee ;
Full fair the course, white-swelling waves enfold it,
　　Four pedestals uphold it o'er the sea.

All eyes' delight, that Plain of Silver glorious,
　　Whereon victorious hosts with joy engage,
Swift coracle and chariot keen contending,
　　A race unending run from age to age.

White the bronze pillars that this Fairy Curragh,*
　　The Centuries thorough, coruscating prop.
Through all the World the fairest land of any
　　Is this whereon the many blossoms drop.

　　　* Plain, as the Curragh of Kildare.

And in its midst an Ancient Tree forth flowers,
  Whence to the Hours beauteous birds outchime ;
In harmony of song, with fluttering feather,
  They hail together each new birth of Time.

And through the Isle smile all glad shades of colour,
  No hue of dolour mars its beauty lone.
'Tis Silver Cloud Land that we ever name it,
  And joy and music claim it for their own.

Not here are cruel guile or loud resentment,
  But calm contentment, fresh and fruitful cheer ;
Not here loud force or dissonance distressful,
  But music melting blissful on the ear.

No grief, no gloom, no death, no mortal sickness,
  Nor any weakness our sure strength can bound ;
These are the signs that grace the race of Evin ;
  Beneath what other heaven are they found ?

Then mayhap Silver Land shall meet thy vision,
  Where sea gems for division leap to land.
The monstrous Deep against the steep is dashing ;
  His mane's hoar lashing whitens all the strand.

Great wealth is his and bright-hued treasure-showers,
  Who links his hours, Land of Peace, with thine.
To strains of sweetest music is he listening,
  He drains from glistening cups the choicest wine.

Pure golden chariots on the Sea Plain fleeting
  Give joyful greeting to the golden Sun ;
Pure silver chariots on the Plain of Sporting,
  With chariots of pure bronze consorting, run.

Swift steeds are on the sward there, golden yellow,
  While crimson steeds to fellow them are seen ;
And some with coats of sleek far-shining azure
  Stretch at full measure o'er the racing green.

A Hero fair, from out the dawn's bright blooming,
  Rides forth, illuming level shore and flood ;
The white and seaward plain he sets in motion,
  He stirs the ocean into burning blood.

A host across the clear blue sea comes rowing,
  Their prowess showing, till they touch the shore ;
Thence seek the Shining Stone * where Music's measure
  Prolongs the pleasure of the pulsing oar.

It sings a strain to all the host assembled ;
  That strain untired has trembled through all time !
It swells with such sweet choruses unnumbered,
  Decay and Death have slumbered since its chime.

Evna of many shapes, beside the waters,
  Thy thousand daughters many-hued to see—
How far soe'er or near the circling spaces
  Of sea and sand to their bright faces be—

If even one approach the music thrilling
  Of wood-birds trilling to thy Land of Bliss,
Straightway the beauteous band is all resorting
  Unto the Plain of Sporting, where he is.

Thus happiness with wealth is o'er us stealing,
  And laughter pealing forth from every hill.
Yea ! through the Land of Peace at every Season
  Pure Joy and Reason are companions still.

Through all the Isle's unchanging summer hours
  There showers and showers a stream of silver bright ;
A pure white cliff that from the breast of Evin
  Mounts up to Heaven thus assures her light.

Thrice fifty distant Isles of fame to Westward,
  Seaward or coastward in the ocean lie ;
Larger those Isles by twice or thrice than Erin,
  And many marvels therein meet the eye.

Long ages hence a Wondrous Child and Holy,
  Yet in estate most lowly shall have birth ;
Seed of a Woman, yet whose Mate knows no man—
  To rule the thousand thousands of the earth.

His sway is ceaseless ; 'twas His love all-seeing
  That Earth's vast being wrought with perfect skill.
All worlds are His ; for all His kindness cares ;
  But woe to all gainsayers of His Will.

          * An Irish vocal Memnon.

The stainless heavens beneath His Hands unfolded,
  He moulded Man as free of mortal stain.
And even now Earth's sin-struck sons and daughters
  His Living Waters can make whole again.

Not unto all of you is this my message
  Of marvellous presage at this hour revealed.
Let Bran but listen from Earth's concourse crowded
  Unto the shrouded wisdom there concealed.

Upon a couch of languor lie not sunken,
  Beware lest drunkenness becloud thy speech !
Put forth, O Bran, across the far clear waters,
  And Evin's daughters haply thou may'st reach.

It will be seen at the end of this poem that Christian
influences were being obtruded upon Pagan thought.
Everything points to a pre-Christian origin of this tale.   But
St. Patrick and his successors evidently enjoyed these old
Pagan tales, realising their beauty and the nobility of thought
which often characterises them, and pressing them into the
service of the Church by means of such interpolated
passages as the above poem contains.

As a matter of fact the Pagan over-sea voyage idea was
so deeply rooted in the Irish mind that the Monkish writers
readily took it over and converted it to their own purposes,
and we thus pass on to semi-Christian visions, such as the
well-known *Voyage of Maeldune*, which Tennyson, at my
suggestion, made his own, after studying the first complete
English version of it given by Dr. Joyce in his *Old Celtic
Romances*.   Other voyages of the kind are *The Navigation
of the Sons of O'Corra*, and the *Voyage of Snedgus and
Mac Riagla*.   The legend of St. Brendan, as told in Irish
literature, differs both from the Latin version and those of
France and Germany.   Matthew Arnold's poem is based on
·these foreign versions and introduces the incident of Judas
Iscariot being allowed out of Hell for one day in the year,
owing to an act of humanity when on earth.   The following
curious hymn of St. Philip, which must be my last poetical

example of early Irish Vision Literature, is an instance of
the influence of pre-Christian Wonderland. I have translated
it from the *Liber Hymnorum*, edited by Professor Atkinson
and Bishop Bernard :

THE HYMN OF ST. PHILIP.

From the Early Irish.

Philip the Apostle holy
　At an Aonach * once was telling
Of the immortal birds and shapely
　Afar in Inis Eidheand dwelling.

East of Africa abiding
　They perform a labour pleasant ;
Unto earth has come no colour
　That on their pinions is not present.

Since the fourth Creation morning
　When their God from dust outdrew them,
Not one plume has from them perished,
　And not one bird been added to them.

Seven fair streams with all their channels
　Pierce the plains wherethrough they flutter,
Round whose banks the birds go feeding,
　Then soar thanksgiving songs to utter.

Midnight is their hour apportioned,
　When, on magic coursers mounted,
Through the starry skies they circle,
　To chants of angel choirs uncounted.

Of the foremost birds the burthen
　Most melodiously unfolded
Tells of all the works of wonder
　God wrought before the world He moulded.

Then a sweet crowd heavenward lifted,
　When the nocturn bells are pealing,
Chants His purposes predestined
　Until the Day of Doom's revealing.

　　* A fair or open air assembly.

Next a flock whose thoughts are blessed,
　　Under twilight's curls dim sweeping,
Hymn God's wondrous words of Judgment
　　When His Court of Doom is keeping.

One and forty on a hundred
　　And a thousand, without lying,
Was their number, joined to virtue,
　　Put upon each bird-flock flying.

Who these faultless birds should hearken,
　　Thus their strains of rapture linking,
For the very transport of it,
　　Unto death would straight be sinking.

Pray for us, O mighty Mary !
　　When earth's bonds no more are binding,
That these birds our souls may solace,
　　In the Land of Philip's finding.

DR. JOYCE'S IRISH WONDER BOOK

OLD world geographies, as Dr. Joyce points out, generally contained a chapter on the Mirabilia or Wonders, whether natural, preternatural or artificial, of each of the countries described; yet in spite of the claims of all other climes from the days of Herodotus down to those of the latest of our tellers of travellers' tales, De Rougemont and Cook, he gravely maintains that for such marvels "no other country in Europe," at any rate, "is fit to hold a candle to Ireland." Certainly it would be hard to beat his records of strange happenings in *The Island of Saints*, though there are perhaps incidents in the *Voyage of Maeldune*, his own *Wonders beyond Thule*, which eclipse those of Antonius Diogenes, and which are at any rate more grotesquely strange than the marvels which he now sets before us. For example, take these two specimens from his *Old Celtic Romances :*

As soon as it was light they saw land and made toward it. While they were casting lots to know who should go and explore the country, they saw great flocks of ants coming down to the beach, each of them as large as a foal. The people judged by their numbers and by their eager, hungry look, that they were bent on eating both ship and crew ; so they turned their vessel round and sailed quickly away.

Their multitudes countless, prodigious their size ;
  Were never such ants seen or heard of before.
They struggled and tumbled and plunged for the prize,
And fiercely the famine fire blazed from their eyes,
  As they ground with their teeth the red sand of the shore.

What an opportunity for Lord Avebury had he been living at the time! He certainly would have beaten no cowardly retreat from the contemplation of these Brobdignag *ecitones praedatores.*

Nor can Dr. Joyce parallel upon Irish *terra firma* his elephant-hided monster of *The Wall-circled Isle* who :

> Threw up his heels with a wonderful bound
> And ran round the isle with the speed of a hare,
> But a feat more astounding is yet to be told ;
> He turned round and round in his leathery skin ;
> His bones and his flesh and his sinews he rolled—
> He was resting outside while he twisted within.
>
> Then, changing his practice with marvellous skill,
> His carcase stood rigid and round went his hide ;
> It whirled round his bones like the wheel of a mill—
> He was resting within while he twisted outside.

After such a wonder beyond Thule, how wanting in distinction are these instances of Welsh wonders which we have lately come across.

> I heard it stated yester morning that a ship of lead swam on the breakers, that a ship of copper sank to the bottom of the sea—that is one of the seven wonders. I've heard it stated that the sweet dove was on the sea keeping a public tavern, with her tiny cup to taste the liquor—that is another of the seven wonders.

Four other wonders of a similar type are described, and the Welsh folk-lorist then concludes :

> I've heard it stated that the swallow was in the sea, putting on a horseshoe with her hammer of gold and silver anvil, and there are the seven wonders for you.

What are these and pellet-making partridges and a self-acting sickle and a book-reading moon and even a cart-loading pig to an island of red-hot animals from whom Maeldune and his men snatched, not roasted chestnuts, but the juiciest of apples, or what are they to " An island which

dyed white and black," and from which the voyagers fled lest
they should share the fate of the white sheep which turned
black when flung across a hedge and become all niggeryfied
on the spot.

Yet Dr. Joyce's New Wonders of Old Ireland will hold
their own even against such marvels as these, though many
of them are at the great disadvantage of being supposed to
be true.

Here we have a new set of wonderful islands and in
especial Inishglora, off the coast of Mayo, whose air and soil
preserve dead bodies from decay. There they were left
lying in the open air retaining their looks unchanged and
growing their nails and hair quite naturally, " so that a
person was able to recognise not only his father and grandfather, but even his ancestors to a remote generation." Such
powers of recognition seem quite an Irish inspiration.

Nennius, as well as Giraldus and the Norse Kongs
Skuggio, are the chroniclers of this wonder. Were these
wonderful bodies mummies of their forbears laid out in
sight of their descendants at periodical tribal gatherings?

The Irish came from the East and an early colony may
have embalmed their dead.

The splitting of Mutton Island near Miltown Malbay
into three is a natural wonder, not only recorded in all the
principal Irish annals as having occurred on St. Patrick's
Eve in A.D. 804, but still vividly imprinted upon local
tradition. Evidently this disruption was caused by a shock
of earthquake, and to a similar cause may be attributed what
were regarded as the miraculous disappearances of lakes,
Lee and Seeoran, in A.D. 848 and A.D. 1054 respectively.

The record in A.D. 864 on the turning of Loch Leane in
West Meath to blood for nine days, and that of a shower of
blood in A.D. 875, are easily explicable in the latter instance*
by the whirling up into the air, as Dr. Joyce points out, " of
water, coloured deep red by millions of little scarlet fungi
and its descent to earth in distant places, and in the former

case by a sudden growth and no less sudden disappearance of these minute scarlet fungi about Loch Leane."

The tidal well of Corann is fabled to have been set going by St. Patrick. For when driving the demon reptiles into the Atlantic and so working one of the Irish wonders, the Saint was so overcome by the foul, fiery breath of one of them, that in an agony of despair he struck his fist "against the solid rock, whereupon a well of sweet water burst forth from it."

"That this well ebbed and flowed, keeping time with the sea, is of course the creation of the people's imagination," writes Dr. Joyce, "but it is a fact known beyond doubt that it sometimes rises and falls in a remarkable and unaccountable way."

We are here reminded of the alternate flow of hot and cold water in an African spring, as described by Herodotus and ridiculed by his critics, as was his account of the Pigmies, though the existence of both marvels have been recently established. Herodotus no doubt was occasionally imposed upon by the Egyptian priests and others for their own purposes, and Giraldus Cambrensis, one of the authorities for his Irish Wonders quoted by Dr. Joyce, had good reason for taking some of them for granted and applying others to suit the purpose of the Norman invaders.

As a Churchman, Gerald Barry supports such tales of wonder as that of St. Colman's ducks, which not only refused to be boiled but even avenged any injury or disrespect to the Church or clergy by deserting their pond, which thereupon became putrid, so destroying its use for man or beast. Not till the offender was punished did the ducks return and their pond become clear and wholesome again.

Giraldus also records this charming story, which all bird lovers would like to believe :

On one occasion St. Kevin of Glendalough had his hands stretched out in prayer, palms up, through the little window of his cell, when a blackbird laid her eggs in one palm and sat on them. When the Saint at last observed the bird, after his prayer, he remained motionless in pity ; and in gentleness and patience he held on till the young ones were hatched and flew away.

Giraldus professed to hold the popular belief in the man-wolves of Ossory who, according to ancient Irish writings, were human beings who passed seven years of their lives as wolves, ravaging sheep folds and devouring cattle in pairs and then returning to their human forms whilst another wolf-pair took their place for a similar period.

Giraldus is never wanting in a good story when it serves his purpose, and he tells " a very circumstantial one " about a wolf who came up to a benighted priest and his youthful companion, and addressing them in very good Gaelic told them there was no danger to them from him and his comrades, and after spending the night in converse with them by their fire, thus answered an inquiry of the priest as to whether, in his opinion, the hostile people, the " Anglo-Normans," who had lately landed in Ireland, would hold the country for any length of time.

The anger of the Lord has fallen on an evil generation, and on account of the sins of our nation and the monstrous vices of the people, he has given them into the hands of their enemies. This foreign race shall be quite secure and invincible so long as they shall walk in the ways of the Lord and keep His Commandments, but we know that the path leading to sinful pleasures is easy and human nature is prone to follow ill example ; so if this strange people shall hereafter learn our wicked habits from living amongst us, they will no doubt, like us, draw down upon themselves the vengeance of divine Providence.

The sanctimonious wolf then went off with himself.

Of course Giraldus, as Dr. Joyce pithily puts it, invented this story, "for the double pious purpose of favouring his Anglo-Norman friends and having a good hearty slap at the Irish people." But the wolf's prophecy as to what would happen if the Normans became more Irish than the Irish is curiously suggestive. Dr. Joyce's authorities for his wonders, besides Giraldus and Kongs Skuggio's *The Royal*

Mirror, written about A.D. 1250 in the Norse language, are *The Book of Ballymote,* a large manuscript volume full of miscellaneous pieces in the Irish language, copied into that book towards the end of the 14th century, an ancient manuscript (H. 3 17) in the library of Trinity College, Dublin, the third part of Roderick O'Flaherty's *Ogygia,* and Sir James Ware's *Antiquities of Ireland.*

Much of this material is all but unreadable and much of it is meaningless, and Dr. Joyce deserves great credit therefore for dishing up this pemmican, as he calls it, in such a palatable form as the above extracts from his volume prove him to have done.

But let us record just a few more of his wonders. The Island of Loch Cre or Inishmameo had three wonderful properties. No one guilty of any great sin could die in it; the body of no unrepentant sinner could be buried in it; and no woman or the female of any animal could enter it. It is unfortunate that St. Kevin did not take up his quarters there and so escape having to protect his privacy by woman-slaughter. It is a greater pity that the island has quite lost its misogynistic defences and is no longer a safe asylum for the Prime Minister and the Chancellor of the Exchequer from the assaults of the suffragettes.

Aviation is so much with us nowadays that the following marvel, recorded by Kongs Skuggio, may really have been only a foreshadowing of what is to be expected from Sabbath-breaking air-craftsmen. "On a Sunday, while the people were at Mass in Clonmacnoise, there dropped from the air, hanging from a rope, an anchor, the fluke of which caught in an arch of the Church door. The astonished people looked upwards along the rope and saw a ship floating on top. One of the crew leaped overboard and dived and swam down to loosen the anchor, when some of the congregation seized and held him while he struggled to free himself; till the bishop, who happened to be just then present, directed them to let him go; for, as he said, if held

down he would die as if held under water. They let him
go and up he floated, when the crew cut the rope at the top
and the ship sailed away out of sight." The old Norseman
gravely adds, of course as he heard the story :—"and the
anchor has since lain in Clonmacnoise Church as a witness
that the event really occurred."

Dr. Joyce appears to have been reading Mr. Wells when
he was transcribing this story from the Norse, for he calls
attention to the circumstance "that the original narrator
of this wonder believed the crew of the ship to have been
the inhabitants of the upper air . . . who had ventured for
once on an unusual voyage of discovery down to the earth."

The last wonder described by Dr. Joyce is the Lia Fail,
or Coronation Stone of Tara, on which the ancient kings of
Ireland were crowned and "which uttered a shout whenever a king of the true Scotic or Irish race stood or sat on
it." This stone, so ran the tradition, was brought out of
Lochlann or Scandinavia by the Dedannan conquerors and
served as their Coronation stone and that of the Milesians
who conquered them in turn. Scottish writers affirm that
when the Scotic princes, Fergus, Angus, and Lorne, the
three sons of Erc of Dalriada in North Antrim, conquered
western Scotland in 503 A.D., Fergus, with the consent of
the King of Ireland, caused the Lia Fail to be brought over
to Alba (Scotland) and had himself crowned on it, there
being an ancient prophecy that, into whatsoever land the
Lia Fail was brought, there a prince of the Scotic or Irish
race should be crowned, a prophecy which Hector Boece,
the Scottish writer, presents in this Latin form :

> Ni fallat fatum, Scoti, quocunque locatum
> Invenient lapidem, regnare tenentur ibidem.

On account of this prophecy, writes Dr. Joyce, "the stone
received the name of Lia Fail, which according to the
Scotch authorities means the stone of Destiny, and upon a
stone supposed to be the true Lia Fail, the Scottish kings

were crowned at Scone, and the Kings of England, since
the time of our James I., have been crowned in Westminster Abbey.

Unfortunately for the truth of this legend, Dr. Petrie
has proved that the Lia Fail was in Tara four centuries
after the time of the alleged removal to Scotland. Antiquaries of the late tenth and early eleventh centuries affirm
that the stone was in Tara, and indeed the poet scholar
Kineth O'Hartigan, who died in the year 975, visited Tara
with the object of describing it. After mentioning in detail
several monuments which he found still existing there, he
states that he was actually standing on the Lia Fail:

> The stone which is under my two feet,
> From it is called Inis Fail ;
> Between two strands of strong tide,
> The Plain of Fal (as a name) for all Erin.

Fal was the proper name of the stone of which the genitive
form is Fail as it appears in *Lia Fail*. The word Lia
means a stone, and Lia Fail is literally the 'stone of Fal.' "

Dr. Petrie attempts, in his Essay on Tara, to identify as
the true Lia Fail a pillar stone now standing on the Forradh
of Tara, as the present writer can vouch, taken, as he asserts,
from The Mound of Hostages in 1821 and placed to mark
the grave of some rebels killed in 1798. But Dr. Joyce
controverts Dr. Petrie's view, having been assured by one
of the men who helped in the removal of the stone in
question, that it was not brought from the Mound of
Hostages where the true Lia Fail was recorded to have
stood, but from the bottom of the trench surrounding the
Forradh itself, where it had been lying prostrate for genera-
tions. Furthermore, Dr. Joyce wisely observes that the
pillar stone believed by Dr. Petrie to be the Irish Coronation stone is of a size and shape quite unsuitable for standing on during the ceremonies of installation and coronation ;
and seeing that the stone weighs considerably more than a

ton it would be impracticable to carry it about, as the legends say the Dedannans carried the Lia Fail in their overland journeys in Scandinavia, Scotland and Ireland and on oversea voyages in their hide-covered wicker boats. Dr. Joyce's conclusion, therefore, is that the true Lia Fail remains still in Tara buried and hidden somewhere in the soil; probably in the position where the old writers place it on the north side of the Mound of Hostages.

Here is indeed an opportunity for such energetic Irish antiquaries as Sir Henry Bellingham or Mr. Francis Joseph Bigger; indeed, what have they been about not to have unearthed the true Lia Fail before King George's Coronation, and there put it to the test which the Westminster stone has ignominiously failed to stand, for there is certainly no record of that impostor having "let out a shout" since kings of the true Scotic and Irish race have been crowned upon it in the Abbey.

Dr. Joyce's volume contains other good things besides the wonders of Ireland. His genius for investigation has enabled him to identify some of Spenser's Irish Rivers whose names have hitherto puzzled the poet's commentators. He gives us two striking folk tales of horror in *The Destruction of Tiernmas* and *Fergus O'Mara and the Demons*, his short biographies of Ireland's three patron saints, St. Patrick, St. Brigit, and St. Columkille, and of her scholar saint Donatus, Bishop of Fiesole, are good reading, as are his contrasted sketches of an Irish and Norman warrior, Cahal O'Conor of the Red Hand and Sir John de Courcy; and lastly he tells a pathetic tale of his native Glenosheen in the dialect of the Limerick peasantry of seventy years ago, which might have been written by William Carleton himself, so human is its interest and so vivid is its colouring.

FOLK SONG

An Address delivered before the Cymmrodorion Section of the Welsh National Eisteddfod of 1906 at Carnarvon, and brought up to date

There seems to be a general impression that the folk songs of the British Isles have been already collected, and are all to be found within the covers of old song books or on the broadside ballad sheets published in London and the larger provincial towns. There could be no graver error. Hundreds, not to say thousands, of British and Irish folk songs remain uncollected, if we are to judge by the results obtained within the last few years under the auspices of the Folk Song Societies. Mr. Cecil Sharp has collected 500 songs in Somerset and Devon, but mainly in the former county, and declares that very many more tunes might still be collected in these counties. A hundred songs have come before the Folk Song Society from Leicestershire alone, and Mr. Vaughan Williams has dealt with a vast body collected by him in East Anglia. In his preface to his collection of sixty-one folk songs he writes :—"Although the field covered by the tunes in this Journal is in one sense very large, in another it is very small, since it is only a small part of each county which I have searched for songs, and the time spent has been of necessity very short. What results might not be obtained from a systematic and sympathetic search through all the villages and towns of England? And yet this precious heritage of beautiful melody is being allowed to slip through our hands through mere ignorance or apathy." I may here say that the Folk

Song Society was founded at my suggestion in 1898, for the purpose of collecting and publishing folk songs, ballads and tunes. Its first meeting was held at the rooms of the Irish Literary Society of London, of which I was then honorary secretary, and it is now on a secure basis. Its president is Lord Tennyson, its vice-presidents Sir Hubert Parry, who may be said to represent England and Wales, Sir Alexander Mackenzie standing for Scotland, and Sir Charles Villiers Stanford being the Irish representative. Mr. Frederick Keel is honorary secretary, and the committee has amongst its members such distinguished folk song collectors as Sir Ernest Clarke, Mr. Frank Kidson, Mr. J. A. Fuller Maitland, Miss Broadwood, Mr. Cecil Sharp, and Dr. Vaughan Williams. Lady Gomme, the leading authority on old English singing games, is its honorary treasurer. The society publishes in its Journal, of which sixteen parts have appeared, such contributions of traditional songs as may be chosen by a committee of musical experts, and from time to time holds meetings at which these songs are introduced and form the subject of performance, lecture and discussion. A legal opinion having been obtained upon the subject, the society guarantees that all versions of songs and words published in their Journal are the copyright of the collectors supplying them, and are printed on behalf of that collector, whose permission must be obtained for any reproduction thereof.

Ireland, with its Home Rule tendencies, felt, however, that her own folk song affairs needed special treatment, and an Irish Folk Song Society has been started under the secretaryship of Mrs. Milligan Fox, who has recently made a valuable find of manuscripts and memorials relating to Edward Bunting, from whose three collections Thomas Moore took so many of his Irish melodies, and is, like Mr. Hughes, the first joint editor with her of its Journal, an enthusiastic and successful folk song collector.

Before this Irish Folk Song Society was formed, our Irish Literary Society, after negotiations with Sir C. V. Stanford, published the Petrie collection of the ancient airs of Ireland, which had fallen into his hands—a gathering of nearly 2,000 tunes of which not 200 had been previously given to the public. This collection is, I believe, the largest ever got together by a single individual, and is of extraordinary interest.

Meantime, moreover, the officials of the Feis Ceoil, an Irish National musical festival much on the lines of the Eisteddfod, have been gathering Irish airs from the pipers and fiddlers attending its meetings by means of the phonograph, and the Gaelic League, which encourages traditional singing in Irish, has also got together a considerable body of hitherto unpublished airs.

Finally, as far as Ireland is concerned, I can report the publication of two other great bodies of fresh Irish melodies. My old friend Dr. Joyce, who has done so much for Irish history, archæology, romance and music, has issued, with Messrs. Longmans, the great long-lost collection of Irish airs gathered by Pigott and Ford, a Cork musician of the last century, which the doctor had at last run to earth and purchased. He has also included in his volume selections from Professor Goodman's fine collection of Munster airs, so that his volume contains nearly a thousand unknown Irish tunes, chiefly from the counties of Cork, Kerry, Limerick, Leitrim and Sligo. He has besides shown me a pile of yet unpublished folk songs.

Crossing over from Dublin to Holyhead, I met the collector of another vast body of Irish music, Mr. O'Neill, for long the distinguished chief of police in Chicago. This folk song enthusiast, beginning by setting down the Irish airs learnt at his Irish-speaking mother's knee, and then through a course of years tapping the memories of fellow-countrymen who had drifted to Chicago from all the four corners of the Green Isle, has succeeded in putting together some 1,850 airs, of which at least 500 have never before been in print. The great value of this collection consists in the number of instrumental airs which

it contains.   Levy's book of The Dance Music of Ireland is
dwarfed beside it.

About nineteen years ago Mr. W. H. Gill, brother of the
Northern Deemster, came to me with an inquiry as to the
possible Irish origin of some Manx folk songs which he had
collected.   It turned out that, after failing to secure more
than a dozen fresh folk songs in the Isle of Man, he had
altered his methods of research, and had thus collected 250
airs, some of English, some of Scotch, some of Norse, and
some of Irish origin, yet all domesticated in little Ellan
Vannin.   Besides these, Mr. Speaker Moore has got together a considerable body of hitherto unnoted Manx airs.

There is no concerted effort being made to collect the
many unpublished airs still floating in the Highlands, though
I have heard of a couple of male enthusiasts who have been
thus engaged within recent years ; but Miss Murray, an
American lady of Scotch descent, has collected no less than
150 airs of a most distinctive character in the Hebrides, and
a charming article on the subject from her pen is contained
in a recent number of the *Celtic Review*, and more recently
Mrs. Kennedy Fraser has brought out a delightful collection
of Hebridean airs finely harmonised and with Gaelic and
English words to them.   I think I have conclusively proved
that the treasures of our recently published, unpublished
and even uncollected folk songs are surprisingly large.

By what methods have these folk songs been gathered ?
Let us listen to the experiences of some of the collectors
named above.   Mr. Henry Berstow supplied Miss Lucy Broadwood, the second secretary of the Folk Song Society, with most
of her Sussex songs.   He was sixty-eight years old in 1893
when he sang them to her.   He was a native of Horsham,
which, up to that year, he had never left for a night, except
once for a week.   He is well known in Sussex and parts of
Surrey as a bellringer, and also in great request as a singer.
He is proud of knowing 400 songs, and keeps a valuable
list of their titles.   He once, by request, sang all his songs

to an inquiring stranger. It took a month to do it, but many of these he refused to sing to Miss Broadwood, considering them to be unfit for ladies' ears, and though by their titles they promised to be amongst the very oldest ballads, he could not detach the tunes from the words, and the airs have therefore remained unnoted. He learnt, as he said, very many of these old songs and "ballets" from shoemakers, who were always singing at their work. Others he learnt from labourers, who often could not read. For many a day he tried to learn an old song from a certain carter, but the man was shy and would not sing it, because he thought Mr. Berstow wanted to laugh at his "burr" (Sussex for "accent"). At length Mr. Berstow laid a deep plot. A confederate lured the carter into an alehouse, where Mr. Berstow sat hidden in an inner parlour. Flattered by his treacherous boon companion, the carter presently burst forth into his favourite "ballet," and Mr. Berstow listened, learnt and sang the song from that day forth.

The first secretary of the Folk Song Society, Mrs. Kate Lee, was emboldened to attempt an even more desperate enterprise. To get hold of some folk songs which she knew were reserved for the ears of the frequenters of a country inn in The Broads, she obtained admittance as a waitress at the ordinary table, and when the diners had settled down to beer, tobacco, and song, she got those precious folk songs into her head, and kept them there for the benefit of the society.

Except in the remote glens, amongst primitive peoples, few folk songs remain to be gleaned from the younger generation, but Miss Murray has been fortunate enough to make a remarkable collection, chiefly among the young island girls of the Hebrides. They were very shy about crooning before her, and could hardly be got to believe that the airs she set down from their chanting were what they had been reciting. To them *the words only* gave a suggestion of music, and they had therefore unconsciously assimilated the wild and uncommon airs to which the tunes

were matched. Like Mr. Berstow, they could not detach
the tune from the words, and but for the latter the airs
would have been lost.

In less primitive places, folk songs are preserved by
elderly and old people alone. This is true for Mr. Sharp's
collection, his singers ranging from sixty to nearly ninety
years of age, and Mr. W. H. Gill has had the same
experiences in the Isle of Man. The Manx are a shy race,
and he had much difficulty in coaxing the old tunes out of
them. Friendliness, combined with judicious *backsheesh*, in
the way of snuff, tobacco, tea, and ale, unloosened their
tongues and revived their memories. He extracted one
excellent tune from a one-legged man who had played the
fiddle in his youth, and could not be got to remember the
air in question till he had propped himself up against the
wall, and had drawn his crutch for a long time across his
shoulder, as if playing upon the long-disused instrument.
With the air thus recovered in his head, he found himself
able to hum it to Mr. Gill.

I myself picked up a long lost Irish air under curious
circumstances at Harlech. I was at work in my study,
when my ears were saluted by an unmistakably Irish tune
played on a hand organ. The air was unfamiliar to me,
and I accordingly went out and asked the organ grinder
about it. "It is *The Beautiful City of Sligo*," he replied.
"I have played it on the road for forty years, and my father
had played it as many before me. He bought the organ at
the sale of a gentleman's property in Liverpool." The
tune had become rather blurred, owing to the age of the
instrument, but by putting the organ grinder at a little
distance on the terrace outside my house, and whistling the
air as he played it through the window to my wife as she
sat pencil in hand at the piano, I succeeded in recovering
it. The air was set by Sir Charles Stanford to a lyric of
my own, suggested by the traditional title, and is now one
of Mr. Plunket Greene's most successful songs.

Dr. Stokes, in his Life of Petrie, describes how that famous archæologist and delightful man collected folk songs in the Isle of Arran. Hearing that a certain household in one of the islands " had music," he visited it, when the day's work was done, with his friend, Eugene O'Curry. He found an expectant group of the islanders round the turf fire, and the proceedings began by the singing of a tune which Petrie wished to add to his repertory. O'Curry first took down the Irish words, which, of course, helped to establish the measure of the air, then Petrie began to note the tune, stopping from time to time to make sure that he had got the correct version of each strain, and then getting the singer to repeat it again throughout. Having thus secured the air, he would play it on his violin, an instrument of singular sweetness and power, as few others could have played it. The effect upon a music-loving people was electrical. Young and old broke out into expressions of eager delight, and after an encore a new air was similarly dealt with.

What is the origin of folk song? Evidently there is a musical instinct in the young of all races. How early do we note our children crooning of their own accord when in a contented or happy frame of mind? As with the child, so, I believe, with the early races. Calls to cattle, street and country cries with intonations, such as the " jodling " of the Tyrolese, strike one as amongst the probable beginnings of folk songs.

The songs of occupation would seem to be extended instances of these primeval chants. The occupation suggests certain measures; thus the rocking of the cradle, the blow of the hammer on the anvil, the sweep of the oars in the water, the turning of the spinning wheel—each invites a rhythmic chant, monotonous at first, but afterwards taking on melodic cadences which become tunes.

And here the genius of various languages comes in, as has been pointed out by Francis Korbay, the Hungarian musician, in an article in *Harper's Magazine*. The length of the Hungarian words tends to a peculiar rhythm, classically known as the " choriambic," and the Hungarian folk songs are all stamped with that peculiar measure. In great contrast to these airs are the folk songs of The Principality, which are largely trochaic in measure, especially when of instrumental origin, and with a tendency to dissyllabic line endings, sometimes three times repeated, an effect helped doubtless by the cadences which are peculiar to Welsh harp music.

This mention of the harp suggests that to that instrument narrative poems were chanted or cantilated, often at great length. Words then were of prime consequence, and the bard, even upon the battlefield, would recite the achievements of his fathers, as an incitement to his chieftain. It is stated indeed that the bard thus chanted on the old Irish battlefields, surrounded by a group of harpers, who accompanied him, almost with the effect of a military band. Thus, no doubt, arose the clan marches, and where the chiefs fell fighting, the lamentations over fallen heroes common to the Gaelic and Cymric branches of the Celts.

It would not appear as if chorus songs were of early origin, though there is a hint or two of something of the kind in early Irish literature. In the Fenian tales there is occasional reference to the Dord, which would appear to be a concerted cry or chorus, a cry of warning, if not a war cry. And in some of the early Irish airs, such as " 'Tis pretty to be in Ballindery," there is an indication of a chorus. Later on, in Irish and Highland music, we find chorus songs of occupation, called "Lubeens" amongst the Irish and "Luinings" amongst the Highlanders. These seem to follow solos and alternate improvised utterances in song, such amœbean contests as we find in the eclogues of Theocritus and Virgil, and in Welsh airs with choruses such as "Hob y Deri Dando."

I have suggested that each language has its own rhythmic genius ; its accent, brogue, burr, or whatever you call it, is part of this, and a clever musical Scot told me he was prepared to show how the Scotch intonation affected Scotch music. If this be so, it is obvious that a popular air carried from one country to another will become modified by the rhythmical genius of the race amongst which it is domesticated. A case in point is the air known in Ireland as the " Cruiskeen lawn," an air of considerable antiquity, and, I believe, sung in an early form to one of Sedulius's Latin hymns. That air was played to me at the Moore Centenary by a Swedish musician many years ago as a Norse air. It no doubt passed into Norway when Dublin was the capital of the Norse empire, and the tides of music flowed strongly between Ireland and Scandinavia. That same air is regarded by the Welsh as one of their National melodies, namely, " The Vale of Clwyd," and it is famous, in another form, in Scotland as " John Anderson, my jo, John." A beautiful tune, " The Cobbler of Castleberry," known now as " The Cuckoo Madrigal," is evidently an English air twisted into an Irish shape, and a Welsh hymn on the New Jerusalem is an English sacred air thrown into a much finer Welsh form.

All this suggests a fascinating aspect of folk song from what might be called the point of view, not of comparative philology, but " comparative philophony." The root of an air would be looked for probably amongst Oriental peoples, like the Indians and Persians, who, according to Dr. Petrie, have set our Irish slumber tunes and ploughmen's whistles agoing. Thence it would be traced in its various developments amongst different nationalities, till it reached a point of alteration which would make it unrecognisable to any but those who had thus followed it step by step from its primitive source. All this, of course, has to be systematically followed up, but what a joy to a great musical grammarian !

Early Scotch musical manuscripts, and some of Bunting's

earliest printed Irish tunes, show folk airs in a very elemental condition.   The musical grammarian might very well trace these growing up into beautiful Scotch and Irish melodies.   He would also find them degenerating in course of time into poor variants.   How are we to account for these processes, and for the corresponding improvement and deterioration of the words to which these folk songs were sung ?   Surely, that very word " folk-song" gives the key to the explanation.   One of the folk chants a song to a rude tune on a rude instrument.   It is taken up, improved in rhythm, improved in air, and often benefited by an improved instrument—a harp of thirty strings, for example, as opposed to one with a dozen.   A consummation is finally reached.   A musical genius arises.   Under his cultivation the simple rose of the hedgeside blossoms into the perfect garden flower.   And to match this beautiful melody, perfect words are needed, if indeed thay have not inspired the absolute air.   A Thomas Moore or a Robert Burns, with his " Minstrel Boy" or his " Scots wha hae wi' Wallace bled," crystallises the melody for ever.

Other airs are not so fortunate.   Partnered by vulgar or meaningless or dissolute words, they drop out of favour, and many of these are at this very moment hiding their heads among the Welsh vales and mountains.   Even Moore's instinct was not unerring, and some of his melodies have ceased to hold the public, because the words written to the airs have proved to be of an ephemeral kind.

Again beautiful, though distinctly secular tunes, are pressed into the services of the churches.   Many of the Welsh love songs, I am told, are now used as Welsh hymns, and to restore them to their former use would probably be regarded as desecration.   Some of the Welsh rollicking airs, too much associated in the past with the tavern and rowdy revelry, are now altogether discountenanced, while their instrumental use as dances, such as are favoured in Ireland and Scotland, is a thing of the past in Wales ;

though a whisper reaches me that school children are obtaining permission to use their limbs in a way for which there is good scriptural precedent, and, perhaps, some of the good old Welsh dance measures may yet be revived. The child is the father of the man and the mother of the woman. But, above all, there is a dangerous tendency to alter the musical accents of characteristic Welsh airs on the part of some Welsh musicians, whilst some modern Welsh lyrists violate the very principles of Welsh rhythm by breaking up the musical measures which were themselves suggested by that rhythm.

The suggestion contained in the preface to the *Cambrian Minstrelsy* that this collection of about 180 Welsh airs is a complete compendium of Welsh song, in the sense that every Welsh air possessing permanent value has been included in it, appears to me to be an ill-advised utterance on the part of the editors of that undoubtedly interesting collection.

I am given to understand that Mrs. Mary Davies, who as Mary Davis won so many laurels of song, possesses a MS. collection of Welsh airs unknown to the editors of the *Minstrelsy*, in which there are many hitherto unpublished airs, some of them of great beauty. I understand, too, that my friends Sir Harry Reichel and Dr. Lloyd Williams, of University College, Bangor, have between them quite a couple of hundred of Welsh airs, many of which are of permanent value. I am glad to find also that it is the practice of the Bangor College authorities not only to rescue from oblivion characteristic Welsh melodies which come in their way, but to mate them to suitable Welsh words, and then arrange them for performance at their University functions. There are several other considerable unpublished collections of Welsh airs, and with this information before me I cannot think that the inquiries of the editors of the *Cambrian Minstrelsy* have been sufficiently searching to justify their statement that there are not 200 Welsh

airs of permanent value in existence. Indeed, that statement is a distinct reflection upon the great and prolific
musical genius of the Welsh, who long before the time of
Geraldus Cambrensis were singing songs in four parts, and
down along the ages, influenced by martial and patriotic
traditions, carried music in the forefront of their fights for
freedom, and at the present day are regarded as the most
actively musical race in the British Isles. Wales, too, has
been generously susceptible to external musical influences
without sacrificing her own musical individuality, and that
she will never lose as long as she adheres to her national
language.

Griffith Ap Cynan, a Welsh King by an Irish Princess,
gathered the Irish and Welsh bards together to regulate the
canon of Welsh National music, and it is stated that from
that day till the times of Llewelyn the canon was kept to.
If this be true, the following statement of Dr. Crotch must
be taken, not with a grain, but with a pillar of salt:
"British and Welsh National music must be considered as
one, since the original British music was with the inhabitants driven into Wales. It must be owned that the regular
measure and diatonic scale of the Welsh music is more
congenial to English taste in general, and appears at first
more natural to the experienced musician than those of the
Irish and Scotch. Welsh music not only solicits an accom-
paniment, but being chiefly composed for the harp is
usually found with one; and indeed in harp tunes there
are often solo passages for the bass as well as for the treble;
it often resembles the scientific music of the 17th and
18th centuries, and there is, I believe, no probability that
this degree of refinement was an introduction of later
times. 'Ffarwel Ednyfed Fychan' is a tune bearing the
name of the councillor, minister and general of Llewelyn
the Great in the 13th century, and yet is remarkable for the
characteristics for which I have mentioned it."

The question of the modes of Welsh music has, I understand, been recently discussed in the columns of *Y Brython* from a very different point of view. Doubtless the old tunes turning up in England do show a connection between the early English and Welsh tunes, but to suggest that England and Wales were distinguished from the Irish and Scots by not using modal tunes at an early period is preposterous. I have had an interesting letter from Mr. Griffith, of the Dolgelly County School, on this very question, from which I make a few quotations : " I would like to call your attention to the efforts to represent the old folks' performances of Welsh music. To name but a few of the points where it fails : the accent, or want of it ; the melodic intervals, often not diatonic, and even wavering, not through ignorance or vocal incapacity ; the grace notes, or more accurately perhaps explanatory or commentatory notes, often highly elaborate and queerly timed with respect to any possible bars, and certain tricks of utterance, perhaps not unconnected with grace notes. If the ordinary trained musician is set to copy down these vocal performances, he will ignore all these things, strictly ruled though they be by tradition, and he will give us but the merest approximation in the polite musical dialect of the day. He has often done even worse in Wales ; looked at the whole thing from a harmony exercise point of view, and calmly altered the most characteristic intervals, as in the case of the old hymn tune 'Bangor,' which has been treated in this way. Now, I think it is important that an attempt should at once be made to represent these vanishing idioms of music on paper. I am convinced for one thing that there is much behind them, a highly developed art, some psychology, and possibly ethnology. In any case, it is a shame to look at them dying, and even to try to kill them, as any successful choir trainer must do, and not to get a record of them. What about the phonograph in this connection ? "

I cordially agree with these views of Mr. Griffith's, with this small reservation. So-called traditional singing is often

corrupt, not only because old rules are imperfectly remembered, but because the introduction of foreign fashions
in the way of variations and flourishes has been imposed
upon the original tradition.   There is an apposite story of
a Hebridean priest, who was so annoeyd by the choric
confusion in his church created by the many variants upon
a hymn tune sung by a Gaelic-speaking congregation, that
he insisted upon its being sung in its simplest modal form,
with all grace notes left out.   The Irish minstrels were
undoubtedly much influenced in the 18th century by an
Italian tendency of this kind, even Carolan showing it in
many of his jigs, planxties, and concertos.   The traditional
singers of the Gaelic League will have to face this fact, and
so, probably, will the Welsh traditional singers of the future,
if they are to preserve their National music in its primitive
purity.

All that I have said leads up to the necessity of every
nation regarding it as a pious duty to collect in the most
perfect manner, to arrange in the most perfect manner, and
to mate to the most perfect words, its own folk tunes.
Wales has yet to do this.   The airs are to collect in
numbers which I believe will prove surprising.   They will
then have to be set in various ways, in the simplest of all
forms for school children and people unable to reach the
highest musical culture ; in art forms for educated amateur
singers and for the professional singers, of whom Wales is
so justly proud.   It will be found, I think, that apart from
the mere arranging of these folk songs for soloists and
choruses in a separate form, Welsh music, when thoroughly
explored on its instrumental and vocal sides, will prove to
indicate theme after theme suitable for treatment in oratorio
or opera, overture or sonata.

Patient, careful investigation will in course of time
enable Welsh musicians to go very near at any rate to
establishing a chronological order of the Welsh tunes, by
internal and external evidence, just as the great English

scholars have pretty well succeeded, after infinite pains, in establishing a chronological order of Shakespeare's plays. At present we have little to go by. Confirmation of historical and traditional events has come through the collection of folk songs even within the last few years. You here in Wales, with your language living in every shire of the Principality, have a far better chance of recapturing the fugitive songs and tunes of your forefathers than we Irishmen, or your English neighbours. For, apart from your linguistic advantage, there is a greater spread of musical knowledge amongst Welshmen, and a greater capacity therefore for taking down your native airs. It has been suggested that a Welsh folk song branch should be affiliated with the Folk Song Society, which acts on an international basis and invites contributions of folk songs from all nations. But whether you accept this suggestion or set up an independent folk song society of your own, I make no earthly doubt that you have enough material to occupy you within your own borders for at least a generation to come. You have to get all the variants of your many Welsh folk songs into your musical museum, and select from them the very best for national purposes. You have to collect the legends with which these folk songs are connected and the local history to which they relate. You have to decide upon the right methods of playing and singing the airs, how many of them are to be left in their old modes, how many adapted to modern scales. You will have to decide as to how many of the Welsh lyrics to which the airs are now sung are worthless from the literary point of view, how many to be restored or improved as Burns and Allan Cunningham restored and improved the Scotch songs. You must do as the Germans are now doing, that is to say, you must treat folk song and the folk lore connected with it practically as well as archæologically.

You must gather its mutilated remains as well as its perfect examples into collections which will serve as illustrative museums.   This material will be available, not only for giving local colour and suitable form to reproductions of old world themes, but would be also available for works of a larger kind, instrumental and vocal.   Much folk lore would be incidentally collected along with the songs, and experts would know into what most fitting hands to place all fresh literary and musical finds with a view to their being first dealt with from an historical, linguistic, and ethnological standpoint, and then, where advisable, adapted for current use.   This treatment of folk songs should satisfy the views of the two schools of collectors, the antiquarian and the artistic.*

* The delivery of this address, which was musically illustrated by a party of singers chosen from the Eisteddfod Choir, was followed by another given by Principal Reichel, of Bangor University College.   The interest created by these addresses led to the formation of the now flourishing Welsh Folk Song Society.

EDWARD BUNTING

Mrs. Milligan Fox, the energetic honorary secretary of the Irish Folk Song Society, while purchasing a harp at a leading London warehouse inquired whether any of the old harpers ever called in there to buy strings. "Well, no," replied the attendant ; " but a gentleman was in here not long ago who bought a harp, and when giving the order said, ' It is only right that I should have a harp in my house, for it was my grandfather who preserved the music of the ancient Irish harpers.' "

Mrs. Fox thus got into communication with Dr. Louis Macrory of Battersea, Edward Bunting's grandson, and eventually obtained from him and from his cousin, Mrs. Deane of Dublin, a large mass of documents relating to their grandfather's famous collections of Irish music. Much of this material had never before been published, and in especial the Gaelic originals of a number of songs collected by Patrick Lynch nearly 110 years ago, during a tour through Connaught.

This find would have alone justified the issue of such a book as Mrs. Milligan Fox's *Annals of the Irish Harpers.* But there is besides much correspondence relating to the publication of Bunting's three collections of Irish airs, harmonised by himself, that throws an exceedingly interesting light upon the period of the Irish Rebellion of 1798 and the decade immediately following it, and is, therefore, eminently deserving of preservation.

Edward Bunting, but for whose collections of old Irish music Moore's melodies would never have seen the light, was the son of an English mining engineer, settled in the north of Ireland in the last quarter of the 18th century. His mother was a descendant of one Patrick Gruana O'Quinn, who had fallen in the Great Irish Rising of 1642. Left unprovided for by his father, he received so good a musical education from his brother Anthony that we find him at the age of eleven acting as deputy to a Belfast organist, Mr. William Ware, and, indeed, so outshining him as a performer that his employer was glad to secure him as a permanent assistant, not only at the organ, but as a teacher of the pianoforte to his pupils throughout the neighbouring county. The zeal of the boy-teacher, reinforced by a caustic tongue, from which he suffered through life, were often productive of ludicrous scenes. As an instance, he afterwards reported to Dr. Petrie, that on one occasion a lady pupil was so astonished "at the audacity of his reproofs that she indignantly turned round upon him and well boxed his ears."

He lodged with and became fast friends of the McCrackens, whose love for Irish folk music as well as the influence of Dr. James MacDonnell, the moving spirit in the Belfast Harper's Festival of 1792, drew him into that collection, study and arrangement of old Irish music which for the next fifty years absorbed all the time he had to spare from his duties as a professional musician.

As Mrs. Fox suggests, it is not improbable that Dr. MacDonnell's Belfast harp gathering was intended by him to divert attention from the great political meeting held in Belfast during the same week by the United Irelanders, with whose methods he was not in sympathy.

Bunting was retained by Dr. MacDonnell to take down the airs played by the nine harpers who assembled on the occasion. He was barely nineteen at the time, but the impression left upon him by that gathering never passed from his mind, and nearly fifty years afterwards he could thus write of it :

The meeting in Belfast was better attended than any that had yet taken place, and its effects were more permanent, for it kindled an enthusiasm throughout the North which still burns bright in some honest hearts. All the best of the old Irish harpers (a race of men then nearly extinct and now gone for ever), Denis Hempson, Arthur O'Neill, Charles Fanning and seven others, the least able of whom has not left his like behind, were present. Hempson, who realised the antique picture drawn by Cambrensis and Galilei, for he played with long crooked nails, and in his performance " the tinkling of the small wires under the deep tones of the bass " was peculiarly thrilling, took the attention of the editor with a degree of interest which he can never forget.

He was the only one who played the very old, the aboriginal music of the country, and this he did in a style of such finished excellence as persuaded Bunting that the praises of the old Irish harp in Cambrensis, Fuller and others, instead of being, as the detractors of the country are fond of asserting, ill-considered and indiscriminate, were in reality no more than a just tribute to that admirable instrument and its then professors.

But more than anything else, the conversation of Arthur O'Neill, who, though not so absolute a harper as Hempson, was more a man of the world and had travelled in his calling over all parts of Ireland, won and delighted the editor. All that the genius of later poets and romance writers has feigned of the wandering minstrel was realised in this man. There was no house of note in the North of Ireland, as far as Meath on the one hand and Sligo on the other, in which he was not well known and eagerly sought after.

For four years after the Harpers' Festival Bunting devoted himself to collecting airs in the counties of Derry and Tyrone, and then passed into Connaught, whither in his own words " he was invited by the celebrated Richard Kirwan of Craggs, the philosopher and founder of the Royal Irish Academy, who was himself an ardent admirer of Irish

native music, and who was of such influence in that part of
the country as procured the editor a ready opportunity of
obtaining tunes in both high and low circles."

As a consequence of this Folk Music Campaign,
Bunting in the year 1796 produced his first volume of sixty-
six native Irish airs never before published.   Shortly before
this, after a picnic to Ram's Island in Lough Neagh, at
which Russell, the Wolfe Tones and the McCrackens were
present, Bunting played " The Parting of Friends," one of
the airs in his collection.   " Overcome by the pathos of the
music, and bursting into tears Mrs. Wolfe Tone left the
room."   The music chosen was indeed singularly appro-
priate, "since tragedy loomed darkly" over the parting
friends; "for two of them the scaffold waited, for a third
death in a condemned cell."

Bunting's 1796 collection fell into Thomas Moore's
hands very soon after its publication.   " Robert Emmet,"
writes Moore, "during those college days, used frequently
to sit by me at the pianoforte while I played over the airs
from Bunting's Irish collection, and I remember one day,
when we were thus employed, his starting up as if from
a reverie while I played "The Fox's Sleep," exclaim-
ing passionately, "Oh, that I were at the head of twenty
thousand men marching to that air."

To this air Moore afterwards wrote his well-known lyric
Let Erin remember the Days of Old.

Eleven years after this Moore and Stevenson included
in their first number of sixteen Irish melodies no less than
eleven from Bunting's first collection, but with no acknowledgment of the source from which they were taken.   Great
bitterness arose out of this unpermitted appropriation, which
was all the more vexatious because Bunting had evidently
intended that the airs in his collection should in course of
time appear as songs and ballads to words by other well-
known lyrical writers of the day.

The period between the issue of Bunting's first and

second volumes was one of great storm and stress for Ireland. It included the risings of 1798 and 1803, in which his friends the McCrackens, Russell and others were implicated, and for their share in which Wolfe Tone, Henry Joy McCracken, Thomas Russell and Robert Emmet suffered death.

Robert Emmet and Thomas Russell were among a group of lyrical writers, which included Miss Balfour and Dr. Drennan, whom Bunting drew around him in order to furnish songs for his second volume which might compete successfully with those of Moore. These songs were founded upon Irish originals collected at the recommendation of the McCrackens by Patrick Lynch, an Irish scholar and schoolmaster who had toured Connaught, folk-song collecting, first by himself, and then along with Bunting. Some of these Gaelic songs were translated, though too artificially, into English lyrics by Miss Balfour and others; Bunting had also made a great but unsuccessful effort to induce Thomas Campbell, the poet, to take a leading part in this work and so come into competition with Moore, but he failed to secure the Scotch poet in this capacity, though Campbell contributed three poems to the collection. Then a most untoward event occurred. Thomas Russell, the *preux chevalier* of the United Irelanders and one of the Irish Folk Song band, was apprehended and executed on the evidence of Patrick Lynch, who, on suspicion of complicity with him, had been fixed upon to identify Russell, and who, in order to save his own neck, had reluctantly given damning evidence against his friend and employer. This, of course, caused Lynch to be dismissed from the employment of the McCrackens, and Dr. McDonnell, who had shown Loyalist proclivities after Russell's rising, was, for the time being, in their black books and Bunting's, though they subsequently made friends with him again.

The band of enthusiastic folk song collectors was then divided, and the publication of Bunting's second volume languished. When it ultimately appeared in 1809, Moore and Stevenson at once proceeded to pillage airs from it, and the poet had a very easy task in excelling the poor translations from Irish originals that served for its lyrics.

Moore, at a later period, was perfectly frank in replying to Bunting's charge that the original airs had been altered by Stevenson to suit his words. In an entry in his diary of July 15th, 1840, he thus writes: "Bunting lays the blame of all these alterations upon Stevenson, but poor Sir John was entirely innocent of them; as the whole task of selecting the airs, and in some instances shaping them to the general sentiment which the melody appeared to me to express, was undertaken solely by myself." "Had I not ventured," he adds in his diary for the same date, "on these very admissible liberties, many of the songs now most known and popular would have been still sleeping with all their authentic dross about them in Mr. Bunting's first volume. The same charge is brought by him respecting those airs which I took from the second volume of his collection."

Bunting married, as an old bachelor, Miss Mary Ann Chapman, the daughter of Mrs. Chapman, a widow and Lady Principal of a school in Dublin. His marriage, which proved an extremely happy one, brought Bunting from Belfast to Dublin. This uprooting of his old connections, though difficult, was wise, for it enabled him to break away from habits of life in which he was becoming confirmed, and which were casual and unwise. His fresh start in Dublin proved satisfactory in every respect. He secured plenty of musical work, and the companionship of men like Petrie, Stokes, O'Curry and others kept up the flame of his enthusiasm for his life work, the preservation and publication of native Irish music. Yet it was not until after a long interval that Bunting in 1840 produced his last collection, and as it proved his *magnum opus*. It was received with high commendation by the leading critics, and assured the editor's lasting fame. It is well described by Robert

Chambers " as a national work of the deepest antiquarian and historical interest. Were we to institute a literary comparison we could say that Moore's Irish melodies had about them all the fascination of poetry and romance, Bunting's collections all the sterner charms of truth and history." He adds, " When we hear Sir John Stevenson's Irish melodies played by a young lady on the pianoforte, or even on the pedal harp, we do not hear the same music which O'Cahan, Carolan and Hempson played. It is as much altered as Homer in the translation of Pope. For the true presentment of this music to modern ears we require the old sets as preserved in the volumes of Bunting and 'the Irish harp' played by an Irish harper." Dr. Petrie concludes his memoir of his great predecessor in Irish Folk Song collecting with these words : " The publication of his last volume was, for the very few years which he survived it, not only a matter of the greatest happiness and consolation to him, but it excited him to devote the leisure of those years to the rearrangement of the old airs and to terminate his labours by leaving behind him a complete, uniform and very nearly perfect collection of Irish music."

Moore's verdict was a very different one :

Received from Cramers and Co. a copy of Bunting's newly published collection of Irish Airs, which they have often written to me about, as likely, they thought, to furnish materials for a continuance of the Melodies. Tried them over with some anxiety, as, had they contained a sufficient number of beautiful airs to make another volume, I should have felt myself bound to do the best I could with them, though still tremblingly apprehensive lest a failure should be the result.

Was rather relieved I confess on finding, with the exception of a few airs, which I have already made use of, the whole volume is a mere mess of trash.

Considering the thorn I have been in poor Bunting's side by supplanting him in the one great object of his life (the connection of his name with the fame of Irish Music), the temper in which he now speaks of my success (for some years since he was rather termagant on the subject) is not a little creditable to his good nature and good sense.

Posterity has reversed Moore's shallow musical judgment. Sir Charles Villiers Stanford has, by an act of historical justice, largely restored Moore's melodies to the forms in which they are presented by Bunting.

" The mess of trash " in Bunting's third volume has, moreover, furnished Sir Charles with many beautiful airs for his own arrangement to lyrics suggested by the spirit and written in the measures of the old Gaelic songs.

Mrs. Milligan Fox and her sister, Miss Alice Milligan, whose Irish scholarship is evident throughout *The Annals of the Irish Harpers*, have taken in hand a good piece of work in dealing with the Bunting MSS. and correspondence as they have done.   But in a future edition the O'Neill and Lynch diaries might be condensed with advantage, and some of the additional space thus secured allotted to further translations from the Gaelic originals to which Bunting's airs were sung.

Limits of space make it impossible to enter into two or three very interesting speculations raised by Mrs. Milligan Fox, which we hope will be publicly discussed.   Was O'Curry justified in discrediting the list of Irish musical terms supplied to Bunting by Arthur O'Neill, who was, by all accounts, an honourable man ?   Was Petrie, as is now generally believed, justified in his contention that the form of Old Irish airs has been more correctly preserved by the Irish Folk singers than by the Irish harpers, to whose records of them Bunting pins his faith ?

Lastly, do not the Irish Harp tunes stand, as a rule, quite apart from the airs of the Irish Folk songs, as the Welsh Harp tunes are proved to stand apart from the airs of the Welsh Folk songs ?   Is it not therefore reasonable to suppose that airs in pentatonic or other incomplete scales which still exist in Ireland and Wales side by side with diatonic tunes dating from the twelfth century, at any rate, take their origin in the main either from the use of early-gapped instruments, or from the secular use amongst the

Irish and Welsh Catholic peasantry of their Church's earliest forms of plainsong? Can any direct connection be set up, as suggested by Petrie, between Persian and Indian lullabies and those of Ireland, and can such early Irish airs as the Plough tunes be proved to have a like connection with the East?

GEORGE PETRIE AS AN ARTIST AND MAN OF LETTERS

GEORGE PETRIE was born in Dublin on the 1st January, 1790, of a Scotch mother and Irish father, though it must be owned that his father was not of Irish stock, although he had cast in his lot with our fellow-countrymen, being the son of a Scotchman settled in Dublin. He was an eminent Portrait and Miniature Painter, and was a man of literary culture as well. He was at pains to give his son the best education available, and therefore sent him to the school of Mr. Whyte, of Grafton Street, and there, sitting perhaps at the same desk at which Thomas Moore and Richard Brinsley Sheridan had sat before him, he acquired that sound knowledge of the English and classical languages which he afterwards turned to such good account when he became a man of letters.

As a boy George Petrie took after his father's taste for Art, and was allowed to assist him in painting miniatures at an early age. Indeed, when only fifteen he gained the Silver Medal for a group of figures in the School of the Dublin Society; hence his father, though he had intended him for the profession of Surgery, was not loath to allow him to follow the bent of his genius and to devote himself to landscape painting, being the more inclined to this course from the fact that the boy was delicate and more suited to an open air than to an indoor life.

One of the early recollections which Dr. Petrie has left on record was of a touching scene, of which when a boy he

was an unwilling spectator.   His artist father had executed
a commission for Sarah Curran, daughter to that distinguished orator and member of the Irish Bar, John Philpot
Curran.   She had been betrothed to Robert Emmet, whose
life paid the penalty of his complicity in the rebellion of
1803; and knowing that Mr. James Petrie had painted
Emmet, she requested that a portrait from memory, aided
by his former studies of her lover, should be painted for
her, and that when completed she might visit his studio
alone.   A day and hour were named by the artist; but his
boy, unaware of the arrangement, was seated in a recess of
the window, concealed by a curtain, when the lady, closely
veiled, entered the room.   She approached the easel, and
gazed long and earnestly on the picture of her lover, then
leaned her head against the wall and wept bitterly.   The
boy, attracted by her sobs, knew not how to act.   She was
quite unconscious of his presence, and before he could
make up his mind what he ought to do, she recovered her
self-control, drew down her veil, and left the room.

At the Drawing School of the Dublin Society Petrie
met with Danby and O'Conor, and these three young Irish
artists became bosom friends.   Up to the year 1809, his
studies as landscape painter were carried on in the counties
of Dublin and Wicklow, and with such enthusiasm that he
would start on foot at nightfall when his day's work was
done, so that by walking all night he might reach, before
sunrise, some chosen spot for study among the Wicklow
mountains.   In the following year he first visited Wales,
and re-visited it a few years afterwards with his friends
Danby and O'Conor.

Dr. Stokes, to whose fine biography of Petrie I am
indebted for the bulk of my information about him, is of
opinion that the influence of these tours in Wales and of
the Welsh scenery can be as definitely traced through
all Petrie's works as that of his Yorkshire surroundings
upon Turner's art.

In 1820, the taste for illustrated Landscape Annuals was at its height, and this helped forward the art of water-colour painting of which Turner was the exponent in England, and Petrie had become the exponent in Ireland; indeed, he supplied no less than ninety-six illustrations to Cromwell's Excursions in Ireland, twenty-one to Brewer's *Beauties of Ireland*, sixteen to Fisher's historical Guide to *Ancient and Modern Dublin*, besides contributing to other works, such as Wright's *Tours* and the Guide to Wicklow and Killarney.

A review of Petrie's Art work in these Landscape Annuals and Guides, published in the *Dublin Saturday Magazine* of March, 1866, criticises Petrie's talents in these fitting terms:

> His refined taste and love of truth influenced him even at the commencement of his career to discard all conventional tricks of Art. He was emphatically our first draughtsman; and so accurate was his pencil that a drawing by Petrie made at any period of his artistic life possesses the value for truthfulness of a photograph. But he was more than a draughtsman, his drawings and pictures were peculiarly imbued with that indescribable charm which for want of a better word has been styled "feeling," and which only genius of the highest order can confer. His simplest sketch assumed the character of a painted poem; a green hillside, a shattered cross, a ruined watch tower, as treated by his genius, became the subject of a picture the indescribable charm of which riveted the attention and set the imagination to work.

But the letterpress illustrated by him in these books of excursions and tours was as a rule so inferior, that Petrie conceived the idea of bringing out a book of the kind both written and illustrated by himself. His tours in Aran and other parts of Ireland so charmingly recorded by him formed the basis for such a work, though he never completed it.

Is it too late for an enterprising publisher to make a selection of Petrie's engravings in the published tour books, combining them with the letterpress in his journal, and that contributed by him to the Dublin and Irish Penny

Magazines?   It would make   a   delightful   and   unique
volume.

As Dr. Stokes points out, " Petrie's Art works may be
divided into two classes; his pictures which are simply
landscapes and those which illustrate National antiquities
in a beautiful setting of natural scenery.   The most striking
characteristics of his landscape works are the power of
conveying simple poetry; the sense of solitude without
gloom; his skilful use of effects with storm and haze in
giving grandeur to scenes otherwise insignificant, and his
delicate, aerial tones and sunlit mists.   Perhaps the highest
effort of his genius as a landscape painter is ' The Home
of the Herons.'   The scene is laid in Lough Atree, and
embraces the little group of islands from which the lake
has derived its name.   These islands are adorned with
trees of naked growth, and the largest island of the group
has been taken possession of by the herons, which have
been allowed to retain it as a sanctuary and a home.   The
day has been wet, but towards evening the clouds have
dispersed, the sun bursts forth, and the mists, rising as
steam from the mountain sides in the western light, form a
rainbow tinted veil of a most ideal loveliness, softening the
rugged outlines of the peaked and barren mountains, and
mingling their distant summits with the delicate blue of the
heaven above.   The delicacy, tenderness, and transparency
in the painting of this picture, the high imaginative power
shown in the treatment of the subject, make it worthy of a
place among the highest efforts of landscape Art in the
Kingdom," and Dr. Stokes thus finely describes what he
considers to be the most remarkable specimen of those of
his works which illustrate our National antiquities :

The subject of this picture is one of the Celtic sepulchural
monuments of Pagan times commonly called Druidical Temples
situated on the Caah Hill near Dungiven in the county of Londonderry.   This circle of monumental stone is one of several still remaining on the mountain, which, according to the tradition of the peasantry

of the district, are the tombs of the chiefs slain in a great battle fought here, and from these the mountain received its name of Caah or Battle Hill.   The tall stones raise their dark forms against the saffron sky, through which the evening star is just appearing and shedding its soft light, while a few cattle stand perfectly motionless on the horizon. The sense of solitude and breathless silence conveyed in this picture, and the deep poetry in the simple treatment of the whole, can be felt only by those who have seen it.

The poetical influence affecting Petrie's Art work is that of Wordsworth, of whom he was a devoted admirer, for in that poet he found " a responsive chord to his own genius —calm, sober, cheerful and meditative."

I will add to the above views of his Art a quotation from an Eloge on Petrie, delivered shortly after his death before the Royal Irish Academy by my father, the late Bishop of Limerick, when he was its President:

" Petrie's pencil was, for many years, put into requisition by those who sought for the most perfect illustrations of Irish scenery and topography.   His drawings were engraved by the most celebrated engravers, Goodall, Higham, Barber, Wickel, Brewer, George Cooke, Greigg, Millar, and Stoners, all of whom remarked of his works, ' beautifully outlined.'   The pictures exhibited by him in London and Dublin attracted the admiration of the most accomplished Art critics.   I have some idea," writes my father, " of the causes of his success.   I believe that it was due in the first instance to the truthfulness with which he represented the grace and harmony of the lines traced by Nature herself in the real landscape.   He seems to have perfectly appreciated their characteristics.   He knew that these lines are produced by natural agencies of various kinds working simultaneously—by forces which shape the outline of a mountain, as well as by those which determine the form of a leaf, it was his nice perception or, call it if you will, an intuitive feeling—of the proper flow of each separate line and of its relation to the other lines in the picture which enabled him to produce drawings almost matchless in delicacy and grace.   His skill as a draughtsman was transcendent, critics allege that as a colourist he was less successful.   It is not given to the same man to excel in every branch of his art.   Still it must be said of him that he showed a fine perception of harmony and balance of colour, even though we may admit that he was sometimes deficient in force.   But the artist who could paint such pictures as his ' Pass of

Llanberis,' his ' Walk in Connemara,' his ' Shruel Bridge,' and ' The Home of the Herons,' has secured for himself a high place in the list of water-colour painters. These are works in which the artistic treatment of the subject manifests an intense love of nature and a familiar acquaintance with the expressions of her everchanging face. And they possess a higher merit. They are not the products of a merely meditative, imitative Art, they are poetical in their conception and full of imaginative power. Petrie had attained to a very distinguished position as a painter, his brother artists in Ireland acknowledged his eminence by conferring upon him the honourable office of President of their National Academy, and artists of the highest repute in England, by their correspondence and their friendship, bore testimony to the respect which they entertained for him as a professional compeer."

Petrie's first contribution to Irish literature, as might have been expected, took the form of art criticism. In his six and twentieth year he wrote a series of leading articles in the *Dublin Examiner*, in which he deals with the condition of the fine arts in Ireland, and more particularly on the attempts which had been made to establish an Academy of Arts in Dublin which had led to the exhibition of works of Irish painters, between the years 1809 and 1816. The exhibitions had proved successful in the first instance, but the Society had split up into two, the Irish and Hibernian Societies of Arts, yet these two bodies came together again and finally coalesced with the Dublin Society.

Public support of Art at first promising had died down, and indeed the general absence of culture amongst the artists and the want of public spirit which had followed the provincialising of the Irish capital consequent on the establishment of the Union were influences greatly adverse to National Art. In five further articles his criticisms became more general. He showed that the decline of European art was due to inferiority in education amongst modern artists, sculptors and architects, as compared with that of earlier workers in these fields of art, and to a tendency to look too much at the business side of art, a view according to which success depended upon a cultivation of the imitative powers ; while Ruskin's dictum that Art is to be considered as a writing or language, the value of which must depend upon what the artist has in him to say, was unrecognised by the public and by the artists themselves. Petrie rightly pointed out the tendency in the training of the schools of the Dublin Society to place the special before the general education of its students, and the consequent product of half educated, illiterate artists. Dr. Stokes comments that this independent spirit and severity of stricture upon the conduct of public men at a time when independent thought was almost a crime and independent action was nearly impossible, was admirable in a young and struggling artist. Yet Petrie lived to illustrate these critical views by his own works as a draughtsman and painter.

He contributed to the Dublin literary journals of 1816 to 1818, but it was not until the year 1832 that, in company with the Rev. Caesar Otway, he started the *Dublin Penny Journal* "on new and exclusively national grounds and with national as well as useful objects in view." Politics and sectarian religion were excluded from the purview of the magazine. The subjects chiefly chosen were, however, such as were most likely to attract the attention of the Irish people next to those of politics and polemics, viz. : the history, biography, poetry, antiquities, natural history, legends and traditions of the country. The journal appeared on the 30th June, 1832, and was conducted with great spirit, ability and success for more than a year, after which it passed into other hands, declined in literary quality and passed out of existence.

Ten years later Petrie became sole editor of another work of the same aim and character, the *Irish Penny Journal*, which he carried on for a year. "There is no more striking evidence of the absence of public opinion or the want of interest in the history of the country on the part of Irish society," writes Dr. Stokes, "than the failure of these two works, and it is remarkable that the principal demand for them was from London and the provincial towns of England."

In literary merit, indeed, they were anything but failures, as might be expected, when it is considered that besides the names of Otway, Petrie and O'Donovan, we have among the contributors to the second work mentioned those of O'Curry, Wills, Anster, Ferguson, Mangan, Aubrey de Vere and Carleton. It is told of Southey, that he used to say, when speaking of these volumes, that he prized them as among the most valuable of his library.

In bidding farewell to his readers of the *Irish Penny Journal*, Petrie observes that the commendations of the press " have not been altogether undeserved, and that the proprietors indulge the pleasing conviction that the volume now brought to a termination will live in the literature of Ireland as one almost exclusively Irish." This hope has been justified. These two volumes, the *Dublin Penny Journal* and the *Irish Penny Journal*, now fetch a high price, and though the illustrations are, to a large extent, antiquated, much of the letterpress deserves reprinting; indeed, not a few of the poems and stories contained in these journals, such as Mangan's *The One Mystery* and some of Carleton's Irish Sketches, have already passed into Anglo-Irish Literature.

As a specimen of Petrie's literary powers at this period a passage from his account of Monasterboice in the *Irish Penny Journal* may be cited :

In its present deserted and ruined state it is a scene of the deepest and most solemn interest ; and the mind must indeed be dull and earthly in which it fails to awaken feelings of touching and permanent interest ; silence and solitude the most profound are impressed on all its time-worn features ; we are among the dead only ; and we are forced, as it were, to converse with the men of other days. With all our frequent visits to these ruins, we never saw a single human being amongst them but once.

It was during a terrific thunderstorm, which obliged us to seek shelter behind one of the stone crosses for an hour. The rain poured down in impetuous torrents, and the clouds were so black as to give the appearance of night. It was at such an awful hour, that a woman of middle age, finely formed, and of a noble countenance, entered the cemetery, and, regardless of the storm raging around, flung herself down upon a grave, and commenced singing an Irish lamentation in tones of heartrending and surpassing beauty. This wail she carried on as long as we remained ; and her voice coming on the ear between the thunderpeals had an effect singularly wild and unearthly ; it would be fruitless to attempt a description of it.

The reader, if he knows what an Irishwoman's song of sorrow is, must imagine the effect it would have at such a moment among those lightning shattered ruins, and chanted by such a living vocal monument of human woe and desolation.

As Dr. Stokes points out, Petrie may be said to be the discoverer of the Aran Islands, at least from the antiquarian point of view. He paid them two visits of considerable duration, the first in the twenties of last century, before the islands had been as much influenced from the mainland as they have gradually become. Indeed, an interesting contrast might be made by a comparison between Dr. Petrie's experiences on the islands and those of Mr. J. M. Synge. It is, as a descriptive writer and painter of character, such as he found it in Aran, that we are here concerned with Dr. Petrie's relation to these islands. Quoting, with three notes of exclamation, Pinkerton's statement that the wild Irish are at this day known to be some of the veriest savages in the globe, Petrie proceeds to show that after visiting Aran out of a desire to meet the islanders who were reputed to be the most primitive people within the five corners of Ireland, he found them to be where uncontaminated, as in Aranmore and Innisheer, a brave and hardy race, industrious and enterprising, simple and innocent, but also thoughtful and intelligent ; credulous, and in matters of faith what persons of a different creed would call superstitious, but, being out of the reach of religious animosity, still strangers to bigotry and intolerance. Lying and drinking—the vices which Arthur Young in his time

regarded as appertaining to the Irish character, formed at
least no part in it in Aran. Not that they were rigidly
temperate, instances of excess followed by the usual Irish
consequences of broken heads did occasionally occur; such
could not but be expected when their convivial temperament
and dangerous and laborious occupations are remembered.
" But," he adds, " they never swear, and they have a
high sense of decency and propriety, honour and justice.
In appearance they are healthy, comely and prepossessing;
in their dress, with few exceptions, clean and comfortable.
In manners serious yet cheerful and easily excited to gaiety;
frank and familiar in conversation, and to strangers polite
and respectful; but at the same time wholly free from
servile adulation. They are communicative, but not too
loquacious; inquisitive after information, but delicate in
asking it and grateful for its communication."

Petrie describes four typical Aran islanders of his day,
Mr. O'Flaherty, one of the two aristocrats of the islands,
the Rev. Francis O'Flaherty, their venerable pastor, Tom
O'Flaherty, who combined the honourable practice of
medicine with the less distinguished calling of a tailor, and
lastly Molly M'Auley, the wise woman, though not in the
sense of being a witch; but space only permits of the
presentation of full-length portraits of the three O'Flahertys,
Mr. O'Flaherty, Tom the Tailor and Father Francis
O'Flaherty.

Mr. O'Flaherty may be justly called the *pater patriæ* of the
Araners. He is the reconciler in all differences, the judge in all
disputes, the adviser in all enterprises, and the friend in all things. A
sound understanding and the kindest of hearts make him competent
to be all those; and his decisions ar enever murmured against or his
affection met by ingratitude. Of the love they bear him many instances
might be adduced, but the following will be deemed sufficient, and
too honourable both to them and him to be omitted.

In 1822 a great number of the islanders had determined to emigrate
to America. A ship lay at anchor at Galway to convey them, and
they proceeded thither accompanied by Mr. O'Flaherty, to aid them

to the last with friendship and advice. Several days elapsed before the vessel was ready to set sail, and Mr. O'Flaherty still continued with them ; but at last the hour to bid an everlasting adieu arrived. They must know the Araners that could fancy the scene that then ensued.

Men and women all surrounded him—the former with cheeks streaming with tears, and the latter uttering the most piercing lamentations ; some hung on his neck, some got his hands or arms to kiss, while others threw themselves on the deck and embraced his knees.

It is no discredit that on such an occasion the object of so much affectionate regard was more than unmanned, and it was a long time before his health recovered the injury, or his face lost the sorrowful expression caused by the grief of that parting.

Mr. O'Flaherty has read a good deal, but thought more, his opinions bespeak at once a noble and liberal feeling and a singularly sound and dispassionate judgment, the grandeur and sublimity of the objects by which he is surrounded seem to have sunk into his soul and formed his character. He is deeply religious, but altogether free from narrow prejudice. All good men are to him alike. His religion has something of a romantic character, and he feels his piety more excited in the little deserted, roofless temple, among the rocks, beside his own house, than it possibly could be in the most crowded and magnificent church. In this solitary ruin he offers up his morning and evening prayers ; and his figure in the centre of the nave looking towards the mouldering altar, in the act of adoration, as I saw it once by chance, will never be effaced from my recollection.

Mr. O'Flaherty's table is for his guests, everything that a man accustomed even to luxurious living could desire ; but, in his own habits, he is singularly abstemious, rarely taking any other beverage than milk, although, when entertaining his friends, he conceals his habits and sets an example of a more free but still temperate enjoyment. His house, however, bespeaks the simplicity of the place, as well as the usages of remote times. It is an oblong, thatched cottage, without a second storey, containing five or six apartments, with a long porch, forming a kind of hall, attached to the centre of the front. The parlour is not boarded, nor do the chairs present the luxury of a soft seat. Mr. O'Flaherty is of the middle stature, blue-eyed, but dark-complexioned and dark-haired. His face is long and oval, and in its expression mild, philosophic and benevolent. His dress is that of the islanders, differing only in the substitution of a heavy cap for the hat usually worn, and boots for their rude sandals.

Here is Tom O'Flaherty :

Tom is not himself an Araner, he came hither after the memorable rebellion of 1798, in which, it is suspected, he was somewhat concerned, and, finding an unoccupied theatre for the display of his varied talents, has continued exercising them ever since, to the perfect satisfaction of all ranks.

Tom, the tailor doctor, is really what many doctors are not, a clever fellow, he has a sharp and clear intellect, and a singularly retentive memory, stored with a variety of information, historical, traditional, genealogical, and topographical, relative to the West of Ireland. He has a romantic imagination, and is never happier, he says, than when wandering about ancient ruins and among lakes and mountains. He is a great talker, a great lover of tobacco, and a great drinker—not a great drunkard—for it would be very difficult to make him drunk, and a great humorist, qualities which are all very Irish. A pint of whiskey he considers a small daily allowance; and on a late occasion, while attending Mr. O'Flaherty in a typhus fever, he was limited to six glasses, he begged that the whisky might be given to him in three equal portions or drams, morning and evening, so that, as he expressed it, "he might feel the good of it."

His humour is dry and original; the following may be taken as a specimen. Expressing my surprise to him one day on the extent of his legendary lore, I inquired of him in what way he had acquired it. This was his answer. "Faith, an' it's easily told. Not being like them poor people (the Araners), you see, but having an independent profession," drawing his arms like a tailor, "I spent my time visiting from one gentleman's house to another, and as I was always sure of welcome, and having had a particular taste for old stories, I always contrived to get myself into the best possible situation for learning them, and faith, I may say, the best part of my life has been spent there." "Where?" I inquired. "Faith, just behind the whisky bottle!" But Tom O'Flaherty had other qualities of a better order. He was remarkable for humanity and active benevolence. In the spring of 1822 some very bad cases of typhus fever occurred in the island, one being that of a stranger lately settled there. The islanders who, like all the poor Irish, have a deep terror of this frightful disease, fled from him; he was without money or friends, and must have perished but for the courage and humanity of Tom O'Flaherty. Tom first removed him on his back from the infected house to a more airy situation, one of the old Irish stone houses which he had prepared for his reception. He then went to Mr. O'Flaherty and peremptorily demanded five shillings. "For what purpose, Tom? Is it a drink?" said the other. "No, trust me with it without asking any questions, I'll make no bad use of it." The money was obtained, and immediately sent off to Galway for the sick man. With this assistance, in addition to his own resources, he was enabled to bring the poor man successfully through the fever.

He visited him several times each day, sat with him, washed him, and
performed all the duties of a humane and skilful nurse. At the same
time he would never let either his family or friends know that he was
thus employed, but gave them to understand that the man was dead, and
would always proceed from home in a different direction from that which
led to the place of the patient, and reach it unseen by a circuitous
route ; nor is it likely that he would ever have undeceived them if he
had not had the pleasure of bringing back to society the man whom he
had thus rescued from the grave . . . Tom's independent spirit is equal
to his other good qualities. For several days' attendance on me to
various parts of the island I could not induce him to take any remunera-
tion. I was also told that he had a strict regard for truth. I shall
only add one more feature of his character which is peculiarly Irish—
namely, his pride of ancestry. Tom boasts the Milesian blood of the
ancient princes of Connaught. On tracing Mr. O'Flaherty's pedigree
for me one day, I inquired if he, too, was an O'Flaherty, " That I
am," said he, drawing himself up with some expression of pride, " as
good a one as Pat O'Flaherty himself."

Father Francis O'Flaherty is a native of Aranmore and received
his education in a college in Spain. After spending a few years as a
curate in some part of Connaught, he was appointed parish priest of
his native Islands whither he returned never again to leave them, and
has now been the unassisted teacher of his flock for forty years. The
unremittent toils attendant upon such a situation may well be conceived ; but the dangers with which they are here accompanied, and
the courage necessary to meet them, can only be appreciated by a
recollection of the singular and peculiar region to which his duties
belong—namely, a cluster of islands washed by the waves of the Atlantic,
presenting in most places an iron bound coast and separated from each
other by rapid currents that never assume a tranquil appearance and are
seldom entirely free from danger. Courage is, indeed, a striking trait in
the character of this venerable man, and is strongly marked on the lip
and brows of his manly but toilworn and weather-beaten countenance,
a face that a physiognomist would look at for hours with pleasure, so
harmonious are its parts, so steady its expression of serious but mild
thought, and of manly firmness and simplicity. One of his peculiarities
was a too favourable idea of the excellence of human nature in general,
which afforded the surest testimony of the virtues of the simple people from
whom his knowledge of mankind had been derived. In illustration of
his belief that vice or depravity could not exist among mankind except
in the rare and solitary instances, Dr. Petrie was told that one of the
islanders, about to emigrate to America, on applying to a stranger in

the island for written instructions how to act in a world of which he had no experience, received from him a paper containing written advice guarding him against a state of society where he would be likely to meet many ready to take advantage of his innocence and inexperience. Terrified at the dangers thus presented to his imagination, the simple Araner submitted it to Father Frank, that he might be assured whether these dangers were real; and the priest, on reading the paper, indignantly tore it to pieces. "Believe not," said he, "what this man says; he must be a bad man to lead you to entertain so vile an opinion of mankind. Suspect no one. There are, I fear, some bad men in the world, but I trust and believe they are few. But never suspect a man of being so without a sufficient reason."

Father Frank is poor. The unglazed windows of his humble cottage and the threadbare appearance of his antique garments bespeak a poverty beyond most that of his flock. He is, in fact, altogether destitute of the comforts that should belong to old age. This is not the fault of his parishioners, by whom he is ardently beloved; they would gladly lessen their own comforts to increase his, and have frequently tried to force on him a better provision, which he has as often refused. "What," said he on a late occasion to Mr. O'Flaherty, who was remonstrating with him on this refusal, "what does a priest want more than subsistence? And that I have. Could I take anything from these poor people to procure me comforts which they require so much more themselves? No, no, Pat, say no more about it."

GEORGE PETRIE AS AN ANTIQUARY

"From his schoolboy days," writes my father, "Petrie took an interest in the monumental remains which fell under his observation in the neighbourhood of Dublin; and as his sketching tours led him afterwards into remote parts of the county where dismantled castles and ruined churches and time-worn crosses, besides furnishing subjects for his pencil, excited his curiosity respecting their history and age, his early predilections for antiquarian pursuits must have been drawn out and fostered.

Nevertheless, he might perhaps have continued to devote himself exclusively to the practices of his art as a painter, if a ramble in company with some friends through the western counties of Ireland had not brought him in 1818 face to face with the ruins of the Seven Churches at Clonmacnoise. There, indeed, he saw a group of ecclesiastical remains, interesting in their architectural features and picturesquely placed on the sloping shore of our great western river; and he perpetuated the scene by making it the subject of one of his most exquisitely painted pictures. But these ruins excited a still deeper interest in his mind, regarded as memorials of men who lived, and the civilisation which subsisted on the spot 1,000 years before.

Looking around him in that great cemetery he was the first to recognise to what an extent it was filled with inscribed monuments, recording the names of distinguished persons who had been buried there in former times. It was a favourite place of sepulchre for kings and chiefs, for bishops and abbots, for men of piety and learning, from the sixth to the twelfth century. Applying himself first to the copying of these inscriptions, he made drawings of above three hundred of them. But as few of them had been previously noted or explained in any previous work, he was obliged to investigate for himself the histories of the persons whose names were thus preserved. With a view to the accomplishment of this object, he commenced, and from that time continued, the formation of such a collection of documents, whether in manuscript or in print, as he hoped would lead to the illustration of the monuments. After his visit to Clonmacnoise Petrie became an archæologist, devoting as much time and attention as he could to the study of Irish history and antiquities." And it was time he did so, for when, after his death, Margaret Stokes, with the help of her brother Whitley, published Petrie's Christian inscriptions, its first volume contained the illustrations of 165 Clonmacnoise sepulchral inscriptions, of which no less than sixty-one seen by Petrie are now lost, buried for the most part, Professor Macalister believes, in modern graves with the object of sanctifying them.

Here in Petrie's own words are some glimpses of the impressions made upon him by Clonmacnoise :

Let the reader picture to himself a gentle eminence on the margin of a noble river, on which, amongst majestic stone crosses and a multitude of ancient grave-stones, are placed two lofty round towers and the ruins of seven or eight churches, presenting almost every variety of ancient Christian architecture. A few lofty ash trees, that seem of equal antiquity and sanctity, wave their nearly leafless branches among the silent ruins above the dead. To the right an elevated causeway carries the eye along the river to the ruins of an ancient nunnery, and on the left still remain the ruins of an old castle, once the palace of the bishops, not standing, but rather tumbled about in huge masses on the summit of a lofty mound or rath, surrounded by a ditch or fosse, which once received the waters from the mighty stream, now no longer necessary. The background is everywhere in perfect harmony with the nearer objects of this picture ; the chain of bare hills on either side, now sere and wild, but once rich with woodland beauty, shut out the inhabited country we so lately left, and the eye and mind are free to wander with the majestic river in all its graceful windings in an uninhabited and uninhabitable desert, till it is lost in the obscurity of distance ! Loneliness and silence, save the sounds of the elements, have here an almost undisturbed reign. Sometimes, indeed, the attention is drawn by the scream of the wildfowl, which inhabits this solitary region, or the shot of the lonely sportsman. At other times we could hear the measured time of the oar, or rather paddle, of a solitary boat, long before the little speck in the water became visible ; and the melancholy song of the shepherd or the milk-girl, might sometimes be heard in the boggy flat, although the singer was too remote to be visible. To such sounds I have been glad to turn for company during the course of the day.

This is but an outline of Clonmacnoise, such as may be intelligible to general readers. The deep interest which this astonishing place afforded in detail, can only be appreciated by the enthusiastic painter or accomplished antiquary. The former will understand the kind of delight with which I was inspired by those groups of pilgrims, clothed in draperies of the most picturesque form, and the most splendid and varied colours. The aged sinner, supported by his pilgrim's staff, barefooted and bareheaded, his large grey coat, the substitute for the forbidden cloak or mantle, sweeping the road, his white hair floating on the disregarded wind ! The younger man, similarly attired, whose face betrays the deepest guilt, hurrying along with energetic strides. The females of all ages, to whom uninquiring faith and enthusiastic devotion seem natural and characteristic ; but, above all, the young and beautiful girl, with pale face, blue eyes, long black eyelashes, and dark hair, whose look betrays no conscious guilt, in the midst of her sighing prayers, but rather a feeling of love and devotion ; who, notwithstanding her religious duties, is not so entirely unconscious of the power of her beauty but that she can spare an occasional glance towards the strangers who are endeavouring to fix her figure on their paper or on their memories—a figure, as a friend well observed, that no one but Raphael could draw.

Happy England ! Well may she boast of her clean and ornamented cemeteries, and well may she glory in her national mausoleum. What a contrast do the former offer to the neglected and unsightly grave-yards of Ireland, and how striking and impressive the living splendour

of the latter, as compared with that which contains the best blood of
Ireland !

Both are situated on the banks of mighty rivers, but that which
reflects the lofty towers of the one, shows them surrounded with the
splendour of the proudest city of the world, and it bears along its
surface the busy hum of a free and happy people. While the equally
noble stream which washes the banks of the other, pours its mass of
waters through a desert, and reflects no object but the passing cloud
and "The round towers of other days"; and its silence is only disturbed
by the occasional wail for the dead, or the scream of the lonely wild
bird that haunts its waters. The temples of the first are still fair and
perfect, for they have been since their foundation objects of perpetual
care ; those of the other are almost gone, for they have been for nearly
the same period of time the objects of sacrilege and plunder, till its
sanctuaries, no longer worth violating, were consigned to the elements
and time to complete the work of ruin.

There is not, perhaps, in Europe a spot where the feeling heart
would find more matter for melancholy reflection than among the
ancient churches of Clonmacnoise. Its ruined buildings call forth
national associations and ideas. They remind us of the arts and
literature, the piety and humanity, which distinguished their time, and
are the work of a people, who, in a dark age, marched among the
foremost on the road to life and civilisation, but who were unfortunately
checked and barbarised by those who were journeying in the same
course and ought to have cheered them on.

Petrie was now to show his great capacity as an organiser
of archæology as well as an individual worker in its cult.
He was elected a member of the Royal Irish Academy and
set to work at once in conjunction with other distinguished
members to raise the Academy from that state of torpor in
which it had remained for the previous quarter of a century.
As an instance of the apathy which had prevailed in its
management it may be mentioned that the King of
Denmark had some time before presented the Academy
with a fine collection of stone implements. These had,
however, been allowed to lie unnoticed and uncared for.
Similar antiquarian gifts to the Academy had actually been
deposited in the Museum of Trinity College for want of a
fitting place for their exhibition within the Academy's walls.
Indeed, Petrie told my father that between the time when

he first saw them, and that when, as a member of the Council, he rescued them from future danger, nearly one-half of these articles, and those the most precious, had disappeared. From this epoch dated a period of fruitful activity in the Academy Committee of Antiquities, the meetings of which had been actually suspended for the seventeen years previous. My father was then secretary, and he and Petrie and others helped forward the acquisition of the various collections, such as the Underwood Collection and those of Dean Dawson and Major Sirr, the assemblage of which in the Academy's museum has given it a national character.

Inspired by Petrie's scientific spirit in his method of dealing with antiquities, the great Irish mathematician MacCullagh purchased the Cross of Cong, and made that splendid donation to the Academy, besides contributing most generously towards the purchase of the Tara golden torques. Petrie's contributions towards the Academy's library were perhaps even more important.

"Whenever," writes my father, "opportunities afforded of acquiring Irish MSS., he exerted his influence to induce the Academy to purchase them. The grant placed at his disposal for this purpose being often inadequate, he ventured more than once at his own risk to secure MSS., the value of which he understood better than anyone, and which he knew ought to be added to the Academy's collection. Thus at the sale of Edward O'Reilly's MSS., after the Academy's grant of £50 had been exhausted, he purchased for himself some of the O'Cleary's MSS., and afterwards gave them up to the Academy at cost price. Having had the good fortune under similar circumstances to become the possessor of the autograph copy of the second part of *The Annals of the Four Masters* he generously surrendered it to the Academy for the sum he had given for it, although, immediately on its becoming known in the sale room what the MS. was, he was offered, in the first instance, £100 over and above the purchase money, and was afterwards pressed to name any sum that would induce him to resign it. In acknowledgment of the generosity and zeal evinced on this occasion by Petrie, the Academy passed a resolution declaring him a member for life."

Petrie contributed many papers to the transactions of the Academy, for three of which he was awarded its gold medal. These were his *Origin and Uses of the Round Towers*, afterwards expanded into his famous work on the subject; his essay on *Military Architecture in Ireland*, and his essay on *Tara Hill*. The second in order of these still remains unpublished.

The essay on the Irish Round Towers by which Petrie has made a world-wide reputation, calls for our interested attention. These remarkable towers had attracted the observation of all Irish antiquaries, but the most astonishing difference of opinion had been displayed in the views taken of them. They had been described as Danish or Phœnician in origin, and had been considered by some to be fire temples; by others, places from which the Druidical festivals were proclaimed; by others, again, they were supposed to be astronomical observatories or phallic emblems or Buddhist temples. Lastly, to come to supposed Christian uses, some theorists held them to be Anchorite towers; others insisted that they were penitential prisons.

The antiquaries who held these views belonged to the old deductive school. Petrie was an inductive archæologist. No doubt, as my father writes :

There is something romantic in the notion of their being monuments belonging to a race wholly lost in the mist of antiquity, and there is something imposing in the parade of Oriental authorities and the jingle of fanciful etymologies in which Vallancy and his disciples so freely dealt. But I have never yet met any intelligent man who has taken the pains to read through and understand Petrie's essay and who has also gone out of his study and examined round towers with his own eyes, and compared their masonry and architectural details with those of the ancient ecclesiastical structures, beside which they often stand, who is not ready to give his frank assent. I am speaking of the most remarkable essay that was ever produced by an Irish antiquary. You will therefore permit me to remind you what those conclusions were : (1) that the towers are of Christian and ecclesiastical origin, and were erected at various periods between the fifth and thirteenth centuries ;

(2) that they were designed to answer at least a two-fold use—namely, to serve as belfries and as keeps or places of strength in which the sacred utensils, books, relics, and other valuables were deposited, and into which the ecclesiastics, to whom they belonged, could retire for security in cases of sudden predatory attack ; (3) that they were probably also used when occasion required as beacons and watch towers. If it were possible to overthrow or seriously to modify the conclusions at which Petrie has arrived his essay would still continue to be a pattern deserving the close imitation of writers undertaking to treat of similar subjects. It is philosophic in its method ; its style is clear and graceful without being pedantic ; it is copious in reference to original authorities ; and, what is rare in works of a controversial nature, it is remarkable for the good temper and good taste with which the writer treats the reasonings of his opponents.

Moreover, Petrie has proved beyond doubt in this great ecclesiastical essay that churches exist in Ireland that go back to the fifth century, that others exhibiting decorated details were founded in Ireland before the Norman Conquest, that there are evidences of the decorations of shrines from the ninth to the fifteenth century, that the principal cross at Clonmacnoise indicates that the Irish artists in the tenth century were experienced and imaginative sculptors, and that while the ornamental work of the ancient churches differs remarkably from that seen on the Norman buildings of England, it is in perfect accord with that of the Irish illuminated MSS., jewelled reliquaries, sculptured crosses and inscribed tombstones. He thus disposed for ever of the aspersions upon the barbarity and want of civilisation imputed to the early and mediæval Irish by writers such as Pinkerton.*

A second prize of £20 was given to Mr. O'Brien who skilfully supported the contention that the Round Towers were of Danish origin, and Sir William Betham wrote a most virulent attack against the decision of the Council, maintaining that O'Brien's view was the correct one. To Sir William's letter Petrie replied with great

* *Churches and Oratories.*

dignity, but with hitting powers of which he had not been suspected.*

The circumstances, my father points out, which must be considered the most important in Petrie's life as giving definiteness to his labours and completely developing his powers, was his employment to take charge of the Topographical Department of the Irish Ordnance Survey in the year 1833. The occasion for his services arose thus. In the construction of the maps it was a matter of primary necessity to determine the orthography of the names of places; but it also proved to be a matter of extreme difficulty.

Various. modes of spelling were found to be sanctioned by common usage. Reference, therefore, had to be made to documents of all kinds; and an inquiry involving comparison between the existing and the ancient state of the country had to be instituted; in fact, questions relating to the spelling of a town-land or a parish frequently gave rise to elaborate researches, which were not disposed of until it had been ascertained that the name was indicative of some early sept, some ecclesiastical establishment, or ancient chief. Thus the co-operation of the historian, the antiquary and the philologist was found to be essential. The work was under the direction of Lieutenant, afterwards Sir, Thomas Larcom, who conceived the idea of drawing together every species of local information relating to Ireland, and embodying it in a Memoir accompanying the Ordnance Survey maps.

Here, as the head of a literary staff, Petrie had the assistance of several persons who possessed a good knowledge of the Irish language, and to whom he communicated his own methods of systematic inquiry and the refinement of a more extended scholarship. It was from Petrie that John O'Donovan and Eugene O'Curry received the training which enabled them afterwards to contribute in so many ways to

* *Illustrations of Round Towers.*

that great development of Irish literature which took place between 1840 and 1866. " Thus Petrie became the informing spirit and great instructor of a School of Archæology, not only laying down the principles but exemplifying upon a large scale the application to Antiquarian Science of the principles of a philosophic induction. He first showed how to make the contents of our Irish MSS. available for the purposes of antiquarian research. He had large collections made from passages bearing upon questions of topography, history, architecture, and so forth, and he took pains to satisfy himself that the true meaning of these was furnished by scholars having a competent knowledge of the Irish language. He explored almost every part of Ireland himself, filling in sketch books with careful drawings of ancient remains ; and it was by means of a comparison of these with one another, and with the notices of them contained in ancient documents, that he established general and solid conclusions respecting their nature.

It is true that the literary and ecclesiastical history of Ireland had received important elucidations from the labours of Archbishop Ussher, Sir James Ware and Colgan, but before Petrie's time little had been done to illustrate our topography, our prehistoric monuments, our military and ecclesiastical architecture." Thus writes my father. But a great disappointment awaited all believers in the value of the great antiquarian work being done for the Irish Ordnance Survey by Petrie and his staff, which included besides O'Donovan and O'Curry, O'Conor and Mangan. A full, accurate and intensely interesting memoir of the county of Derry was published, and hailed with delight and pride by all patriotic Irishmen. But unfortunately the very finish and detail of the work caused its interruption. The question became a Treasury one, and all Irishmen know what that means. The Memoir of Londonderry had hardly appeared when difficulties arose as to the cost of its publication. As Dr. Stokes writes, this led to a partial suspension of the topographical survey, and finally its operations were put an end to by the Master-General of the Ordnance. The staff were discharged, and the vast mass of material, comprising among other things, upward of four hundred quarto volumes of letters and documents relating to the topography, language, history, antiquities, productions and social state of almost every county in Ireland, were directed to be kept in the Central Office of the Survey.

Here is Mr. Wakeman's sketch of the work and workers of the Ordnance Survey led by Mr. Petrie himself :

How well do I recollect my first sketching journey, when employed on the intended Ordnance memoir. Dr. Petrie was the head of that particular department of the survey to which I was attached. In the little back parlour in Great Charles Street we used to meet daily ; by we, I mean John O'Donovan, Eugene O'Curry, Clarence Mangan, P. O'Keefe, J. O'Connor, besides two or three more. The duty of the office was to collect every possible information, antiquarian or topographical, about that particular portion of the country which was at the time being surveyed. All sorts of old documents were examined, old spellings of names compared and considered. O'Donovan and O'Curry, even then the first Celtic scholars of the age, settled the orthography of the towns, villages, baronies, or other divisions of land, so that the Ordnance map might be as correct, in a literary sense, as they undoubtedly were as surveys. At the same time Petrie's great work on the *Ecclesiastical Architecture of Ireland*, as also his admirable essay *On the Antiquities of Tara Hill*, were being completed. Indeed, we lived in such an atmosphere of antiquarianism, that a thousand years ago seemed as familiar to us as the time when we first donned breeches. For my own part, I felt as if I had a personal acquaintance with Niall of the Nine Hostages, or Con of the Hundred Battles (or bottles, as poor Mangan humorously mis-styled the hero), or with Leogaire, who would not mind the exhortations of St. Patrick, but insisted on being interred, sword in hand, in his rath at Tara, with his face turned to the east, as bidding defiance to the men of Leinster. Petrie, as head of the office, superintended everything ; and the mass of antiquarian and topographical information collected far exceeded the expectations of the most sanguine. A miserable system of false economy caused the memoir to be abandoned ; and, from the character of the matter collected, we can judge how great has been our loss that the work had not been continued for at least a few years longer. I should like to dwell a moment on the scene of that very happy time when we used to meet in Dr. Petrie's back parlour. There was our venerable chief, with his ever-ready smile and gracious word ; then poor Clarence Mangan, with his queer puns and jokes and odd little cloak and wonderful hat, which exactly resembled those that broomstick-riding witches are usually represented with, his flax-coloured wig, and false teeth, and the inevitable bottle of tar-water, from which he would sip and sip all day—except when asleep, with a plain deal desk for a pillow. By-the-by, it was in that office Mangan penned his since famous ballad, *The Woman of Three Cows*, and I verily believe the composition did not occupy him half an hour. Mangan was a man of many peculiarities. In addition to the curious hat and little round cloak, he made himself conspicuous by wearing a huge pair of green spectacles, which had the effect of setting off his singularly wan and wax-like countenance with as much force as might be accomplished by the contrast of colour. Sometimes, even in the most settled weather, he might be seen parading the streets with a very voluminous umbrella under each arm.

At this time O'Donovan was about thirty years of age. As in the case of almost every man who has risen to distinction, he was an unwearied worker, never sparing himself, and evidently holding his occupation a labour of love. With all employed in the office he was a general favourite, and in the intervals between his most serious business would often give us some of his experiences as a traveller, telling his tale in a rich emphatic manner peculiarly his own.

Then there was O'Connor, the companion of O'Donovan in very many of his topographical expeditions, a man of kindly feeling, and possessed of a very considerable amount of information on Irish subjects. He died early, however, and without having given more than a promise of taking a high place amongst those who have made Irish history and antiquities their peculiar study. I must also mention P. O'Keefe, perhaps at that time the most learned and accomplished of all men employed in Petrie's department of the survey. His duties were very similar to those of O'Donovan, and his loss to the survey, when he retired to a non-literary or antiquarian life, was considerably felt.

At the time I write of, Eugene Curry had really commenced that course of application to the illustration of ancient Irish history which has gained for him the proud appellation of the Chief Brehon and Lexicographer of Ireland. He, too, belonged to our staff, and, during the summer time, was engaged chiefly in travelling and collecting information about old names and places for the use of the Ordnance authorities.

Years passed away, and then, through the exertions of Viscount Adare, afterwards Earl of Dunraven, a large and remarkable meeting was held in London, at which it was agreed that a deputation should wait upon Sir Robert Peel and press upon him the resumption of the interrupted Ordnance Survey work.   Sir Robert consented to appoint a Commission to take evidence and report on the entire question.   This Commission, consisting of Lord Adare, Mr. Young, a Lord of the Treasury, and the Clerk of the Ordnance, Captain Boldero, took evidence, on the strength of which they unanimously recommended the resumption of the Ordnance Survey work on the lines upon which it had been previously conducted.   But as happens with Irish Commissions only too often, its Report bore no fruit, and in the estimates for the following year no notice was taken of the Survey so far as its topographical and historical department was concerned.   The vast stores of unpublished information were deposited in the offices of Mount Joy Barracks, but on application from the Royal Irish Academy for the custody of a portion of these records, more than one hundred volumes of manuscripts with eleven volumes of antiquarian drawings, fully indexed and bound, were presented to the Academy in November, 1860.   A warm vote of thanks was paid to Sir Thomas Larcom, the Academy recognising the gift "as the most valuable accession ever made to their library," and expressing the belief that scholars engaged in historical and topographical studies would largely avail themselves of the materials thus liberally placed within their reach.   To this store some of our antiquaries have certainly gone, notably Dr. Joyce, who must there have found material for much of the matter contained in his delightful *Irish Names of Places*.

Dr. Stokes's comment on the action of the English Government in this affair is as follows :

In its endeavours to draw closer together the ties of friendship between the countries and to foster goodwill and peace, the educated mind of England has felt and complained of the want of reliable information as to the social state and history of the Irish people. Here would have been the knowledge so wanting, undisturbed by politics, passions or sectarianism.

But it was unhappily rejected while the means through the agency of which such success had been obtained was broken up and scattered abroad.

Looking at the relative conditions of Great Britain and Ireland, at the social relations of the countries, at the ignorance of the Irish as well as the English public, of the true history and resources of Ireland, and at the desire expressed by all classes for the completion of the work, it is hardly too much to say that this step was an error in statesmanship of the greatest magnitude.

During this Ordnance Survey period of Petrie's career he wrote a number of delightful letters to Larcom, Dunraven and O'Donovan, keeping them in touch with the work as it progressed, advising or correcting his subordinates, always in the best humour, and even when, as in the case of O'Donovan, a little feeling was excited, it was soon smoothed down by his unfailing justice and tact. Here are just a few extracts from his correspondence :

My dear Larcom, The whole of this ancient territory of West Connaught is as yet the region of romance, with its solitary lakes and mountains, its—

Desert isles and fairy lands forlorn,

the simplicity and honesty of its inhabitants, the costumes of the women so exquisitely beautiful and simple—exactly as if they had stepped out of the pictures of Raphael or Murillo. By the way, I never saw so much beauty of female form in a wild district before as I have met in this, and what is very remarkable, their hands are quite aristocratic, small and elegantly formed in the highest degree. Burton, the artist, who is one of our party, is almost mad with delight. He is a charming fellow, and his company adds greatly to the pleasure of my journey.

Here is an extract from a letter to Lord Dunraven,

combating the suggestion that he was dilatory over his preparation of the work of the Round Towers :

> I assure you solemnly that I never worked so hard and un-remittingly in my life as I have at this for the last eight or ten months. I go to work every day immediately after breakfast, and never stir till four or half-past four o'clock, when, if the weather be fine, I turn out for a little exercise before dinner. Then in the evenings I generally read to prepare myself for the day following. I refuse all invitations to go out lest it might interfere with my habits, and when I tell you that within the last fortnight I refused going with Stokes to Iona, which I have long desired to visit, and with Smith and Kane to the County Wicklow for a few days, you will, I trust, give me some credit for firmness and devotion to my work. But the truth is, though I say it as should not, the said work is a great labour, and particularly from my anxiety to make it accurate on all points.

This is an interesting passage, for it explains much, at any rate, of the causes which led to the belief that Petrie was somewhat of a *dilettante.* The fact was that he was extremely hard to please over his own work, and his con-scientiousness was such that it occasionally delayed his literary labour to a degree that provoked the remonstrance of even his friends. This charge of dilatoriness has thus been answered on Petrie's behalf by my father :

> Petrie may not have been blameless in this regard, but I think that valid excuses may be offered in mitigation of the censure which has fallen upon him. In the first place, his health was always delicate and his temperament sensitive, thus his total working power was less than that of many other literary men ; his intense intellectual energy was out of proportion with his physical strength, and besides all this he was intentionally slow in his work, whether with the pencil or the pen, because he was cautious and truthful and in the highest degree fastidious.

In 1840 Petrie received the gold medal of the Academy for his essay *On the Antiquities of Tara Hill.* This essay, printed in the eighteenth volume of Transactions of the Royal Irish Academy, was a portion of the memoir intended to accompany the Ordnance Survey map of the county of Meath. I adopt my father's summary of it. Its subject, as the title indicates, is partly antiquarian, and partly historical; and it deserves special notice, because the latter element is developed more perfectly in it than in any other of Petrie's writings. Having gathered from our most ancient manuscripts every notice contained in them of the Hill of Tara—a spot celebrated by foreign as well as native writers as the chief seat of the Irish monarchs, from the earliest dawn of their history down to the middle of the sixth century—he proceeds, in the first instance, to analyse those which record events connected with the civil and ecclesiastical history of Ireland, and then goes on to show the exact agreement of the monuments still remaining with the descriptions of raths and other structures mentioned in ancient topographical poems and tracts as having formely existed at Tara. The first portion of the paper touches upon several subjects of great interest. Such, for instance, is the account of the compilation and promulgation of laws by Cormac Mac Art, in the middle of the third century; and the compilation, two hundred years later, of the *Seanchus Mor*, in the time and at the instance of St. Patrick. The hints which he has given in this paper will afford valuable help towards the settlement of some of the most perplexing questions connected with our early Irish history. Though we may feel sure that the catalogue of 142 kings who are recorded as having reigned at Tara prior to its desertion in the year 565 is largely mythical, we should be rash in totally rejecting all the statements for which we have no better authority than bardic legends. Petrie has pointed out the probability of some of these, and adduced confirmations of them, derived from independent and trustworthy sources. One of the most curious parts of the essay on Tara is that in which he discusses the perplexing difficulties which beset the history of St. Patrick—I might rather say, of the Saints Patrick, for there were certainly two of the name—and proposes to identify the second St. Patrick with Palladius. The recent investigation of this subject by Dr. Todd has brought its difficulties into a clearer light; but the solution of them seems still almost beyond our reach. The second portion of the essay furnishes a striking instance of the use to be made of antiquarian research in establishing the authenticity of documents. The *Dinn Seanchus*, a well-known topographical work of great antiquity, contains tracts and poems relating to Tara, some of which describe with considerable minuteness the buildings which formerly stood there. With the buildings so described Petrie was able with complete certainty to identify the crumbling remains which are still apparent. Such a confirmation of the accuracy of the accounts disposes us to attach more credence than we should otherwise have given to statements respecting the uses to which the various structures were applied, and all the details respecting the mode of life of their ancient occupants. The truth of these very ancient testimonies being corroborated in certain points, the probability of their being in the main trustworthy is increased in a high degree.

The results arrived at by Petrie on the subject of Irish Military Architecture were equally important and enlightening, and these may be thus briefly summarised. That Cambrensis was wrong in denying castles to Ireland before the Norman occupation, such castles having been erected, though in small numbers, shortly before that occupation, and among these the Castle of Tuam. These castles were round and not as lofty as the Round Towers.

Petrie, in opposition to current belief, held that the Danes built few castles in Ireland, but that older forms of defensive architecture under the names of Caisel, Rath, Lis, Dun, Cathair, Mur and Tur existed in large numbers before' the first Danish invasion; that the Cathairs exceed all other Irish fortifications in interest and historic importance, and that they occur constantly in the west and south of Ireland, and are probably of Greek origin.

As Count Plunkett has so well pointed out, Petrie

was not merely a man of scientific spirit, he was also a poet. He had the intuitions of the seer, and he divined what he afterwards proved by link after link of careful investigation.

His main contentions have been upheld, and even in matters of detail his views have been confirmed by subsequent antiquaries in the most surprising manner.

GEORGE PETRIE AS A MUSICIAN AND AMONGST HIS FRIENDS

How early Petrie's love for Irish music had been is shown by this anecdote communicated to me by Dr. Joyce, as it had been related to him by Petrie himself:

When Petrie was a boy he was a good player upon a little single-keyed flute.

One day he and some young companions set out for a visit to Glendalough, then in its primitive state of solitude. While passing Luggelaw they heard a girl near at hand singing a beautiful air. Instantly out came paper and pencil, and Petrie took it down, and then played it on his little flute. His companions were charmed with it ; and for the rest of the journey—every couple of miles when they sat down to rest, they cried, " Here, Petrie, out with your flute and give us that lovely tune." That tune is now known as Luggelaw, and to it Thomas Moore, to whom Petrie gave it, wrote his words (as lovely as the music), *No, not more welcome*, referring to Grattan's pleadings for his country.

And this brings us to George Petrie's famous collection of Irish music, in the gathering of which he had been engaged with passionate interest from his seventeenth till after his seventieth year.

At first he freely gave these folk airs to Thomas Moore and Francis Holden, and even offered the use of his whole collection to Edward Bunting. But finally, for fear that the priceless hoard might be neglected or lost after his death, and also as a protest against the methods of noting and dealing with the airs pursued by Edward Bunting and Moore and Stevenson respectively, Petrie agreed to edit his collection for " The Society for the Preservation and

Publication of the Ancient Music of Ireland," which was founded in December, 1851.

One volume of this collection, comprising, however, only about a tenth part of it, saw the light in 1857. A supplement contains thirty-six airs, some of which Dr. Stokes tells us were sent to Petrie by personal friends, such as Thomas Davis the patriot, William Allingham the poet, Frederick Burton the painter, and Patrick MacDowell the sculptor; "whilst physicians, students, parish priests, Irish scholars and college librarians all aided in the good work. But most of Petrie's airs have been noted by himself from the singing of the people, the chanting of some poor ballad-singer, the song of the emigrant—of peasant girls while milking their cows, or performing their daily round of household duty—from the playing of wandering musicians, or from the whistling of farmers and ploughmen." And this description by Dr. Stokes is typical of the method by which the airs were obtained, in this instance on the islands of Aran :

Inquiries having been made as to the names of persons " who had music," that is, who were known as possessing and singing the old airs, an appointment was made with one or two of them to meet the members of the party at some cottage near to the little village of Kilronan, which was their headquarters.

To this cottage, when evening fell, Petrie, with his manuscript music-book and violin, and always accompanied by his friend, Professor Eugene O'Curry, the famous Irish scholar, used to proceed.

Nothing could exceed the strange picturesqueness of the scenes which night after night were thus presented.

On approaching the house, always lighted up by a blazing turf fire, it was seen to be surrounded by the islanders, while its interior was crowded by figures, the rich colours of whose dresses, heightened by the firelight, showed with a strange vividness and variety, while their fine countenances were all animated with curiosity and pleasure.

It would have required a Rembrandt to paint the scene. The minstrel—sometimes an old woman, sometimes a beautiful girl or a young man—was seated on a low stool in the chimney corner, while chairs for Petrie and O'Curry were placed opposite, the rest of the crowded audience remaining standing. The singer recommenced, stopping at every two or three bars of the melody to permit the writing of the notes, and often repeating the passage until it was correctly taken down, and then going on with the melody exactly from the point where the singing was interrupted. The entire air being at last obtained, the singer, a second time, was called to give the song continuously, and when all corrections had been made, the violin—an instrument of great sweetness and power—was produced, and the air played as Petrie alone could play it, and often repeated.

Never was the inherent love of music among the Irish people more shown than on this occasion; they listened with deep attention, while their heart-felt pleasure was expressed, less by exclamations than by gestures; and when the music ceased, a general and murmured conversation, in their own language, took place, which would continue till the next song was commenced.

When Dr. Joyce was quite a young man he sent Petrie some beautiful folk songs which he had, as a lad, collected in his native Glenosheen. Petrie was delighted with these, and Joyce became a frequent caller at the doctor's house and heard his songs sung by Petrie's daughter Mary, who in her youth was very beautiful; Sir Frederick Burton's picture of "The Blind Girl at the Well" is an admirable likeness of her at that period. "How well," writes Dr. Joyce, "I recollect the procedure when I returned to Dublin from my vacation. One of the first things was to spend an evening with the whole family, the father and the four daughters, when Mary went through my new collection on the piano with the rest listening, especially Petrie himself, in wrapt delight, as she came across some exquisite air he had not heard before. But of all the airs he was most delighted with 'The Wicked Kerry Man,' now in my *Ancient Irish Music*, page 84."

Some further airs drawn from the Petrie collection, after the publication of the volume of 1857, have apeared in the form of piano arrangements by Francis Hoffmann, and in vocal settings in *Songs of Old Ireland*, *Songs of Erin*, and *Irish Folk Songs*, published by Boosey and Co., and in *Irish Songs and Ballads*, published by Novello, Ewer and Co. Now, however, the entire collection of about 1,800 airs in purely melodic form, exactly as they were noted down by Petrie—a vast treasure-house of folk song, has been published by Messrs. Boosey and Co., for our Irish Literary Society under the editorship of Sir Charles V. Stanford.

And now for Petrie among his friends.

Here is a sketch by one of them, Samuel, afterwards Sir Samuel Ferguson, showing him amongst his friends of the Royal Irish Academy at one of their meetings :

The Provost of the University presides.   His son, the distinguished Humphrey Lloyd, sits near him.   That animated individual with the eager eye and broad forehead, who is reading the formula from the demonstrating board, is Sir William Hamilton, the illustrious mathematician and astronomer.   This intelligent-looking personage, whose countenance combines so much gravity and liveliness, is the Archbishop of Dublin.   There is Petrie—he with the Grecian brow, long hair, and dark complexion—the accomplished antiquary ; and here is Pim, the introducer of railroads into Ireland.   Here sits the scientific Portlock, with Apjohn, our leading chemist ; and this is Stokes, the great physician of the lungs. . . .   And who are these who have just entered—one with a light step, huge frame, sharp Irish features and columnar forehead ; the other lower in stature, of a paler complexion, large featured, with the absent aspect of a man of learning?   They are Carleton, author of the *Traits and Stories of the Irish Peasantry*, and Anster, the translator of *Faust*.

I may here say that on the only occasion on which I myself met Petrie, Dr. Anster was of the company, other men of note being Leopold von Ranke, the historian of the Popes (my father's brother-in-law), my father himself, Dr. Ingram, Dr. Mahaffy, and Dr. Dowden.

"In the choice of his friends," writes Lady Ferguson, "he was uninfluenced by political considerations, or any narrow feeling of sectarianism, a quality which none but those who know Ireland can sufficiently admire or estimate. Loving his country and feeling for her wrongs, he was liberal in politics, though from angry passions he ever held aloof.   At once a loyalist and a patriot, a combination which, in these days, is in some minds unintelligible, he saw the real obstacles to his country's weal, in her want of healthy public opinion and self-respect, and gave the labour of his life to overcome them." And to quote my father, in this connection, " he largely helped towards achieving the great problem of our day—the reconciliation of the cultivated intelligence and loyalty, with the popular aspirations and the sympathies of the country."

William Stokes, Petrie's biographer and father of Whitley and Margaret Stokes, was in his day one of the foremost physicians of the world. "He was a rarely gifted man," writes Lady Ferguson, " a man of genius, and yet eminently practical. A lucid writer, a profound and most accurate clinical observer, he was early recognised as a master in his profession. But he was also a skilful practitioner, at once full of kindness and sympathy, observant of every symptom, and rich in resource. At the bedside he inspired confidence, and often affection. As a teacher he was constantly followed by crowds of admiring students. Like most men of real power, he had many interests and pursuits outside of his professional sphere. He was a keen archæologist, a true lover of his country. The tenderness of his nature and his brilliant wit and humour were only manifested on occasion, for his manner was often abstracted, but his domestic affection and his love for his chosen friends never failed. It was not everybody that could win his friendship," as Petrie had done. And I can speak to a similar friendship between him and my own father, and between him and Lord Adare, afterwards the Earl of Dunraven, Sir Thomas Larcom, and of course Whitley and Margaret Stokes. Frederick Burton was also a close friend, and O'Curry and O'Donovan, first his assistants on the Ordnance Survey, were always afterwards his friends. Who indeed of note in Ireland at that day was not a friend of " dear Petrie," as he was universally called by his intimates.

"In 1857," writes Lady Ferguson, "the British Association met in Dublin, and the Ethnological section went on an excursion to Aran of the Saints. Stokes, Petrie, Burton, O'Curry were of the party, and remained behind with Ferguson, who secured a roomy cottage and wrote to his wife to join him with their nephews, a servant and a well-stocked hamper. Dr. Stokes wrote for his wife, son and daughter.

The combined party chartered a hooker with its crew and retained, as guide, the local antiquary," doubtless Tom O'Flaherty, whose portrait, drawn by Petrie, has already been presented.

" The friends, so congenial in their tastes, passed a few weeks of entire enjoyment.

They sailed from island to island, taking with them on board the hooker all the local singers of whom they could hear. The music they sang was noted by Petrie and rendered on his violin—the Irish words recorded by O'Curry and translated by Whitley Stokes. Burton painted the peasants and their children, and he and Ferguson and Margaret Stokes sketched the ruins and other antiquarian objects, while Whitley Stokes worked at the ancient inscriptions. The weather was propitious, and the friends thoroughly enjoyed the out-of-door life, the pure air, and refreshing sea-breezes.

An incident of their sojourn which might have had serious results may be recalled to memory. They had landed on Inismaen, leaving one man only in charge of the hooker, and, taking the rest of the crew on shore to carry their dinner to the pagan fort on the summit of the island, proceeded to explore Inismaen. When the meal was over and the hamper repacked, they descended, towards evening, to the place where they had left the hooker ; but no boat was visible on the wide horizon. At last, at a great distance, off the coast of Connemara, the vessel was descried slowly making for Inismaen. It was apparent that many hours must elapse before the boat could arrive, and as the sun had set, and no shelter was possible, dancing for the sake of warmth was resorted to by the shivering party. At last the hooker, manœuvred by its one man, arrived. He, when left in charge, had lighted his pipe, and under its soothing influence had fallen asleep. The boat drifted with the tide, and was almost on the rocks off the mainland when the sleeper was aroused by shouts from another vessel. With great difficulty he navigated his way back. It was almost midnight when the party were under weigh for Aran Mor. The ocean was luminous; the track of the curragh—a light canvas boat in which to land—was a veritable line of light. Every movement of its oars seemed to cleave through molten fire, and to reveal marvels of nature before undreamt of. The lustrous waves beneath, the silent stars overhead, the dim outline of the rocky shore, and its utter solitude, impressed and solemnised our spirits. It was an adventure not to be forgotten."

And here is another engaging account of a holiday

ramble in which Petrie and his friends took part. Ferguson and his wife, absent on their vacation rambles in 1864, were joined in Sligo by their young English friends, Henry and William Winterbotham, afterwards Parliamentary Secretary for the Home Department and Member for Stroud, respectively. "I come to Ireland for the enjoyment of your society," wrote the elder brother; "and whenever you are pleased to delve I am ready to hold the hod," a reference to Sir Samuel Ferguson's antiquarian digging.

Here, too, came the Rev. Hercules Dickinson, later to become Dean of the Chapel Royal, Petrie, Dr. James Henthorn Todd, the famous scholar and antiquary, Dr. Stokes and his daughter Margaret.

"Notwithstanding the dreary and tempestuous weather," writes Lady Ferguson, "the group of friends had much enjoyment in congenial society, added to the interest of the antiquities and scenery. The fine cliffs, which at Slieve League rise to the height of 1,800 feet above the Atlantic, are belted with lichens of brilliant hues. But in the autumn of 1864 the country, the crops, and the inhabitants suffered from the almost continuous rains, which made the chief food of the people—the potatoes—more than usually wet and waxy. Sickness supervened, and when it became known that a great physician was sojourning at the hotel, Stokes was besieged every morning with petitions that he would visit the sufferers in their cabins. The doctor, ever ready to assist the poor, would take down all addresses, return to the breakfast table, crumble some bread, crush a few lumps of sugar, and to these add a little white powder—probably some preparation of soda or magnesia—which he carried in a tiny box. With these ingredients he made pills, which he placed in his waistcoat pocket. We started every day for some scene of archæological interest, where all but the doctor and the present writer were set to sketch the various objects. They then proceeded on a round of medical visits. The sufferers were generally aged peasants. 'A weakness about the heart,' an 'oppression on the chest,' and rheumatic pains, were the ills of which they chiefly complained. Dr. Stokes's manner was full of sympathy. He listened, with his hand on the pulse, to all they had to say, with the utmost patience. Then he prescribed, invariably the same remedy. With the pills—which were to be taken at stated intervals—he produced half-a-crown, with strict instructions to apply it to the purchase of mutton chops, one of which was to be eaten daily. When rallied by his

companion on the uniform treatment ordered for every complaint,
' My dear friend,' he would say, ' in whatever way these poor people
describe their sensations, their ailments spring from the same cause—no
change of diet, and their only food a wet root. The chops will do
them good so long as they last. As for their rheumatism, it is slightly
intensified by the wetness of this season—that is all.' He would
discourse, as we made our way across meadows, bogs and streams,
from one poor habitation to another, on the philosophy of health and
disease, and extort the admiration and respect of his listener by the
wide range of his knowledge and the depth of his sympathy for the
suffering and sorrowful condition.

The labours of the day were closed by a festive dinner, ending with
a bowl of punch, untouched by the juniors, but enjoyed in moderation
by the seniors. Conversation, flavoured with ' Attic salt,' genial
humour, and sparkling wit, combined to make the repast

> The feast of reason and the flow of soul.

Then came the solace and refreshment of music. Petrie's violin was
placed entreatingly in his hands by one of the younger members of the
party, whose reverent and affectionate attentions to the elders were
touching to witness, and soon

> Amid the strings his fingers strayed
> And an uncertain warbling made,
> And oft he shook his hoary head.
> But when he caught the measure wild,
> The old man raised his face and smiled."

Petrie was not only a friend of humanity but devotedly
fond of animals, horses, dogs, cats and, indeed, as I may
say, of all living creatures. Dr. Stokes tells this very
characteristic story of him in this connection.

" During Petrie's residence in Charles Street, the kitten of
his favourite cat had its leg broken, when he rushed out for
one of his friends—then a practising surgeon, but failed to
find him; he then called on another, but had hardly
knocked at the door, when, for the first time, the singularity
of his position struck him; for a moment he thought of
leaving the door, but waited to apologise for calling. The
door was opened, he was forced to come in, the candles
were lit in the study, and the servant, regardless of Petrie's
remonstrances, ran upstairs for his master, who was in bed.

In a few minutes the surgeon came down, carrying his boots in his hand, and assuring him that no apologies were necessary, he donned his hat and cloak, and accompanied him to the house, when Petrie, almost dumb with confusion, at last took courage to tell the nature of the case ; the good-humoured answer was—' Well, let me see the patient, at all events.' He was brought to the kitten, the limb was carefully put up, and the surgeon, refusing his fee, promised to call next day; but as Petrie went to show him to the door, the old cat, who had been watching the entire pro-ceeding, sprang on the table, and carried her kitten to the corner of the room. She then proceeded to undo all the bandages, deliberately taking out pin by pin, while Petrie watched in amazement, and the splints being removed, she commenced licking the part, and thus continued with hardly an intermission for some days and nights, when a cure was effected without the slightest deformity ! "

Petrie's manifold services to his native land were soon to end. During the spring of 1865, feeling that his time would not be long, he devoted himself to cataloguing his museum, now included in the National Museum of Ireland. This he did with an energy which led him to give up his usual exercise, and on the 17th January, 1866, after an illness that entailed no suffering and was unattended by any failure of intellect, he peacefully expired in the arms of his children. "He died," as his biographer writes, "as a Christian man should do, not in triumph, nor yet in gloom, but in calm resignation to the will of Him Who doeth all things well."

His remains were followed to the tomb by the members of the Royal Irish Academy ; they rest in a grave without an epitaph in the cemetery of Mount Jerome.

But I am glad to believe that these three lectures * to his

* This and the two papers on George Petrie which immediately precede it in this volume were delivered at Alexandra College, Dublin, as the three " Margaret Stokes Memorial Lectures " for 1912.

memory and that of his dear friend, co-artist, co-antiquary and co-musician, Margaret Stokes, are likely to prove the cause of the erection of a worthy monument over the remains of our greatest Irish Antiquary, "dear Petrie," as we can all now unite to call him.

I conclude with a character sketch of Petrie by my father, contained in the Eloge, which, as its President, he delivered before the Royal Irish Academy shortly after his friend's death:

Petrie united qualities which are seldom possessed by the same individual; he had the enthusiasm and the imaginative power which are essential to the artist; he also possessed the sagacity and calmness of judgment which are commonly supposed to be characteristic of the man of science. There was in him a singular gracefulness, combined with masculine force. He was sensitive, without being morbid; he was playful, but never wayward; he was candid in criticism, but never gave a gratuitous wound to the feelings of an opponent. "He exerted," as has been well said, "an influence which prompted and encouraged many minds in liberal ideas—in genial and tolerant social views—in the elegancies of native accomplishments, and in that appreciation of the generous criticism which discovers the good achieved rather than the shortcomings in works of literature and of art—an influence which gave a rare charm to his society."

He often declared that though always a poor man, his life had been one of great enjoyment, greater than falls to the lot of most men, and that his chief happiness was in the society of so many loving, lasting, and intellectual friends.